Sustainability in Tourism

Ian Jenkins • Roland Schröder (Eds.)

Sustainability in Tourism

A Multidisciplinary Approach

Coordinator: Andreas Lax (M.A.)

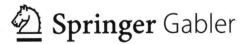

Editors
Ian Jenkins
Les Roche Gruyere University
Bulle, Switzerland

Roland Schröder
BiTS – Business and Information
Technology School ggmbH
University of Applied Sciences
Iserlohn, Germany

ISBN 978-3-8349-2806-1   ISBN 978-3-8349-7043-5 (eBook)
DOI 10.1007/978-3-8349-7043-5

The Deutsche Nationalbibliothek lists this publication in the Deutsche Nationalbibliografie; detailed bibliographic data are available in the Internet at http://dnb.d-nb.de.

Library of Congress Control Number: 2013940768

Springer Gabler
© Springer Fachmedien Wiesbaden 2013
This work is subject to copyright. All rights are reserved by the Publisher, whether the whole or part of the material is concerned, specifically the rights of translation, reprinting, reuse of illustrations, recitation, broadcasting, reproduction on microfilms or in any other physical way, and transmission or information storage and retrieval, electronic adaptation, computer software, or by similar or dissimilar methodology now known or hereafter developed. Exempted from this legal reservation are brief excerpts in connection with reviews or scholarly analysis or material supplied specifically for the purpose of being entered and executed on a computer system, for exclusive use by the purchaser of the work. Duplication of this publication or parts thereof is permitted only under the provisions of the Copyright Law of the Publisher's location, in its current version, and permission for use must always be obtained from Springer. Permissions for use may be obtained through RightsLink at the Copyright Clearance Center. Violations are liable to prosecution under the respective Copyright Law.
The use of general descriptive names, registered names, trademarks, service marks, etc. in this publication does not imply, even in the absence of a specific statement, that such names are exempt from the relevant protective laws and regulations and therefore free for general use.
While the advice and information in this book are believed to be true and accurate at the date of publication, neither the authors nor the editors nor the publisher can accept any legal responsibility for any errors or omissions that may be made. The publisher makes no warranty, express or implied, with respect to the material contained herein.

Printed on acid-free paper

Springer Gabler is a brand of Springer DE.
Springer DE is part of Springer Science+Business Media.
www.springer-gabler.de

Foreword

David S. Graves

CEO, Laureate Hospitality, Art and Design Education

For many families around the world, the highlight of each year is an annual holiday trip. Whether travelling by airplane or camper, cruise ship or train, pleasure travel for relaxation and family bonding has become culturally institutionalised. But travel and tourism are much more today than an annual trip to the seaside. Long-haul flights halfway around the globe are fully booked with business travellers creating new enterprises; health tourism is exploding with cross-border medical procedures being performed in rapidly rising numbers; and religious travel continues to drive a significant portion of tourism in some countries. A key question being asked from many quarters is whether such tourism is sustainable.

But what is sustainability? Definitions vary wildly, with little common agreement. In fact, there are many scholarly studies on the subject of sustainability, a wide variety of books offer popular discourse on the perils of lack of sustainability, and a vast array of media reports from all viewpoints have created a staggering level of confusion.

Part of the confusion arises from the highly complex nature of the subject. Few books on sustainability have been written with a multi-disciplinary approach. The selections in this compendium offer an extensive review of sustainability from a carefully considered range of viewpoints. The authors represent a variety of disciplines, including economics, geography, marketing, media, sociology, environmental science, accountancy and hospitality. Each chapter explores the business of tourism and hospitality from a unique viewpoint, considering its relevance to the health of national economies and the significant role that tourism plays as a major generator of GDP worldwide.

Under the broad umbrella of sustainable development, this book examines sustainable tourism by taking into account factors such as media, business profitability, educational inclusiveness, political and community needs, medical tourism and aspects of sustainable labelling and marketing. Some authors suggest the spectre of climate change can be seen as an energiser of sustainable polices. Several chapters present empirical evidence and case studies, whereas others have a more philosophical and theoretical basis. However, each author offers insights into methods that industry and governments might employ to create more sustainable practices and policies.

Finally, the authors have noted the need for universities, and in particular business schools, to be leaders in disseminating concepts of corporate social responsibility, a key element of which is sustainability. Laureate Education is a worldwide network of colleges and universities that are committed to the concept of sustainability being incorporated into all university curricula. With nearly 700,000 university students in 30 countries, about one-third of whom are studying business, we believe it is possible to have a global influence on the future direction of business enterprises through enlightened curricula. It is our hope that this book, which includes authors from the faculties of several Laureate institutions, will contribute knowledge and practice to help create a more sustainable world.

Contents

Edmund A. Spindler
The History of Sustainability
The Origins and Effects of a Popular Concept 9

Ian Jenkins
Sustainability and Climate Change 33

Thomas Rieger
Sustainability and Health Tourism 53

Robert S. Bristow
Sustainability and Eco-health tourism 69

Thomas Meuser & Carola von Peinen
Sustainable Tourism
"Wish you weren't here" 85

Britt Ventriglia & Ruth Rios-Morales
The Shift toward Sustainability in the Travel Trade Industry 103

Henri Kuokkanen & Ruth Rios-Morales
Developing Sustainable Competitive Advantage in the
Tourism Industry: a financial conceptual model 123

Andy Middleton
Managing Ecological Balance 137

Mark Piekarz & Michelle Callanan
Politics, Community Tourism and Sustainability 159

Roland Schroeder & Oliver Hahn
Media and Sustainable Tourism 177

Ian Jenkins
Education and Copernicus 192

David Horrigan
Sustaining Sustainability 210

Index 221

About the Authors 223

The History of Sustainability
The Origins and Effects of a Popular Concept

Edmund A. Spindler

Introduction

Rarely has a concept gained status as rapidly or with such profound implications as the term 'sustainability'. Within a relatively short period of time it has become a loose/rather nebulous metaphor for describing current issues. A rather unwieldy, catch-all term, it can be found across a wide range of topics. It has become an extremely popular term, particularly in connection with economic activities. In the field of ecologically oriented economics, it has significantly reinvigorated research and has become the starting point for a new approach. There is even talk of a paradigm shift, with sustainability viewed as a "driver of innovation" (Hollmann-Peters, 2011, p. 18). The growing debate over global environmental problems (Chasek *et al.*, 2006) has highlighted and further strengthened this trend.

> "Hence, the term 'sustainable development' seems to be enjoying immense popularity. No speech about the future of our society is complete without it, it serves as a slogan used by politicians, regularly keeps lawyers occupied, is a hot topic among scientists and increasingly discussed by the board of directors of corporations" (Reidel, 2010, p. 96).

The term sustainability is often used in an undiscerning and loose way and has turned into somewhat of a "container term" (Vogt, 2009, p. 111; Reidel, 2010, p. 98); it has become a buzz word, and one that is worth reflecting on. At any rate, sustainability has developed into the "categorical imperative of contemporary responsibility for Creation" (Vogt, 2010, p. 7) and the 21st century has been chosen as the "century of sustainable development" (Kreibich, 2011, p. 47). Additionally, Switzerland was the first country to add the term *sustainability* to its constitution in Article 2 (since January 1, 2000): "The Swiss Confederation supports the common welfare, the sustainable development, the internal cohesion and the cultural diversity of the country" (Grober, 2010, p. 204).

"The concept of sustainable economic management has become a political key word in recent years. Anybody who wants to achieve something, has to demonstrate that he or she intends to do it in a sustainable way" (Diefenbacher et al., 1997, p. 21). In the academic sector this is already a topic which is being addressed (de Haan, 2007; Kless, 2010). The University of Applied Science in Eberswalde, for instance, is now called the "University for Sustainable Development" and uses the advertising slogan "our name says it all" (www.hnee.de). One of its master's degrees on offer is "Sustainable Tourism Management".

Sustainability is no longer a niche topic. "The concept of sustainability will always have its relevance. Sustainability has become the subject for a contemporary assessment of progress and responsibility, freedom and culture" (Bachmann, 2010, p. 2). Linguists and scientists can therefore claim that the concept of sustainability has been well established globally in politics, the economy and our society (Reidel, 2010). However, whilst the term is becoming increasingly popular, doubts have also been raised about whether the promised harmonization of ecological, social and economic goals, associated with sustainability, is actually achievable. Also because the term has entered the vocabulary of advertising language in German, where *nachhaltig* is e.g. also used for shampoos that remove dandruff (Grober, 2010).

Sustainable development is a multi-faceted term—"a buzz word and imported word" but also a "disparaging and praising term at the same time" (Reidel, 2010, p. 97 and p. 99).

But what is the origin of the term, what is behind it and how is it used?

The following text will outline some milestones in the evolution of the terms "sustainability" and "sustainable development", as evidenced by discussion of the relevant literature.

A recent concept with a long history

Sustainability or sustainable development has its roots in all cultures. A lake in South America is evidence of this; its name, Manchau gagog changau gagog chaugo gagog amaug, means: "We fish on our side, you fish on your side and nobody fishes in the middle." This is "obviously a simple instruction for the sustainable use of vital resources" (Schreiber, 2004) and demonstrates that sustainability is a survival strategy. This is also evident in the management of commons (Chasek *et al.,* 2006), which shows commitment to sustainability, a sense of responsibility and respect for nature.

Ever since antiquity, a shared understanding of the concept of sustainability has existed, particularly in rural cultures (Vogt, 2009). The roots of the term can be traced back to the world of hunting, where hunters and gatherers were keen to secure their livelihood. "The old German word for 'sustenance,' used to describe those supplies that were saved for times of need" (Reidel, 2010, p. 102).

The term 'sustainable' or rather 'to sustain' has been "shown to be a derivation of the noun "sustenance" (actually retain, what one retains) used towards the end of the 18th century" (Vogt, 2009, p. 116). In everyday parlance, 'sustainable' is nowadays still used in the sense of 'enduringly effective'. Also the Bible requires mankind to take care of the earth and to look after it; this could be seen as an early proof of Sustainability (Grober, 2010).

Roots in the German Forestry Industry

In the 18th century, sustainability was laid down first as a principle of the German forestry industry. The first documented idea of sustainability was written by the Saxon mining director Hans Carl von Carlowitz (1645-1714) from Freiberg (Saxony). In his book *Sylvicultura Oeconomica* (or the *Economic News and Instructions for the Natural Growing of Wild Trees*), published in 1713, he suggests a form of forestry where only so much wood should be cut as can be re-grown through planned reforestation projects. He talks about "sustainable use of forests" and pleads for "forest management that allows for a continuous, perpetual use of timber" (Schretzmann et al., 2006, p. 68). What makes the work of Von Carlowitz particularly remarkable is that it was written with a focus on economics. He had obviously already recognised that the forest could not be saved by the forestry industry alone but rather by the economy as a whole. Ulrich Grober (2010, p. 94) calls this a "societal task". This holistic view is characteristic of the concept of sustainability, which is why a "process" (Chasek et al., 2006, p. 425) or a process-oriented definition of the term is discussed in the text.

Another pioneer of the sustainable forestry industry is mining director Georg Ludwig Hartig (1764-1837) from Gladenbach, Germany. He wrote in his *Instructions for the Taxation of Forests* in 1804: "There will be no sustainable forest industry if lumbering in the forests is not based on sustainability. Every wise forest authority must assess the use of the state's forest without delay and in such a way that our descendants can obtain at least as much gain from them as today's generation does" (www.hessen-nachhaltig.de).

As a result, sustainability in the forest industry or sustainable forest management is not an independent objective. It is, rather, the core principle of an economic forestry operation based on the following components (Schretzmann et al., 2006, p. 69):

- **Durability**
  Resources and functions of the forest are to be secured in the long term.
- **Responsibilities to Society**
  Society's interest in the forest can lead to restrictions relating to rights of use.
- **Economics**
  Necessity of economic forestry with systematic protection of natural resources in order to achieve optimal economic benefits.
- **Responsibility**
  Sense of responsibility for the significance of the forest for future generations.

This concept of sustainability or sustainable development in forestry has been used for many other global environmental issues and has become a fundamental principle in all areas of the economy and society. Sustainability is essentially about the preservation of natural capital. "The natural stock of resources needs to remain stable and mankind has to learn to live from its yield rather than its over-exploitation" (Diefenbacher et al., 1997, p. 24). This notion also plays a crucial role in the fishing industry (Carnau 2011), and even in development aid sustainability is achieved when a stable state is reached and a certain degree of autonomy has become apparent (Vogt, 2009). "This illustrates that in many areas the concept has developed far beyond the original forestry and ecological framework" (Vogt, 2009, p. 117).

"Living off the interest rather than the capital" can be considered the general motto of sustainability today.

From a view point of terminology, the concept of Sustainability is not an exact definition of Sustainability but to determine, what should endure and to link spatio-temporal levels, which must result in policy building of Sustainability. The basic idea is that a system is sustainable, if it survives and endures on a long term basis. How concrete these measures are must be determined individually (Carnau, 2011).

Grober (2010) therefore considers the idea of Sustainability not as a concept developed by technocrats or by the *Woodstock Generation* but as part of the worlds cultural heritage.

"The principle of sustainability spread via the College for Forestry in Freiberg near Dresden to Germany and in the US. In 1780 it appears for the first time in an encyclopaedia of forest sciences. A forestry regulation from 1795 explicitly refers to future generations by limiting the use of the forest to the extent that posterity would be allowed the same utilisation of resources. In forestry regulations of the 19th century the concept of sustainability is expanded and defined as the optimal planting of trees in soil that is suitable for that purpose and the use of mixtures of crops, including relevant care of their soil. Therefore, sustainability goes beyond setting limiting principles" (Vogt, 2009, p. 115).

Based on this historical development, sustainability appears to many as a 'German speciality' (Schretzmann, 2011). However, the concept is "not uniquely German" (Vogt, 2009, p. 115), but in the context of Enlightment to be seen form an international perspective. (cf also Grober, 2010) and has to be viewed within an international context of Enlightenment. Sustainability is a "life principle" (Vogt, 2009, p. 117) respectively and "ethical principle" (Grober, 2010, p. 266) that is characterized by transparency, participation and an enlightened, process-related (holistic) view. It requires a "mature individual" (consider Immanuel Kant) who can take an interdisciplinary approach to how he/she thinks and works. It is this holistic view that makes the term sustainability so versatile, which is why it is very well suited for, and easily adopted by, cross-cutting issues such as "environmental protection" and "environmental precaution". "Sustainability is often understood as a new type of environmental policy but it is more than environmental protection. It takes into account the responsibility for future generations (inclusive justice) and also for people living today (distributive justice)" (Freericks *et al.*, 2010, p. 250).

Sustainability in environmental policy

As well as the (historical) forestry industry, the 'new environmental policy' gave sustainability a new boost. This boost came with the publication of the 1962 book *Silent Spring*, by Rachel Carson. Thanks to this eco-classic, environmental protection became an important interdisciplinary topic and society's environmental awareness rose globally.

As a result of the environmental debate, the US adopted the National Environmental Policy Act in 1969. This law was enforced on January 1, 1970 and caused a global furore, particularly its requirement for a comprehensive Environmental Impact Assessment (EIA) for large projects with public participation. This concept was subsequently introduced in Germany and elsewhere in Europe. According to Article 2 of EIA law, EIA identifies, predicts and evaluates the effects of a project—with participation of citizens—on:

1. Humans, including human health, animals, plants and biological diversity
2. Soil, water, air, climate and landscape
3. Cultural goods and other material assets, as well as
4. The interaction of all of the above goods.

This cross-sectional, trans-sectoral and cross-media approach goes beyond current environmental policy, which is focused on sectors, and makes environmental protection an eco-systemic challenge that serves as a base for an environmental management system and also for sustainability management (von Hauff, 2010; Bay, 2010). Sustainable development in this sense is an "environment policy perspective that emphasizes the necessity to reconcile present and future economic needs through protection of the environment" (Chasek et al., 2006, p. 425). This also means the "Courage of Less" (Grober, 2010, p. 270) as Sustainability is basically a strategy of self-restriction and reduction.

As a first conclusion it could be stated, following Albert Schweitzer that Sustainability is the ability to think and plan ahead (Grober, 2010).

The new global environmental policy has been considerably influenced by the UN Environmental Conferences (Figure 1). This is also where the term sustainability was coined and where it gained significant popularity (on the chronology of global environmental events and on milestones in environmental policy) (see Chasek et al., 2006, pp. 417-422).

UN Environmental Conferences
1st Environmental Conference in 1972 in Stockholm
2nd Environmental Conference in 1982 in Stockholm
3rd Environmental Conference in 1992 in Rio de Janeiro
4th Environmental Conference in 2002 in Johannesburg
5th Environmental Conference in 2012 in Rio de Janeiro (Rio+20)

Figure 1: UN Environmental Conferences

In the context of the UN Conferences, the concept of 'sustainability' was defined relatively independent of its conceptual history based on forestry management. The principle previously known as the 'ecological economic principle of nature management' was now expanded to a comprehensive model linking 'environment' and 'development' (Vogt, 2009, p. 117). The concept of sustainability has continued to develop in a process that has now taken on a life of its own (Diefenbacher *et al.*, 2006). This is particularly the case in discussions about development policies relating to sustainable ways of fighting poverty or to the equitable distribution of natural resources. The UN Conference on Environment and Development was initiated as a result of a new North-South dialogue. Professor Vogt writes concerning this: "The concept of sustainable development has gained ethical and political significance that goes beyond the specific ecologic aspect" (Vogt, 2009, p. 117). It is interesting to note that sustainability has raised the important question of 'distributive justice'.

In 1972, the first worldwide environmental conference was held in Stockholm on a Swedish initiative and with the support of the US. 114 countries (not including the former USSR) – a novelty in the history of the UN – and numerous NGOs (nongovernmental organizations), altogether 1,200 delegates participated in the UN Conference on the Human Environment. They adopted an instrumental declaration that contained fundamentals for dealing with the global environment and an action plan regarding international cooperation on environmental protection as well as principles concerning the foundation of UNEP. "The most important outcome of this conference was the foundation of the United Nations Environmental Programme (UNEP) based in Nairobi" (Diefenbacher *et al.*, 1997, p. 40).

UNEP provided global environmental policy with a voice and also with a continuity that led to the organisation of a UN environmental conference every ten years.

"In the first half of the eighties, sustainable development became a buzzword for an alternative paradigm. Its use became more popular at conferences that brought together NGOs and government officials in the US and elsewhere. In 1987, the publication of "Our Common Future", the report of the World Commission on Environment and Development (better known as the Brundtland Report, after the Chairman of the Commission, the former Norwegian Prime Minister Gro Harlem Brundtland), made the term 'sustainable development' widely known and provided the impulse to replace the dominant paradigm with the new paradigm. (...) The Brundtland report defines sustainable development as development that is 'in harmony with both present and future needs'" (Chasek *et al.*, 2006, p. 49).

The Brundtland Commission was to establish the most significant definition of sustainability in politics, describing sustainable development as development that "meets the needs of the present without compromising the ability of future generations to meet their own needs" (Diefenbacher *et al.*, 1997, p. 41; Deutscher Bundestag, 1998, p. 28).

Another outcome of the Brundlandt Report is the subsequent decision by the UN General Assembly in December 1989 to organize a conference called the United Nations Conference on Environment and Development (UNCED, to be held in Rio de Janeiro, Brazil, in 1992).

Rio and its Consequences

Informally known as the Earth Summit, the UN Conference on Environment and Development of 1992 has become a symbol of the shared responsibility of all the world's nations. Approximately 200 countries in the world attended, 178 participated in the conference. They pointed out the urgent need for action to preserve the Earth's natural resources and laid the foundations for a qualitatively new and significantly more intense degree of co-operation in environmental and developmental politics. It could be said that Rio laid the groundwork for global governance in "Earth Politics" (von Weizsaecker, 1992, p. 9).

Here, the terms of "Global Governance" (Carnau, 2011, p. 34) are introduced, which should not be confused with "Global Government" (Grober, 2010, pp. 218-220).

The Earth Summit was very productive, adopting six documents that were declared the most important areas of action in a global environmental and developmental policy (Schretzmann *et al.*, 2006, p. 71-72; Vogt, 2009, p. 119):

- Rio Declaration on Environment and Development (known as the Rio Declaration)
- Forest Principles
- Framework Convention on Climate Change
- Convention on Biological Diversity
- Convention to Combat Desertification
- Agenda 21.

An action plan and the final document of the conference, Agenda 21 set as an objective the adoption of those measures required for environmentally sustainable development, both locally and globally, to ensure viability for future generations. Agenda 21 makes more tangible the Rio Declaration, which consists of 27 principles intended to guide future sustainable development around the world; for instance, it states in principle 4: "In order to achieve sustainable development, protection of the environment must constitute an integral part of the process of development and cannot be regarded in isolation" (BMU, 1992, p. 45).

In the 40 chapters of Agenda 21, tourism management is largely omitted, but this gap was closed in 1997 at the Rio+5 congress, where the Commission on Sustainable Development (CSD), which had been founded in 1993, was assigned the task of engaging in 'Sustainable Tourism' during its annual meetings. The result was the adoption of the Global Code of Ethics for Tourism (1999), which was created in cooperation with the UNWTO (World Tourism Organization), a specialized agency of the UN based in Madrid, Spain. The following definition was established: Sustainable tourism "satisfies criteria of social, cultural, ecological and economic sustainability. Sustainable tourism has a long-term focus, i.e. relating to today's and future generations, it is ethically and socially just, culturally appropriate, ecologically sustainable, as well as economically rational and productive" (Freericks et al., 2010, p. 249). "Based on this definition a comprehensive action programme was devised that outlines aims, measures and relevant players. A year later, the topic of 'environmentally sustainable tourism' officially became an item on the agenda at the 7th CSD meeting" (Freericks et al., 2010, p. 249).

"Humanity stands at a defining moment in history. We are confronted with a perpetuation of disparities between and within nations, a worsening of poverty, hunger, ill health and illiteracy, and the continuing deterioration of the ecosystems on which we depend for our well-being. However, integration of environment and development concerns and greater attention to them will lead to the fulfilment of basic needs, improved living standards for all, better protected and managed ecosystems and a safer, more prosperous future. No nation can achieve this on its own; but together we can—in a global partnership for sustainable development."

(Extract from the preamble to Agenda 21)

It can be noted that "Rio represents the worldwide recognition of a vision of sustainability that systematically links environmental protection and the fight against poverty as two interdependent elements and thus enables the transition from an end-of-pipe policy of remediation to an integral policy for the future" (Vogt, 2009, p. 119). The implementation of sustainability in politics was dealt with at the UN Conference on Sustainable Development (UNCSD), held in

Johannesburg in 1992. "It was not about new objectives but finance, precise deadlines and binding agreements to allow for implementation of the Rio resolutions" (Vogt, 2009, p. 120).

Here, a new concept concerning the implementation of sustainability was discussed called Public-Private-Partnership (PPP). This allows corporations to act as a contracting party of the state so that common environmental goals can be achieved according to the idea of "cooperation instead of control". This 'soft' instrument was subject to some criticism, however, and contributed to the outcomes of the conference in Johannesburg receiving little positive response. But Professor Vogt points out that: "Despite all the justified criticism, the role of the UN Conference on Sustainable Development in Johannesburg should not be underestimated: Due to its obvious contradiction between aspiration and reality it has become a public memorial to tasks left undone. "It prevented the complex documents of the Rio conference from disappearing from the agenda of world politics and serves, in spite of all the opposition, as a benchmark for eco-social responsibility" (Vogt, 2009, p. 121).

The 5th UN Conference on Sustainable Development, taking place in Rio de Janeiro from June 4 to 6, 2012, will have to deal with this issue of serving as a "memorial" and to ensure once more that the concept of sustainability has a permanent place on the political agenda. At Rio+20, the big Earth Summit of 1992 will be commemorated and current political matters will be discussed. At the centre of the debate will be issues like "Greening the economy" and "institutional reforms such as the further development of UNEP" (see www.uncsd2010.org and www.earthsummit2012.org).

Sustainable Development in Europe and Germany

The recognition of the importance of sustainability at a high level internationally has resulted in sustainable development becoming an ongoing mission in European Union (EU) politics (Diefenbacher *et al.*, 1997). The Lisbon strategy, developed in March 2000, has made sustainable development in the EU a strategic objective. At the Gothenburg Summit in June 2001, environmental aspects were added to the strategy entitled "Sustainable development in Europe for a better World: a European Union strategy for sustainable development" (Vitols, 2011, p. 23). The 27 EU states are committed to this strategy; they have to support the policy of sustainability and implement the environmental regulations of the various action plans.

In Germany, the Advisory Council on the Environment (SRU), established in 1971, carried out an in-depth analysis of the concept and effects of sustainability in its environmental report published in 1994. It suggested its own translation of sustainability: "sustainable, environmentally compatible development" (Diefenbacher *et al.*, 1997, p. 44; Vogt, 2009, p. 125-126). The SRU's 1994 annual review states: "The Advisory Council on the Environment is hoping that the formula *sustainable, environmentally compatible development* will make the concept of sustainability the main focus in future environmental politics and also anchor it in the public's consciousness." And it continues: "The concept of sustainability has led to the insight that the areas of economic, social and environmental development are interdependent and cannot be analyzed independently or played off against each other. In order to secure humanity's development, these three components have to be regarded as a necessary unity that needs constant re-building" (SRU, 1994, p. 46). Based on these profound statements, it is clear that sustainability has become an enduring issue in Germany – a permanent feature of its political landscape.

The Study Commission of the German parliament has also made its contribution by publishing a total of three extensive reports on sustainability. It defines the English term 'sustainable development' as "sustainable, environmentally compatible development" and also states: "The principle of sustainable, environmentally compatible development is a concept that takes into equal account environmental problems generated primarily by past production patterns and lifestyles in industrialized countries and the needs of developing countries and future generations" (Deutscher Bundestag, 1994, p. 30). On an executive level of the Federal Government, the Council for Sustainable Development (RNE) has been active since April 2001 (www.nachhaltigkeitsrat.de). The RNE includes 15 individuals from the public sector; these are appointed by the German government for three years and focus intensively on topics related to sustainability or sustainable development in politics, the economy and society. Statements by and campaigns and events organized by RNE are highly regarded and enjoy wide acceptance among the general public.

In April 2002, a national sustainability strategy entitled "Perspectives for Germany. Our Strategy for Sustainable Development" was developed with the participation of the RNE. The aim was to issue "management guidelines" for acceptable conduct in politics and society. "The ten management rules of sustainability describe the demands on ecological, economic and socially balanced development. This includes, for instance, the participation of all players in sustainable development, sustainable production methods, the use of renewable resources, avoidance of dangers and unwarranted risks to human health as well as ecologically and socially acceptable structural change, low energy and resource consumption, sound public finances, sustainable agriculture and social cooperation. (...) Each topic specified in the management rules was assigned targets and key indicators for monitoring progress" (Vitols, 2011, p. 8).

At present, the RNE is trying—in a wide-ranging dialog—to establish a German Sustainability Code (GSC) for all businesses in Germany. The GSC's effects and its applicability and practicability will initially be tested for one year to ensure successful (legal) implementation. Of particular interest is the concept of a "sustainability pledge" (Bachmann, 2010) that was negotiated with the umbrella organization Deutscher Naturschutzring, or DNR, which covers German nature conservation and environmental protection organizations. With the help of the RNE, the DNR aims to enrich the debate around guidelines, emphasize the importance of a "code for ecological sustainability", and strengthen commitment in sustainability matters. RNE Secretary-General Dr Gunther Bachmann stated: "Sustainability needs a strong guarantor. This guarantor must give direction to the concept and offer assurance that anything claiming to be sustainable is actually sustainable" (Bachmann, 2010, p. 6). The foundation for such a "sustainability pledge" is not only transparent and measurable criteria that may be used for a sustainability certification, but also a new approach in the public debate around sustainable development (keyword "pledge to society").

Parallel to this, and complementing the work done by the RNE, the German Commission for UNESCO is currently hosting the UN World Decade (2005-14) of "Education for Sustainable Development" in Germany, with great success (www.bne-portal.de). The goal is to broadly anchor the principles of sustainable development in the education system.

On a regional and municipal level, sustainability has become an important focus in the implementation of the Local Agenda 21 (Diefenbacher *et al.*, 1997), where detailed information on urban development is provided, demonstrated by the City of Heidelberg.

Sustainability seems to meet with wide approval in society, at least in theory. A reasonable number of associations and NGOs have 'discovered' the subject and made it their mission (cf. eg. www.nachhaltigkeit-ev.de; www.nachhaltigkeit.info; www.stratum-consult.de; www.stratum-consult.de). The term is very versatile and is used in ways that are at times very creative. The catchy slogan "sustainability is change", for instance, was created by stratum®, a consulting company that grew out of an environmental initiative (Haeusler *et al.*, 2009). Among the multitude of other initiatives is the LOHAS-movement (Lifestyle of Health and Sustainability), which has developed a philosophy of life based on health and sustainability (www.lohas.de; www.lohas.com).

Description and essence of sustainability

"Concepts without perceptions are empty, perceptions without concepts are blind."

Immanuel Kant

The first graphical displays of Sustainability developed one and two column models (Carnau, 2011). The focus was on the three goals of ecology, economy and social affairs (Figure 2). This "sustainability formula" (Vogt, 2009, p. 102) had a significant impact on the environmental debate in the '70s and '80s. "In theory, the principles of sustainability have been agreed upon in 1992, and effort has been made to implement them, but in actual fact hardly any progress has been made towards these objectives" (Vogt, 2009, p. 102). And Vogt continues:

> "The paratactic understanding of the three-pillar model that ecology, economy and social equity are equally weighted interrelated pillars threatens the guideline function of the principles defined. They are used to hide contradictions and differences instead of finding a consensus on core issues, goals and priorities. (...) Sustainability will remain a meaningful concept only where it continues to be an environmentally focused concept, and where a systematic integration of environmental issues into other sectors of politics, economy and society is achieved" (Vogt, 2009, p. 142).

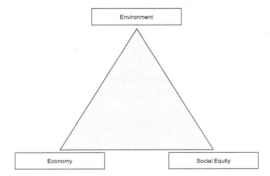

Figure 2:   The Triangle of Sustainability

The 'triangle of sustainability' was further developed into a 'magic triangle' (Deutscher Bundestag, 1994, p. 54) with the following dimensions: environmental dimension, economic dimension, and social dimension (Figure 3). It became the symbol of the German parliament's Study Commission entitled "protection of the human and the environment".

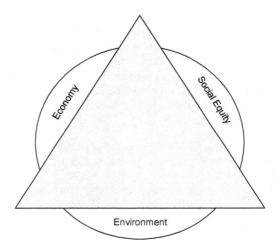

Figure 3:   Dimensions of Sustainability

"In the magic triangle of sustainable development, economic, social and environmental objectives face each other" (Deutscher Bundestag, 1994, p. 54).

This "three-dimensionality of sustainability" (Deutscher Bundestag, 1997, p. 170) served as a basis for the design of the commonly used "three-pillar model" (Fig. 4).

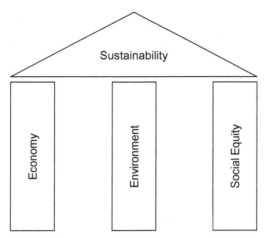

Figure 4:   Three-Pillar Model

Economy, environment, and social equity constitute the three pillars of sustainability and are of equal importance. In practice, interpreting sustainability is often difficult and arbitrary due to the conflicting objectives of the three pillars. Hence, emphasis has been put on those 'natural assets' (Deutscher Bundestag, 1994, p. 31) that led to the environment becoming more high-profile. Professor Vogt writes concerning this: "From an ethical viewpoint the concept of an 'equality' of environment, economy and social affairs—as the three-pillar model is often interpreted—does not make sense because we are dealing with completely different systems, issues and tasks that cannot be directly compared and valued". And he comes to a disappointing conclusion: "Therefore the well-established model of three pillars is rather irritating" (Vogt, 2009, p. 143).

In order to secure ecological efficiency and the natural production system it would be obvious to change the look of the 'environment' pillar because "allocation of resources and reception of waste in particular, are non-renewable services provided by nature, thus limiting the scope of human economic activities" (Deutscher Bundestag, 1994, p. 32).

Former Professor Volker Stahlmann succeeded in resolving the conflicting interests between environment, economy and social affairs by creating an 'edifice' of sustainability that reflects reality more accurately (Figure 5). "The environment is the foundation on which social, cultural and economic pillars are built. Sustainable development represents the roof of the building and is supported by this structure" (Stahlmann, 2008, p. 61).

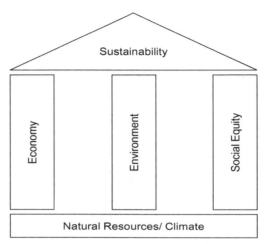

Figure 5: Weighted Pillar Model of Sustainable Development (Stahlmann, 2008), adapted

This further development of the three-pillar model to a "weighted pillar model" gives a much clearer understanding of sustainability. It clarifies the foundation on which sustainable development is based, and how it is supported and safeguarded. That means economizing nature is the sole basis for our Economy (Grober, 2010).

Sector-specific additions to and definitions of the pillars are necessary and permissible. The area of CSR (Corporate Social Responsibility), for instance, asks for a fourth pillar to emphasize the "political and institutional dimension" and to reinforce "the significance of participation and integration" (Vitols, 2011, p. 19; Freericks *et al.*, 2010, p. 347-348). Integration of sustainability into the CSR process is specified by the new ISO-26000, introduced on November 1, 2010 (Bay, 2010; Hardtke and Kleinfeld, 2010).

Figure 6 depicts an example of sector-specific addition to the model which includes 'health'.

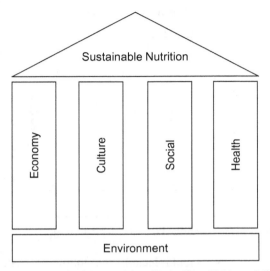

Figure 6: Model of sustainable nutrition (Spindler, 2010, p. 24)

A similar model could be developed for tourism by replacing the "health" pillar with "recreation".

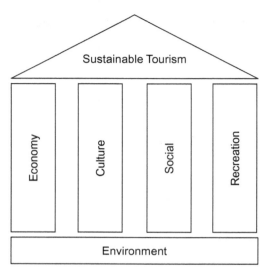

Figure 7: Model of Sustainable Tourism

All models and concepts should include the following basic principles for sustainable development:

- **Intergenerational Justice**
  To satisfy the needs of today's generation without compromising the ability of future generations to meet their own needs.
- **Capacity for Regeneration**
  Not taking more from nature that it can regenerate in a natural ecological cycle.
- **Law of Succinctness**
  To use non-renewable resources only to the extent that an equal substitute in the form of renewable resources can be found or that resource productivity can be increased.

- **Reduction in Risk**
  To minimise potential environmental risks and ensure safety in the manufacturing process and with materials.
- **Absorption Capacity**
  To generate emissions only at a level that nature can cope with over time or that can be transformed into non-toxic substances.
- **Ecological-Economic Value Creation**
  To maintain and promote the ecological potential and biodiversity.

Meanwhile, these principles of efficiency, consistency and sufficiency have been implemented in many projects and activities. In order to clarify the contents of the sustainability concept and sustainable development, many models have been created that include indicators and targets. A good example of this is the "magic circles of sustainability" developed by the Applied Ecology Project of the Regional Office for Environmental Protection in Baden-Wuerttemberg (Diefenbacher, 1997, p. 71).

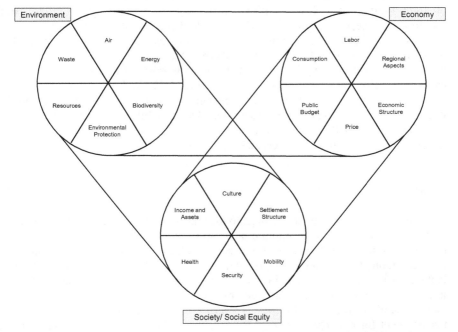

Figure 8:   Magic Circles of Sustainability (Diefenbacher, 1997), adapted

> "The term 'magic circles of sustainability' illustrates that environment, economy and society are interdependent; none of the areas can exist without the others. (...) Each of the magic circles is divided into six different sub-objectives" (Diefenbacher, 1997, p. 73).

The objectives are kept deliberately vague in order to facilitate concretisation by means of an indicator system.

> "We made a conscious decision not to provide any quantitative objectives. On the one hand, this is impossible given our current state of knowledge: we can attempt to indicate in which direction society should go in order to achieve the goal of sustainability —we cannot predict when exactly this might be the case. On the other hand, we are of the opinion that quantitative values for sub-objectives would limit the scope for development in society. It is of particular importance that the different sub-objectives lead to a discussion process involving all players in society about different environmental, economic and social developments in connection with sustainability" (Diefenbacher, 1997, p. 74).

This shows once again that the definition of sustainable development is an ongoing, fluid process. Sustainability is intricately linked to change – similar to a building site the management of which is challenging but ultimately leads to progress. It might be appealing to mention the *collapse* as an antonym of Sustainability (Grober, 2011a; Grober, 2011b). "Sustainability is not a fad" but a "megatrend" (Bachmann, 2010, p. 3). In other words: Sustainability concerns everybody. Everyone can understand sustainability. And everyone can live sustainability every day. It is about constant reflection on sustainability and internalizing it. Only this can lead to a "staged sustainability process", one that is a challenge for all of us. As a conclusion it can be stated: "The discovery of Sustainability continues" (Grober, 2010, p. 268).

Tourism and Sustainability

There is no doubt that tourism belongs to the "most progressive economic sectors" – those sectors with an economic interest in the conservation of ecological homeostasis and which are well placed to achieve "comprehensive ecologic modernisation" (Petermann, 1999, p. 241; Freericks *et al.,* 2010). Although nature is the decisive factor of production in tourism, rigorous sustainability schemes are lacking. And while there is a multitude of "practical approaches to environmental management" (Viegas, 1998 , p. 42 and (older) scientific papers on eco-management for tour operators e.g. Mezzasalma, 1994), few projects have had a specific impact on the concept of sustainability. Despite the many definitions of sustainability (Reidel, 2010, p. 97) there is no authoritative standard definition of sustainable tourism. And the sector has to date failed to produce the kind of compelling graphics needed to illustrate the subject properly.

Petermann notes that "Tourism service providers' enlightened self-interest to generate income from nature may well be an incentive for environmental protection measures. However, this incentive is often too weak and there is a lack of continuity in the willingness to act" (1999, p. 243). Ultimately, the primacy of the (short-term) economy seems to prevail. But one has to realise that what is wrong ecologically cannot be reasonable economically. When it comes to defining the term, it is hoped that sustainable development would play an active part in the practical implementation of tourism policies and take a pioneering role in this field. Sustainability is an existential challenge for tourism. The main issue is to discuss and define targets as well as the processes needed to implement responsible structures. For instance, the tourism sector could help support and promote the recent emergence of "sustainability science" (Reidel, 2010, p. 24). It could lead by example by implementing the all-important precautionary principle and this could be helped by tourism risk management illustrating the impacts of tourism on destinations. Such a 'compass' (Vogt, 2010, p. 7) for *a tourism industry with a clear conscience* would be helpful.

In the field of environmental policy this path has already been taken with the proposal of a "Sectoral Reference Document for Tourism in Europe" (Final Draft, January 2011). This sector-specific reference model for tourism, created for the European Eco-Management and Audit Scheme EMAS (www.emas.de), could serve as a basis for further sustainable development activities and for defining more specific guidelines for sustainable tourism (see 'members-only' area of www.uga.de). There is also a requirement for effective sustainability management and for firmly defined criteria for sustainable tourism (see www.sustainabletourismcriteria.org). Otherwise "the much expected golden future of tourism remains unknown. (...) However, because tourism is dependent on an intact environment and sustainable growth like any other industry, there is a chance of finding means and ways to reconcile economy and environment in the age of globalisation" (Petermann, 1999, p. 251).

This optimistic view of the future can be maintained if tourism faces up to the universal question of sustainability and gives an honest answer to the public: *Always ask yourself what marks you have left in life.*

Perhaps the following quotation best describes the current debate around sustainable tourism:

> "The tourist destroys what he seeks by finding it".
> Hans Magnus Enzensberger (German author and poet)

References

Bachmann, G. (2010): *Verbürgte statt beliebige Nachhaltigkeit.* Unpublished manuscript.
Bay, K.-C. (Ed.) (2010), *ISO 26000 in der Praxis. Der Ratgeber zum Leitfaden für soziale Verantwortung und Nachhaltigkeit,* Munich, Oldenbourg Industrieverlag.
BMU, Bundesministerium für Umwelt, Naturschutz und Reaktorsicherheit (1992), *Konferenz der Vereinten Nationen für Umwelt und Entwicklung im Juni 1992 in Rio de Janeiro,* Bonn, BMU.
Carnau, P. (2011), *Nachhaltigkeitsethik. Normativer Gestaltungsansatz für eine global zukunftfähige Entwicklung in Theorie und Praxis,* Rainer Hamp Verlag, München.
Carson, R. (1962), *Der stumme Frühling,* Beck, München.
Chasek, P. S. et al., (2006), *Handbuch Globale Umweltpolitik,* Partgas Verlag, Berlin.
Deutscher Bundestag (1994), *Die Industriegesellschaft gestalten. Perspektiven für einen nachhaltigen Umgang mit Stoff- und Materialströmen. Bericht der Enquete-Kommission "Schutz des Menschen und der Umwelt – Bewertungskriterien und Perspektiven für Umweltverträgliche Stoffkreisläufe in der Industriegesellschaft"* des 12. Deutschen Bundestages, Economica Verlag, Bonn.
Deutscher Bundestag (1997), *Konzept Nachhaltigkeit. Fundamente für die Gesellschaft von morgen. Zwischenbericht der Enquete-Kommission "Schutz des Menschen und der Umwelt – Ziele und Rahmenbedingungen einer nachhaltig zukunftsverträglichen Entwicklung"* des 13. Deutschen Bundestages, Deutscher Bundestag, Bonn.
Deutscher Bundestag (1998), *Konzept Nachhaltigkeit. Vom Leitbild zur Umsetzung. Abschlussbericht der Enquete-Kommission "Schutz des Menschen und der Umwelt – Ziele und Rahmenbedingungen einer nachhaltig zukunftsverträglichen Entwicklung"* des 13. Deutschen Bundestages, Deutscher Bundestag, Bonn.
Freericks, R. et al., (2010), *Freizeitwissenschaft. Handbuch für Pädagogik, Management und nachhaltige Entwicklung,* Oldenbourg Wissenschaftsverlag, München.
Grober, U. (2010), *Die Entdeckung der Nachhaltigkeit. Kulturgeschichte eines Begriffs,* Verlag Antje Kunstmann, München.
Grober, Ulrich (2011a): „Zauberwort Nachhaltigkeit – warum wir sorgsam damit umgehen sollten.", in *UNESCO heute,* No. 2/2011, pp. 14-16.
Grober, Ulrich (2011b): „Welches Wachstum wollen wir?", in *PSYCHOLOGIE HEUTE,* June 2011, pp. 60-64.
de Haan, G. (Ed.) (2007), *Studium und Forschung zur Nachhaltigkeit,* W. Bertelsmann Verlag, Bielefeld.
Häusler, R. et al., (2009), *Nachhaltigkeit ist Veränderung. Initiativen zum Umweltschutz,* Erich Schmidt Verlag, Berlin.
Hardtke, A., and Kleinfeld, A. (Eds.) (2010), *Gesellschaftliche Verantwortung von Unternehmen. Von der Idee der Corporate Social Responsibility zur erfolgreichen Umsetzung* Gabler, Wiesbaden.
von Hauff, M. (2010), *Öko-Audit. Vom Umwelt- zum Nachhaltigkeitsmanagement,* Verlag Wissenschaft & Praxis Dr. Brauner, Sternenfelde.
Hollmann-Peters, I. (2011), "Innovationstreiber Nachhaltigkeit", *face to face,* April 2011, Mitarbeitermagazin von Beiersdorf, pp. 18-19.

Kless, C. (2010), *"Bildung für Nachhaltige Entwicklung. Deutsche Hochschulbildungsangebote für Nachhaltige Entwicklung im Tourismus, eine Analyse"*. Masterarbeit an der Hochschule für nachhalte Entwicklung Eberswalde (FH).
Kreibich, R. (2011), "Das Jahrhundert der nachhaltigen Entwicklung. Integriertes Roadmapping and Sustainable Value als Methoden zur Durchsetzung nachhaltiger Innovationen", in BAUM (Ed.) *Ressourcenmanagement,* B.A.U.M. Jahrbuch 2011, ALTOP Verlag, Munich, pp. 44-47.
Reidel, J. (2010), *Erfolgreich oder ruinös? Transnationale Unternehmen und nachhaltige Entwicklung – kritische Reflexion aus menschenrechtlicher Perspektive,* oekom Verlag, München.
Schreiber, R. L. (2004), *Neue Wege im Naturschutz. Wie muss Nachhaltigkeit kommuniziert werden?,* available at: www.ask-eu.de (accessed 12 April 2011).
Schretzmann, R. *(2011), Nachhaltigkeit – eine deutsche Spezialität!? Das Internationale Jahr der Wälder 2011,* aid-PresseInfo, 9 March 2011.
Schretzmann, R. *et al.,* (2006), *Wald mit Zukunft. Nachhaltige Forstwirtschaft in Deutschland,* aid-Heft 1478/2006, Bonn.
Spindler, Ines (2010), *Verpflegungskonzept für Schulbauernhöfe orientiert am Leitbild der Nachhaltigkeit,* Bachelorarbeit an der Fachhochschule Osnabrück, Studiengang Ökotrophologie, Osnabrück.
SRU, Der Rat von Sachverständigen für Umweltfragen (1994), *Umweltgutachten 1994. Für eine dauerhaft-umweltgerechte Entwicklung,* Verlag Metzler-Poeschel, Stuttgart.
Stahlmann, V. (2008), *Lernziel: Ökonomie der Nachhaltigkeit. Eine anwendungsorientierte Übersicht,* oekom Verlag München.
Vitols, K. (2011), *Nachhaltigkeit – Unternehmensverantwortung – Mitbestimmung. Ein Literaturbericht zur Debatte über CSR,* edition sigma, Berlin.
Vogt, M (2009), *Prinzip Nachhaltigkeit. Ein Entwurf aus theologisch-ethischer Perspektive,* oekom Verlag, München.
Vogt, M. (2010*), Maßstäbe einer nachhaltigen Unternehmensführung aus der Sicht christlicher Sozialethik und Wirtschaftsanthropologie,* paper presented at the "Erstes Deutsches Eliteforum zur Nachhaltigkeit der LMU München" on 28th October (manuscript).
v. Weizsäcker, E. U. (1992), *Erdpolitik. Ökologische Realpolitik an der Schwelle zum Jahrhundert der Umwelt,* Wissenschaftliche Buchgesellschaft, Darmstadt.

Sustainability and Climate Change

Ian Jenkins

> *'Each generation needs to regard itself not as owning the assets of society but as taking care of them; it has inherited a treasure from the past which it is its duty to pass on, augmented if possible but at any rate not depleted, to future generations'*
>
> Edmund Burke, British 18th Century Philosopher[1]

Preamble

Sustainability is now an important agenda item for tourism (Hall and Lew, 1998). That said, issues of sustainability are complicated by the threat of climate change, presenting the tourism industry with considerable negative impacts. Depletion of resources and the modification of tourist destinations through climate shift, will exacerbate the already strained systems of mass tourism destinations (UNWTO, 2008; Jenkins 2011). Climate change, combined with sustainable development, will inevitably engineer new 'successful' tourist locations, as a result of managers and policy makers developing innovative ways to manage tourist destinations, perhaps changing the tourism industry irrevocably (UNWTO, 2008). Certainly, the development of new forms of tourism, incorporating niche and eco-tourism products, may well herald the demise of the mass tourism market as we know it today.

There will be a need to look at linking the strategies of climate change with those of sustainable development (SD). In many cases there is not, necessarily, a conflict, as the environment and human society are the main focus of both tourism and sustainable development. The difficulty, perhaps, is in trying to synergize the management strategies of both approaches, especially where conflicts might occur. Hence, there appear to be a number of paradoxes that climate change and sustainable development might engender.

It appears that tourism resources will have to be carefully managed, possibly resulting in the decline of mass tourism markets and the emergence of different types of tourism and tourists. Development of niche tourism

---

[1] Quoted by Bryan Magee, Burke the Supreme Conservative, in the book ,The Story of Philosophy

destinations and use of renewable resources with sustainable transport networks now seems to be tourism's future *golden egg* with far more domestic tourism being developed and limits on international travel.

The Predictions of Climate Change

The phenomenon of climate change although presented as being recent, originated in the 1970s when 'environment damage' was on the agenda of a number of important organisations; however, this was very much tangential and evolved from the 'Hippy' and 'Green Movements' of the 1960s. Out of this era emerged organisations such as Friends of the Earth (FOE) and Greenpeace who are currently the driving force in tackling climate change (Greenpeace 2010). These organisations have now become socially acceptable (no longer pariahs) and pivotal to the movement tackling climate change. Interestingly, the main environmental concern of the 1970s was not global warming but global cooling! (Pearce 2010). This highlights, to some extent, the problem of predictive climate modeling and the variables that are relied upon to forecast the future climate (Pearce, 2010). Global warming is now the main dictum of these environmental lobbying bodies and it is asserted by many, that the science of global warming is now proven, although protagonists still exist who challenge this (Pearce, 2010).

As most students of statistics will know, *proven*, is rather an emotive word, suggesting certainty, which in statistics is never wholly the case. However, the body of evidence and the eminent scientists who support this strong assertion of global warming are difficult to argue with (Black, 2010). What becomes apparent is that man's population growth and the concomitant resulting strains on resources, inevitably impacts upon the planet and its assets. As a consequence, global warming has proffered an excellent platform to support the dictum of sustainability and can now be strongly linked to future success of global economies (Scott, 2011).

The science of climate change has produced some useful predictions that can be linked and associated with changes in tourism and its products. The predictions can be summarised as follows:

- Changes in weather patterns
- More droughts
- More severe weather conditions
- Rise in sea levels

All these predictions seem rather simplistic, but have the potential for massive change to economic activity and in particular, tourism. Weather is a primary resource for tourists and tourist choices, therefore changes to weather patterns will engender changes to tourism. The unseasonable snow in Northern Europe in December 2010, demonstrated the chaos this can bring to transport, resulting in the closure of many northern European airports causing huge travel disruption (Millward *et al.*, 2010).

Additionally, the transferability of tourism from one part of the globe to another is now incredibly quick and can cause economic shocks for tourist destinations that do not address many of the issues. One good example of this relates to Alpine destinations. Over the last 20 years they have received unpredictable snow falls, with the resultant transfer of tourists to alternative global destinations. Although not decimating European destinations, the destinations of Canada and USA benefited, while having a profound effect upon the ski tourism market, especially the development of artificial snow, which now seems to be 'standard' for most major ski resorts (Responsible Skiing, 2010). This demonstrates the global nature of tourism and how markets can unexpectedly change from one destination to another and from one year to another.

Growth of Sustainability

The importance of sustainability, as noted in the last section, can be seen as the product of the environmental movements of the 1970s. It has taken some 40 years to get to the phase of development where tourism companies now have to take notice and consider sustainability as part of their product. A quick review of the media will identify clear signs of tourist companies using sustainability as key components of their products, with even air transport eulogising about the importance of sustainability and climate change (Virgin Atlantic 2010). For example, 'responsible tourism' has now become an important tourism maxim, raising concerns about the ethics of tourism products and the transport used to arrive at and travel within destinations. Concerns focus on: flights to long haul locations, use of resources while at a destination and tourism products and experiences. Companies are switching to responsible tourism products reflecting this transformation in the market.

A good exemplar of this change can be illustrated through the product known as 'Five Responsible Tribal Experiences'. This is designed to allow tourists' access to native Indians in South America (Hammond 2010). It is also argued that 'tribal visits can be mutually rewarding and enlightening encounters

– or, they can be excruciating and exploitative, even seriously damaging.' (Hammond, 2010, p. 71). This emphasises the need to manage and consider the impact of tourism on sensitive cultural and environmental destinations (WTM, 2010).

There is evidence that perhaps all sectors of the industry are now considering the notion of responsible tourism, which is linked very closely to the ideals of sustainability. Even major tour operators such as Thomas Cook appear to be fully embracing the need for SD (Thomas Cook, 2011). The 'Virgin Responsible Tourism' awards certainly go a long way in emphasising this development and the need for more and more companies to try and engage with sustainability and climate change (Virgin Holidays, 2011). Nonetheless, there is a paradox here; Virgin's image is associated with transport (aircraft, trains and holidays), which is concomitant to the burning of fossil fuels that contribute to global warming. That said, Virgin is cautious to emphasise that they are trying to ensure a tradeoff between the contribution to climate change through their carbon footprint and the benefits that tourism can bring to guests and hosts (Virgin Holidays, 2010).

What is also apparent when talking to providers is how much consumers are really aware of the importance of sustainability and the types of products that they are consuming: in essence do they care? In a recent research study of adventure tourism operators, although some companies are attempting to address sustainable development, many customers are simply not interested. For example any 'over burdening' of the concept of sustainability on the website or marketing material, has been cited by some operators as simply a 'turn-off' for many consumers (Jenkins *et al.*, 2010). Some companies do not exhibit any clear delineation of sustainability in their products and their websites usually reflect this (Jenkins *et al.*, 2011).

However, at the other end of the spectrum there are also companies that clearly extol the virtues of sustainable approaches. One such company which is clearly evangelical about both the product and the environment is The TYF Group in St David's, Wales, UK. Their website is embedded with environmental controls, sustainability and the impact of climate and its effects on the product that they offer (TYF, 2010). Their philosophy appears to be one of 'educating the client'. Also, as noted above, there are many responsible tourism companies that try to ensure that the customer does have a truly sustainable experience from their tourism adventures (Jenkins and Clark, 2010; TYF, 2010).

To a greater extent the growth of National Parks has also reflected the importance that society is now putting upon nature and sustainable methods of delivery (Wheeler, 2005; PCNP, 2010). Certainly, in the UK conservation is 'king' over recreational activities and the need to preserve the environment for future generations. This has also been reflected in the way that National Park policies are trying to incorporate elements of employment and sustainable communities as guardians of the parks and living organisms rather than fossilised museums (ENPA, 2010). Interestingly, TYF is located within the Pembrokeshire Coastal National Park, which may be one reason why the Company is geared towards sustainability.

Eagles and McCool's (2000) model of sustainability (see Figure 1) illustrates admirably the complex and interactive relationship between tourism and the environment. Here again there is clear emphasis on the economic benefits and costs that tourism brings to a community, which appears to be an essential element in the model of National Park sustainability. This is often lost in some of the images and debates about tourism, where the emphasis is on the environment rather than the notion of employment and also employment practices. A clear linkage here is the perception of community involvement in tourism and sustainability measures, highlighting the importance of employment; especially that of local employers and the idea of equity of employment for locals. By employing local residents and ensuring that monies go to them, money is maintained within the community and the impact of leakage from tourism reduced (Zeppel, 1998). The ideology of sustainability is also related to the use of local goods and services again ensuring employment within the locale. This is also beneficial to climate change as it reduces the carbon footprint of transporting goods and services. However, one comment that was given to the author by a tourism operator, relates to cost-benefit of using local goods (Jenkins *et al.*, 2010). It is evident that buying locally is not *always* the most cost effective. Simply buying bread locally for an adventure centre, can add thousands of pounds to the running costs rather than sourcing from a supermarket.

Sustainability also raises the issue of how food is produced and transported together with the carbon footprint it produces. In addition, there are moral issues relating to how some goods are produced; for example the use of child labour, unfair wage structures and poor working conditions. Once more, considered action should be given to the goods that foster sustainable practices in developing countries, rather than simply cost benefit analysis to the company. One such company that seems to consider climate change and sustainable development is Patagonia, where the emphasis is upon the production of goods from recycled clothes and other carbon reduction measures (Patagonia, 2011).

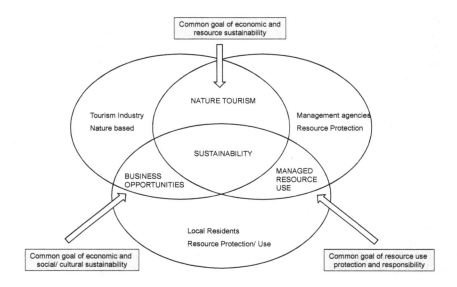

Figure 1: Shared goals for sustainability in the tourism industry, the community and park resources (Eagles and McCool, 2000), adapted

Clearly the importance and growth of sustainability in tourism has created new ways of thinking about and using, resources for tourism. These new paradigms would not have come about were it not for the revivifying gaze on the environment and how the planet might be sustained for future generations. The growth of sustainability has also permeated into less obvious establishments related to tourism, such as universities. The Copernicus network (Copernicus Campus, 2005) and also government authorities (HEFCE, 2009) such as the EU, now expect these organisations (universities) to be sustainable not only in their buildings, but also their educational courses (Copernicus Campus, 2005).

Paradox of Climate Change

Evaluating the latest news reports seems to imply that climate change has never previously occurred. As is evident from historical records, there has always been climate change and the emergence and extinction of species is not a new phenomenon. Without climate change human beings would not be here on earth and climate change catastrophes probably allowed humans to evolve. That said, the current debate appears to hinge upon the speed of exponential change rather than change itself (UNWTO, 2008). As with all change there will be some winners and some losers; but to what extent will this really affect present tourism products and tourists? As with all predictions this is difficult to calculate but what can be recognised are some aspects of trends, indicating a shift in the consumption patterns of tourist products. Ironically climate change has also emphasised the need for sustainable policies (Scott, 2011) and these policies need to go beyond the simply environmental. If anything, climate change has enhanced the sustainability agenda. Yet it is difficult to ascertain to what extent the public and consumers are convinced of the immediacy of the affect of climate change on their everyday lives and concomitantly their holidays (see above text on consumer attitudes).

A growing contributor to climate change is that of air transport, now allegedly at 2-5% of global carbon emissions (depending on which statistic you accept). It is also predicted that this form of transport will grow over the next 50 years (RAE, 2005). If society were to limit growth or encourage reduction in transport how would this affect the tourism industry? To encourage the growth of domestic tourism would result in a reduction in GDP for poorer countries that rely heavily upon tourism and would have substantial economic consequences for development, growth and sustainable development in those countries. Yet, if carbon reduction targets are not reached the weather systems of the globe may change to the extent that current products of tourism, based on climate, would be completely different, resulting in massive disruption to mass tourism patterns (UNWTO, 2008). For example, increased tropical storms and the extension of the storm season in tropical regions would affect current mass tourism destinations, reducing demand and thereby restricting tourism income or if the patterns continue, changing tourism flows entirely.

Returning to consumption of seasonal goods seems to be sensible, rather than transporting goods thousands of miles. So climate change or the prevention of climate change is certainly a supporter of sustainable development relating to the consumption of local goods (Scott, 2011). It is asserted that this must be a sound approach for the support of global local communities. But again a paradox arises: if developing countries do not export their goods globally, how are they to grow economically without global trade?

New Management Paradigms

Sustainable management appears a key element in the future of establishing SD and a reduction in climate change. Put simply, it is about the efficient and effective control of resources; optimising the enjoyment of tourists, while maintaining the environment (natural and human, social/economic) in a way that future generations can enjoy the benefits that society currently enjoys.

It is asserted that levels of management for sustainability are seen on a number of geographical scales: global, national, regional and community. The polemic is possibly how these interact with each other and who should manage which resources?

Pender and Sharpley 2005 (see Figure 2) note three types of management, not necessarily on a geographical scale but more on the resource side of the tourism industry. Firstly, physical resources; secondly, management of visitors; and thirdly, the management of sustainable developments. As can be seen from the model the idea seems to be that the guiding principles of sustainability are to be incorporated as follows:

Principles of sustainable tourism development: a summary

- "The conservation and sustainable use of natural, social and cultural resources is crucial. Therefore, tourism should be planned and managed within environmental limits and with due regard for the long-term appropriate use of natural and human resources.
- Tourism planning, development and operation should be integrated into national and local sustainable development strategies. In particular, consideration should be given to different types of tourism development and how they link with existing land and resource uses and socio-cultural factors.
- Tourism should support a wide range of local economic activities, taking environmental costs and benefits into account, but should not be permitted to become an activity which dominates the economic base of an area.
- Local communities should be encouraged and expected to participate in the planning, development and control of tourism with the support of government and the industry. Particular attention should be paid to involving indigenous people, women and minority groups to ensure the equitable distribution of the benefits of tourism.
- All organisations and individuals should respect the culture, the economy, and the way of life, the environment and political structures in the destination area.
- All stakeholders within tourism should be educated about the need to develop more sustainable forms of tourism. This includes staff training and raising awareness through education and marketing tourism responsibly of sustainability issues among host communities and tourists themselves.

Sustainability and Climate Change 41

- Research should be undertaken throughout all stages of tourism development and operation to monitor impacts, to identify problems and to allow local people and others to respond to changes and to take advantage of opportunities.
- All agencies, organizations, businesses and individuals should co-operate and work together to avoid potential conflict and to optimize the benefits to all involved in the development and management of tourism."

(Pender and Sharpley, 2005, p. 269)

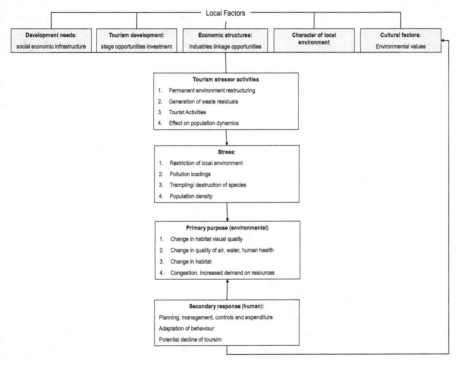

Figure 2: A model of the study of the tourism-environment relationship (Pender and Sharpley, 2005), adapted

Pender and Sharpley's model reflects the principle of amelioration which can be developed and help identify the needs of all stakeholders to form coherent sustainable policies. Added to this, there is now the spectre of climate change and how this will affect the elements of each of these principles. Perhaps management needs to be related to who has the greater influence: 'top down or the bottom-up', that is to say experts or communities. The debate over the importance of giving gravitas to communities and their interests has been a long running one, but the often forgotten maxim is that a community is not homogenous and often has divisive and competing interests. Consequently, the community does not always 'know what is best' for the location. The community level is further complicated by macro climate change policies and how these might affect micro scale management (community level). This is certainly an important issue (linkage between Macro and Micro Scales) if climate change is to be halted or seriously addressed. Amelioration of global, national and local tourism is required to ensure cohesive and agreed management policies at destinations. How power and executive control is devolved will be a crucial point for success.

Mass versus Niche Tourism

Perhaps the main emphasis is to reduce the consumption of mass tourism and move to micro or niche tourism markets (Cusicka *et al.,* 2010). But can the current mass tourist be persuaded to pay more and have fewer holidays? This might be the outcome of a move to a niche tourism market. Would this be the outcome of reducing mass tourism? The economic model of mass tourism is akin to that of supermarkets where volume rather than price and quality is important. Clearly, there is an impetus to move to a more qualitative experiential experience than the current mass tourism model of *volume* rather than *quality*. It is argued that the low volume high quality paradigm is based upon certain principles that would benefit all:

Principles such as appropriate pay, use of local rather than global resources, developing renewable energy. Moving to smaller scale tourism will, to some extent, have limited and more manageable impacts upon the environment and possibly encourage the development of local skills, based upon the cultural tenets of the destination; further supporting local communities (Cusicka *et al.,* 2010).

This change seems a positive one for destinations that are environmentally and culturally sensitive, but how would this work in cities and urban areas, or is there indeed a need for this? By their nature cities are quite robust at absorbing tourists. Studies have shown that little animosity to tourists is to be found in large cities and the contribution that tourism makes is important but not necessarily a dependent source of GDP (Financial Info., 2012).

The balance between mass tourism and niche tourism is certainly shifting and it appears that the rise of niche tourism is growing (Novelli, 2005; Jenkins, 2006). Moving to more sustainable niche product led markets could be helpful in reducing climate change. The milieu of niche tourism is to some extent far more controllable than that of mass tourism; but could niche tourism also be more vulnerable? By its very nature niche tourism is possibly less competitive, as its character is to be highly specialized, therefore having narrow market appeal (Jenkins, 2006). It is suggested that education of tourists to these possible product changes, might be necessary; but how can this be achieved? Educating tourists is asserted as being somewhat controversial and difficult to accomplish especially in a market led economy.

There is an assumption that mass tourism is still linked to less well educated tourists. Mass tourism could also be linked to those corporations who see tourist damage being a part of the products, choosing quick profits over longer term gains through sustainable products. Consequently, it is asserted that the mass tourism market is likely to have more difficulty changing consumers' attitudes and expectations. However, the example of cigarettes is a useful one. 50 years ago it would have seemed highly unlikely that cigarette smokers and their damaging smoke would eventually become pariahs. So why not mass tourism? Surely the spectre of global warming and climate change has greater imperative than the humble cigarette? The pillorying and shunning of companies and products that are not sustainable could be a useful policy instrument and act to encourage positive sustainable policies for mass tourists.

Hence, the policy to reduce mass tourism and emphasise the development of niche tourism seems a sagacious response to the delivery of sustainable developments and the reduction of climate change. It simply needs determination and policies (legislation if necessary) to do this. An interesting perspective is that niche tourism does not necessarily mean a small number of tourist visitors, it can be in the millions (Jenkins, 2006) which seems to some extent a paradox and perhaps this component of niche tourism needs to be clearly redefined towards a more common understanding of what a niche tourism market is: small, specialised and limited (Jenkins, 2006). Surely, the development of niche tourism would support the key principles for sustainable development, far more than the current mass tourism market, which in some destinations has little regard for the environment, or the economic and social values of employees and community.

Problems of Persuasion

The essence of the current climate debate and the sustainability vernacular seems to be that of persuasion. It is evident that neither climate change nor SD are ever very far from the news and the importance of both is consistently emphasised (Black, 2010). However there appears to be little evidence illustrating what the consumer really thinks about these two issues. To what extent do ordinary citizens worry about climate and ensuring that future generations are not adversely affected by our current consumption of resources?

The media is trying to produce a case for immediate action which can be seen from a number of perspectives such as a focus on unseasonable weather and linkage with climate change. Yet consensus on this is not clear as illustrated by a number of organisations, the public and companies. The climate summits in Copenhagen and Cancun (2010) possibly illustrate the lack of consensus at government level, consequently how much less consensus at consumer and citizen's level? (Black, 2010). This seems reemphasized in the latest and significant summit of Rio+20, where once again little, if any, progress has been made. Black notes, 'Environment and development charities say the Rio+20 agreement is too weak to tackle social and environmental crises. Gro Harlem Brundtland, author of a major UN sustainable development report 25 years ago, said corporate power was one reason for lack of progress.' (Black, 2012).

This seems a very bleak outlook and emphasises a pressing need for ensuring reduction in carbon output and conserving/preserving the environment for future generations. It is asserted that persuasion and the need to change people's attitudes and habits are important ways to achieve this.

Attitude change is one of the key success factors in combating climate change and ensuring a more sustainable environment. Attitudes can be changed and economic penalties can certainly be a motivator. An example illustrating this is from the Canton of Fribourg, in Switzerland, which operates a strict recycling regime with a monetary perspective. Official orange bags are the only means of disposing of rubbish that is non-recyclable and these cost approximately £1.50 per bag. The perspective of paying this fee for disposal has certainly galvanised the citizens, including the author, into recycling 80 % of consumer rubbish. Switzerland is often cited as an example of sound environmental policies and it could be argued that other countries could easily follow given the right pressures (Confederation Suisse, 2010).

This simple example perhaps demonstrates the motivation for change to be one of economics and this is also an issue that is constantly identified by sustainable transport experts who point out that the car is still much cheaper than public transport (RAE, 2005). But there are clear examples where cost and legislation can reduce the use of cars. Most major cities of the world now have public transport systems that are overall cheaper and more efficient than using private transport. London has high car parking charges and also congestion charges, which means that unless you are visiting briefly, private transport is clearly more expensive and inefficient to use. Zermatt in Switzerland is an example where private transport is prohibited and seems not to have had a detrimental effect upon the destination or the popularity of the product (Rough Guide, 2006). Perhaps similar policies need to be enacted in other mass tourism destinations.

If attitudes can be changed towards rubbish disposal and recycling, then it seems fair to assume that it would also be possible for future tourists to adopt sustainable attitudes. Perhaps SD should be the main focus at all destinations. Indeed there is evidence to suggest that tourists, while on holiday, can be more receptive to adopting/adapting to new attitudes and ways of thinking (Jenkins *et al.*, 2010).

Interestingly, some destinations have adopted tourist visas and limitations on visitor numbers, for example Bhutan. "With careful planning and management of the industry and the appropriate inputs, the tourism industry in Bhutan could well surpass its economic expectations without eroding the cultural and environment of the country." (Bhutan Excursions, 2010, p. 1)

Why not take this one step further, especially for less popular destinations such as eco-sensitive destinations? Tourist tests for entry could be introduced, the idea being to encourage education and change. This could be particularly relevant for either environmental or culturally sensitive destinations. Perhaps what is needed are environmental and cultural visas which are destination specific, these visas only being issued through the tourist producing evidence of cultural and environmental awareness.

Motivations for Change

Consumers are the driving force in a market economy. However, recent studies with adventure tourism operators and National Park providers manifestly identify moderate to low interest by consumers in sustainability and climate change (Jenkins *et al.*, 2010). Tourists simply want the experiential outcome from the product they have bought and are not really engaged in the practice of sustainability or interested in climate change. It can be postulated that for many these are, to a large extent, abstract concepts with little tangibility. Only if the tourist is affected directly will there be an immediate effect.

As discussed above, changing consumer behaviour is possibly the biggest challenge for sustainability. It can be postulated that attempts to persuade the consumer to change have been met with mute resistance. The FAIRTRADE Certification Mark is an example of attempts to motivate the consumer to embrace sustainable policies but which has taken some considerable time to be accepted.

This symbol is now established worldwide and there has been increasing growth of products with this logo (Fairtrade Foundation, 2010; 2011). Perhaps, what is needed is an independent certification system, similar to the Fairtrade system, for tourism. The consumer will then be aware, that by purchasing this product, there is some sustainable benefit.

Secondly, businesses supposedly produce services and goods for customers, so if customers do not really want sustainable goods why provide them? This is a conundrum that is not easily solved and as has been detailed earlier, some companies are making great efforts to be environmentally friendly and sustainable (TYF, 2010; Virgin Holidays, 2010). Virgin is now offering niche holidays called Human Nature Collections which aim to: "Sample true local flavour, give something back to your host communities, go on truly authentic adventures that take steps to look after the environment and take you away from the crowds. Our Human Nature Collection is all about balancing unforgettable experiences with more responsible travel choices – holidays that are good for the soul!" (Virgin Holidays, 2010, p. 1). This must be regarded as a step in the right direction and a good example of responsible tourism linked to sustainable development, illustrating that tourism can be a vanguard for these types of products.

The notion of Corporate Social Responsibility (CSR) is an important axiom in the sustainability/climate debate if there is to be change by the tourism industry towards embracing climate change. As indicated earlier in this chapter, some companies are clearly now engaging with sustainability and also ensuring that their products and operations are carbon neutral (Kasim, 2009; TYF, 2010). The example of TYF (TYF, 2010) is an exemplar, but it is also evident that this has not been achieved simply through customer demand. The policy seems to have been management driven displaying high CSR emphasising the image the Company wishes to project. Interestingly, in 2008-9 during the global recession the number of TYF's customers was significantly higher than previous years, possibly reflecting that sustainable environmental policies can be also profitable (Jenkins *et al.,* 2010).

Unfortunately, there are also clear examples where the sustainable image of a company can be seriously questioned; the tragic disaster of summer 2010 and the Gulf of Mexico oil spill is one such example of a company, BP, which claims to be an environmentally friendly corporation. The oil spillage is possibly the worst ever in North America and the Company will find it hard to recover from its image as a sustainable energy company that has stated that the environment and tackling climate change is part of its raison d'être (BBC, 2010).

Thirdly, change can also be brought about by governments and the policies that they adopt for the protection of their citizens and the environment that they inhabit (Kasim, 2009). Unfortunately, this is usually the preserve of rich developed nations, although attempts have been made by less developed nations and sustained by agencies such as the United Nations. The establishment of National Parks and the legislation relating to employment and the environment are all worthy actions that can help in the reduction of climate change and the support for sustainable future (PCNP, 2010). The actions of governments to ban certain products and trade goods that are not sustainable are sensible ways to reduce the demand for goods which are endangered or contribute to poor living standards. Ensuring economic support for projects can only be seen as positive and essential resources for establishment of frameworks that will endeavour to support motivations for change (Kasim, 2009). Governments also have an important role to play in being a significant agency for change, through education and the need to educate future generations in terms of climate management and sustainable measures, by supporting universities and their research outputs (Kasim, 2009; Copernicus Campus, 2005).

Fourthly, NGOs are lobby organisations and motivators, able to pressurise governments, citizens and businesses to transform (Wiemers, 2010). As mentioned earlier, Greenpeace, FoE, SAS (Surfers Against Sewage) and Tourism Concern have been successful in introducing important policy decisions and also encouraging the 'powers' to change their approach to environmental and sustainable issues. SAS is a classic example of this and their campaign to ensure the continued cleanliness of the UK's coastal water has been very successful. They can certainly be seen as an organisation that has helped to rejuvenate the UK's seaside for future generations ensuring that many of the beaches are now blue flags (SAS, 2010).

Sadly, it is asserted that the consumer will only change as a result of two extreme measures: firstly, governments and world travel organisations enforcing conformity to carbon reduction targets together with the development of policies that enhance social and cultural sustainability. Secondly, that there is such cataclysmic climate change that the market has to transform to ameliorate the weather patterns which will severely disrupt global tourism and transport systems.

Perhaps, human nature being what it is, the latter will be the most likely outcome, especially as the latest Climate Summits of Copenhagen and Cancun (2010) seemed to reflect a lack of global agreement and action needed to impede the accelerating impacts of climate change (Black, 2010).

Conclusions

Climate change has clearly heightened the debate relating to sustainability and in many respects the two are closely linked. Reduction of man-made climate change can only be seen in terms of a sustainable policy that can benefit future generations. Sustainability is now firmly fixed on the agenda of all governments, tourism organisations and some tourism companies. However, persuading people to change seems a long way off, although there are glimmers of hope. Some companies are clearly encouraging consumers to adopt sustainable measures and attitudes. However, evidence seems to indicate that consumers still feel that the experience of the holiday takes precedence over the importance of sustainability. A move away from mass tourism towards niche tourism seems a sensible way forward, but with emerging economies and developing nations yet to have had their experience of mass tourism will this be a sensible or achievable global policy?

It is hoped governments will act to reduce the effects of man-induced climate change. If this does not happen then the weather will surely force a new regime of tourism upon us; as with past generations adaptation to change will be essential. Possibly the new tourist order will be an exponential growth of local tourism niches, using local products and local labour.

References

BBC (2010), "Gulf of Mexico oil leak 'worst US environment disaster', US & Canada", BBC London, available at: http://www.bbc.co.uk/news/10194335 (accessed 30 May 2010).

Bhutan Excursions (2010), "Tourism in Bhutan and its sustainability", November 5, 2010, Filed Under Articles on Bhutan, Comment, Thimphu, Bhutan, available at: http://www.bhutantour.bt/bhutan-articles/tourism-in-bhutan-and-its-sustainability.html (accessed 20 December 2010).

Black, R. (2010), "Climate change warning at UN Cancun summit", BBC News, London, available at: http://www.bbc.co.uk/news/science-environment-11939768 (accessed 08 December 2010).

Richard, B. (2012), "Rio Summit Ends with Warning on Corporate Power", BBC News, 23 June 2012, London, available at: http://www.bbc.co.uk/news/science-environment-18561223, (accessed 29 June 2012).

Confédération Suisse (2010), Sustainable Development Strategy, Federal Office of Spatial Development ARE, available at: http://www.are.admin.ch (accessed 22 February 2011).

Copernicus Campus (2005), "COPERNICUS-Guidelines for Sustainable Development in the European Higher Education Area", *How to incorporate the principles of sustainable development into the Bologna Process*, COPERNICUS-CAMPUS Sustainability Center, University Oldenburg, Oldenburg.

Cusicka, J., McClureb, B. and Linda Cox L. (2010), "Representations of Ecotourism in the Hawaiian Islands: a content analysis of local media Journal of Ecotourism", Vol. 9 No. 1, March 2010, Routledge, London, pp. 21–35.

Eagles, P.F.J. and McCool, S. F. (2000), *Tourism In National Parks and Protected Areas: Planning & Management*, CABI, Wallingford.

ENPA (2010), *Sustainable Tourism in UK National Parks Case studies – July 2010*, English National Park Authorities Association, London.

Fairtrade Foundation (2010), "Logo", available at: http://www.fairtrade.org.uk/, (accessed 21 June 2010).

Fairtrade Foundation (2011), "Global Fairtrade Sales Increase by 47%", available at: http://www.fairtrade.org.uk/producers/default.aspx (accessed 22 February 2011)

Financial Info (2012), "The City Tourism has Become the New Engine of Economic Growth in Europe", *Financial Info & Financial News*, available at: http://www.financialinfo.co/ (accessed on 24 June 2012).

Greenpeace (2010), "History", Greenpeace, available at: http://www.greenpeace.org/usa/en/about/history/ (accessed 22 February 2011).

Hall, M. C. and Lew, A. A. (1998), *Sustainable Tourism: A geographical Perspective*, Addison Wesley Longman, Harlow.

Hammond, R (2010), "Clash of Cultures", *Geographical*, Vol. 82 No. 6, pp. 71-72.

HEFCE (2009), *Sustainable development in higher education, 2008, update to strategic, statement and action plan*, HEFCE, London.

Jenkins, I. S. (2006), *Postmodern Tourism Niches: UK Literary Festivals And Their Importance For Tourism Destination Development*, PhD Thesis, University of Wales, Swansea.

Jenkins, I. S. (2011), "Risk Management Issues and Challenges", in Jones, A. and Phillips, M., *Disappearing Destinations: Climate Change and Future Challenges for Coastal Tourism*, Cabi, Wallingford.

Jenkins, I. S., Rios-Morales R M and Cevera R. (2011), *Professed Sustainability of Caribbean Companies: Case Study of Internet Evaluation of Company Websites as Vicarious Information Systems for Company Products*, AGA Conference Presentation, January 2011, Martinique.

Jenkins, I. S., Rios-Morales, R. M. and Clark, S. (2010), "Ambiguities of Sustainability and Operations Ascribed to Adventure Tourism Companies that use National Parks as a Tourism Resource: A Comparative Study Switzerland And Wales", EuroMed, Conference Presentation, November 2010, Cyprus.

Kasim, A. (2009), "Managerial attitudes towards environmental management amongsmall and medium hotels in Kuala Lumpur", Journal of Sustainable Tourism, Vol. 17 No. 6, pp. 709–725.

Magee, B. (2010), *The Story of Philosophy*, Dorling Kindersley, London.

Millward, D., Evans, M. and Adams, S. (2010), "UK snow chaos: hundreds more flights cancelled as BAA criticism intensifies", The Telegraph, On-Line, London, available at: http://www.telegraph.co.uk/topics/weather/8213613/UK-snow-chaos-hundreds-more-flights-cancelled-as-BAA-criticism-intensifies.html (accessed 23 February 2010).

Novelli, M. (2005), (Ed.), *Niche tourism contemporary issues, trends and cases*, Elsevier, London.

Patagonia (2011), Materials Recycled Polyester, available at: http://www.patagonia.com/eu/en GB (accessed 22 February 2011).

PCNP (2010), "Pembrokeshire Coast National Park Local Development Plan", ADOPTION STATEMENT, available at: http://www.pcnpa.org.uk/Files/Files/dev%20plans/AdoptionStatement.pdf, PCNP, Pembroke Dock (accessed 8 December 2010).

Pearce, F. (2010), *The Climate Files: The Battle for the Truth about Global Warming*, Guardian Books, London.

Pender, L. and Sharpley, R. (Eds.), (2005), *The Management of Tourism*, Sage, London

RAE (2005), *Transport 2005: The Route to Sustainable Wealth Creation*, The Royal Academy of Engineering, London.

Responsible Skiing (2010), "Skiing and Climate Change", VRIT Associates Ltd. availbale at: http://www.responsibleskiing.com/skiing--climate-change.html (accessed 22 February 2011).

Rough Guide (2006), *The Rough Guide to Switzerland*, Penguin Books Ltd., London.

SAS (Surfers Against Sewage) (2010), "Surfers Warn Water Industry That Pride Comes Before A Fall", SAS, St Agnes, available at: http://www.sas.org.uk/news/2010/11/15/surfers-warn-water-industry-that-pride-comes-before-a-fall/ (accessed 8 December 2010).

Scott, D, (2011), "Why Sustainable Tourist Must Address Climate Change", *Journal of Sustainable Tourism*, Vol. 19, No.1, pp. 17-34.
Thomas Cook (2011), "Sustainable Tourism", available at: http://www.thomascook.com/sustainable-tourism/ (accessed 22 February 2011).
TYF (2010), "People, Planet and Place", TYF, St Davids, available at: http://www.tyf.com/?c=environment (accessed 8 December 2010).
UNWTO (2008), "Climate Change and Tourism, Responding to Global Challenges", World Tourism Organization and United Nations Environment Programme, Madrid.
Virgin Atlantic (2010), "Change is in the Air", available at: http://changeisintheair.virginatlantic.com/, (accessed 22 February 2011).
Virgin Holidays (2010), Human Nature Collection, availbale at: http://www.virginholidays.co.uk/brochures/human_nature/online, Virgin Holidays, Crawley (accessed 8 December 2010).
Virgin Holidays (2011), "Responsible Tourism", Virgin Holidays Ltd., available at: http://www.virginholidays.co.uk (accessed 22 February 2011).
Wheeler, N. (2005), PCNP (Pembrokeshire Coast National Park Authority), Environmental Policy: Declaration, available at: Pembrokeshirecoast.org.uk, PCNP, Aenvironmentalpolicy.doc PCNP, Pembroke Dock (accessed 8 December 2010).
Wiemers, J. (2010), "Climate NGO Partnerships: WWF and Climate Group team up with business", CCC (Climate Change Corporation) London, available at: http://www.climatechangecorp.com/ (accessed 8 December 2010).
WTM (2010), "The World's most Ambitions Campaign, Securing the Future of Travel and Tourism", Programme, WTM Responsible Tourism Programme, London.
Zeppel, H. (1998), "Land and Culture: Sustainable Tourism and Indigenous People", in Hall, M. C. and Lew, A. A., *Sustainable Tourism: A geographical Perspective*, Addison Wesley Longman, Harlow.

Sustainability and Health Tourism

Thomas Rieger

Introduction

The leisure time activities of many people have fundamentally changed during recent decades. Styles of individualisation, different consumer behaviours, consumption of fun and adventure, advanced globalisation, increasing luxury and a new health and body awareness are popular phenomena. These variables can characterise the changes in people's lifestyles and the tourism market has also been affected by these developments. This is especially so with types of health-oriented tourism where there is an increase in market share. Health, Fitness or Well-being have become important criteria for choosing a destination. This has presented new and interesting marketing approaches with remarkable economic potential.

When it comes to health tourism, physical and sporting activities are the main or even mandatory elements and outdoor sport is very popular because of increasing concerns related to the body and the natural environment (Deutscher Tourismus Verband, 2005). In Germany nearly 15 million people are engaged in outdoor sporting activities like hiking, biking, mountain-biking or Nordic-walking (Trittin, 2004). For many people and institutions the combination of outdoor sports and health tourism activities are seen as innate, because health promotion primarily engenders behavioural changes like physical activity, recreation or medical treatments.

Outdoor sporting activities, however, often use protected environmental destinations. Traditional regions are also affected by the enlargement of health related outdoor sports programs developing new tourism models. The continuing increase of this type of tourism will inevitably develop conflicts between customer-oriented products: in this case health or well-being and the use of outdoor resources. Against this background one of the major tasks of health or sports tourism providers is to ensure that their commodities also include a sustainable perspective, so that the regional environment is preserved.

By examining the past, it becomes perceptible that positive and negative effects of different forms of tourism (health tourism, sport tourism, adventure tourism, wellness tourism) are ubiquitous. Jost Krippendorf, in his 1975 publication, mentioned several negative consequences of tourism and its effect on the landscape and he mooted the suggestion of a more sustainable use of environmental resources. Subsequently, terms like 'soft travelling' or 'soft tourism' appeared in several publications (Krippendorf, 1982).

The following discussion, about the compatibility of nature with tourism, results from the acceptance of tourism companies to integrate ecological sustainable products into their portfolio. Environmentalism has become more and more recognised as an important strategic business factor.

The majority of health tourism developments have been primarily based on individual behaviour and lifestyle changes. Health and health promotion does not only mean the development of physical and psychological changes, akin to increasing sporting activities or reduction of mental stress, but also the development of sustaining local traditions and ecological environments. The current chapter illustrates this problem by developing scientific concepts and the use of valuable examples. The development of sporting and outdoor activities under sustainable conditions will also be discussed.

The State of Research

The list of relevant publications and research studies in the field of sustainable tourism has steadily increased in recent years (Butler, 1999; Holden, 2008; Miller, 2001).[1] Meanwhile different management strategies and guidelines have been published to strengthen sustainable development in tourism (Europarc Federation, 2002; Secretariat of the Convention on Biological Diversity, 2004). Many publications indicated, unquestioningly, the positive benefits of sustainability acting to improve tourism, because most of the principles of sustainable development are similar with many of the basic principles of sensible resource and environmental management (Pearce, 1995; Hall and Jenkins, 1995). In the late '80s and early '90s, many authors appeared to have accepted the basic proposition that sustainable development is inherently superior and useful for tourism, and that its adaption will solve many of the negative consequences of tourism impacts. Currently, the discussions are reflective. Several writers have argued that sustainable development is not always possible, nor even always appropriate (e.g. Wheeller, 1993; Wall, 1996). It should always depend on the specific circumstances of the destination. Furthermore, the publications do not speak with one voice concerning several aspects of sustainability. This

---

[1] Despite the large amount of different publications the research field has developed its own journal: the *Journal of Sustainable Tourism*, first published in 1993.

dissonance is demonstrated in finding a definitive definition, and owes its polemics to the lack of agreement and clarity over the meaning of the concept (Butler, 1999). A common sense research approach can be grounded on the notion, that every type of sustainable tourism development should seek a profitable, as well as an environmental and socially acceptable product (Becker *et al.,* 1996).

The field of health tourism is relatively uncharted within the topic of sustainability and literature has been published on this subject (Carrera and Bridges, 2006). Moreover, some papers deal with the economic developments and the potential of health tourism (García-Altés, 2005). The majority of authors agree that health tourism, with regard to different social and health care developments (e.g. demography, demand for more self-responsibility) has excellent growth prospects. Another obvious research focus lies with the reasons why tourists choose a specific destination (country, province, city) in order to make use of health treatments (Lee, 2009).

Analysing the current research, a gap emerges in relation to the important interactions between sustainability and health tourism. Concerning the topic of this chapter relating to sports tourism, it is virtually impossible to find any papers or articles of appropriate quality that evaluate this subject. Hence the idea is to develop a theoretical link between sustainability and health tourism that also incorporates aspects of sports tourism.

Sustainability – Key Elements of a Modern Concept in Tourism

The history of sustainability can be dated back to the 19th century and has its origins linked to forestry. The basic idea was to be profitable without destroying the soil and the local destination (Haber, 1994). The study of Meadows et al., (1972) identified the future of the world economy and sustainability, which could be seen as seminal at the time (Meadows, 1972). The foundations of today's debate are formed by the 'Brundtland Report' from 1987 and the conference in Rio de Janeiro of 1992, together with 'Agenda 21' (Rio Declaration). Since then exponential developments have taken place.

It is asserted that all definitions of sustainability are indistinct. The encyclopaedia of the Foundation Kathy Beys (2006) includes thirty-five definitions and the Foundation for the Rights of the Future Generations (2006) identifies almost sixty-three scientific definitions of sustainability. The definition of the World Commission on the Environment and Development, which is a part of the Brundtland Report, has a definition that is seen as useful to the current debate: "Humanity has the ability to make development sustainable to ensure that it meets the needs of the present without compromising the ability of future generations to meet their own needs" (World Commission on Environment and Development, 1987, p. 43).

This definition seems to be more acceptable and is found in much of the literature, acting as a guiding principle for sustainable development, by integrating its various perspectives. In essence it takes care of the needs of today's generation without jeopardising the options and chances of future generations. It also identifies economic, ecological and social aspects equally (World Commission on Environment and Development, 1987). Germany also strives to harmonise economic profit with the protection of environmental and social livelihoods. The international agenda should also be developed at a local scale.

Trying to develop an acceptable definition of sustainable tourism is also problematic. Butler (1999) lists seven different approaches. The World Tourism Organization (1993, p. 7) defined a useful and acceptable definition. Sustainable tourism is a type of "tourism which meets the needs of present tourists and host regions while protecting and enhancing opportunity for the future". Additionally, Bieger (2007) pointed out that sustainable development within tourism appears as a triangle and can be identified as a development which is based on the assets and not on the substance of the natural environment (landscape, biodiversity), the social environment (culture, identity, cohesion of local inhabitants) and the economy (image, substance of touristic businesses) (See Figure 1).

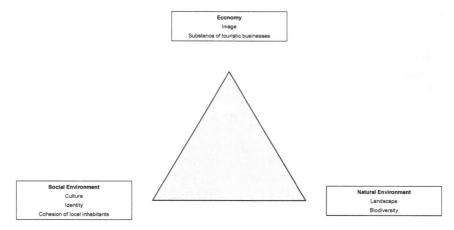

Figure 1:   Sustainable development triangle

Sustainability is an important criterion for future-oriented tourist activities due to the exponential development of tourism activities and the concomitant effects these have on the destination. Using the concept in Figure 1, it is asserted that sustainability in tourism means the harmonisation between the following dimensions: economic productivity, environmental tenability and social compatibleness. The dimensions have to be incorporated in sporting and health tourism concepts, but currently there is little evidence that this is the case.

Tourism and the economic dimension
International tourism is an important income generator of the world economy. Its economic significance is undisputed. In 2009 the global tourism market achieved nearly €611 billion (World Tourism Organization, 2010). Thus even emerging nations need to focus on tourism as a driving force for their economic development. The economic goals related to sustainable development in tourism are as follows (Vorlaufer, 1996): improvement of the balance of payments[2], employment creation, increase in incomes and narrowing of regional disparity[3]. Sustainable tourism also seeks these effects for its economy. These effects primarily depend on the main form of tourism, the size of the economy, the stage of development of the destination and also on the willingness of the government to support tourism (Aderhold et al., 2000).

Tourism and the ecological dimension
An undamaged environment is doubtless an important criterion in the context of sustainable development. For many destinations it is even the centre of their marketing concept. So the protection of the environment must be a self-interest for a tourism product. A fundamental burden on the environment is caused by tourism through infrastructure developments, especially mega tourist projects, which can cover large areas of land, for the development of new resorts or sports

---

[2] In terms of sustainable development the emphasis must lie on the net earnings not on the gross earnings. The net earnings also depend on the payments of the country (e.g. payments for food, beverages, energy, infrastructure, human resources) to maintain tourism. To increase the net earnings and to support sustainable development it is necessary that the country reduces its imports of goods and strengthens its own economy by focusing on home markets (Vorlaufer, 1996).

[3] A balance between the attractive tourist spots and the peripheral areas can be achieved by specific types of tourism (e.g. adventure tourism). Moreover, the government must intervene financially, because the reduction of regional disparity leads to a diversified and dynamic regional economy.

facilities, with the potential for massive ecological damage. Moreover, there are also questions of energy consumption together with waste and effluent disposal (e.g. water supply in dry regions). As well as the infrastructural improvements specific to tourism, there are also related tourist behaviours, which can lead to ecological problems. Several publications identify specific forms of sports tourism as being environmentally damaging. For example, playing golf on a wet green in an Egyptian resort at the Red Sea coast, or some forms of trekking in the Himalayas should be re-evaluated (Hinch and Higham, 2004). However, it is not only the incongruity between some sports tourism activity and the local characteristics, but also the frequency of activity and the density of tourists at a location. Both these factors play important roles in the protection of the environment. An unrestricted growth of both variables has to be managed properly.

Tourism and the social dimension
It is asserted that the social impacts of tourism are the most difficult to identify and manage. Moreover, it is irrefutable that tourism affects the socio-cultural dimension at a destination, because heterogeneous cultures mix at the same destination. This is mainly true for developing countries where the coming together of cultures is very prevalent. Tourists transfer their habits, lifestyles and cultural attitudes to these local communities, which may lead to a process of change in the destination areas. The intensity of influence on the social structure and the value system depends on the relation between the numbers of tourists and inhabitants together with the type of tourism. The differences between destinations make it extremely difficult to evaluate the social-cultural influences. A sustainable approach must manage, reduce and prevent expulsion and cultural expropriation of inhabitants at these destinations (Vorlaufer, 1996).

One theoretical approach to management can be seen through the Global Sustainable Tourism Criteria (GSTC), which include thirty-seven voluntary standards "representing the minimum that any tourism business should aspire to reach in order to protect and sustain the world's natural and cultural resources while ensuring tourism meets its potential as a tool for poverty alleviation" (The Global Sustainable Tourism Criteria, 2009, p. 1). The criteria are linked to four superior categories: sustainable management, social/economic, cultural heritage and environment. The GSTC is a sound concept for the evaluation of sustainability at destinations.

Hence, these criteria could be a useful discriminator to assess the concept of health tourism when compared with sustainable approaches to tourism. The next section illustrates what measures can be adopted to ensure a sustainable product for health tourism.

Specific Characteristics of Health Tourism

The Concept of Health

For many years numerous experts have dealt with the concept of health and evaluated it from different perspectives. It is not possible to discuss all these different approaches because this would go beyond the scope of this article. Nevertheless, it is necessary to introduce a general perspective of health, allowing a better understanding of the basic issues within this chapter.

Klaus Hurrelmann is a recognised researcher in most fields of health and health promotion. He has defined health as "the balanced condition between risk and protective factors which appears when a human being succeeds in coping with the inner and outer demands" (Hurrelmann, 2010, p. 94, author's translation). Hurrelmann distinguishes between risk factors which have a negative influence on the constitution of an individual such as physical, mental, social or ecological variables and individual or structural protective factors, including access to health care.

A closer look at the risk factors reveals the following aspects:

- physical: e.g. disabilities such as obesity, lack of exercise, hypertension, high blood cholesterol levels,
- mental: e.g. negative stress, mental overload,
- social: e.g. unemployment, family-related problems,
- ecological: e.g. pollution, noise pollution, traffic nuisance.

And the protective factors:

- individual: e.g. physique, capability (muscles, cardiovascular system), personality, self-confidence, coping strategies,
- structural: e.g. access to health care (health care systems).

Both factor categories affect the level of coping an individual can make. If the individual is able to manage the risk factors by adapting to protective factors then a healthy balance is reached. Hurrelmann constructs his definition from the health policies of the World Health Organisation (WHO): "Health is a state of complete physical, mental and social well-being and not merely the absence of disease or infirmity" (WHO, 1946, p. 1).

The circumstances of a person play an equal role in maintaining and improving health, as well as an individual's behavioural perspective. Hurrelmann uses the term "outer demands" and furthermore integrates ecological risk and structural protective factors into the concept, whereas the policies of the WHO focus more on a social component.

It seems evident that ecological and social components are basic elements in the sustainability triangle already introduced in previous sections. It also seems obvious that there is a need to compare these basic themes with current existing concepts and approaches of health tourism.

The Concepts of Health Tourism

Health tourism is a popular concept and also one used in many adverts for different products, which are related to specific tourist destinations. Since the late '50s it has been heavily influenced by the aspect of Wellness, which places emphasis on individual lifestyles, and is connected to the option of the 'American way of life' (Dunn, 1959). Carrera and Bridges (2006, p. 447) note that health tourism is "the organized travel outside one's local environment for the maintenance, enhancement or restoration of an individual's wellbeing in mind and body". When it comes to health-tourism there are again many perspectives on this definition. As with sustainability a high degree of complexity appears. Numerous authors have tried to reduce this complexity by evolving different types of health tourism. Smith and Puczkó (2009) give a selective overview of the main health tourism types, including related activities:

- physical healing (medical baths, surgery trips, rehabilitation retreats),
- beauty treatments (cosmetic surgery trips),
- relaxation/rest (pampering treatments, wellness treatments, thalasso therapy),
- leisure/entertainment (sport and fitness activities),
- life/work balance (occupational wellness workshops),
- psychological (mental treatments),
- spiritual (meditation retreats).

The large array of different types of health tourism can be attributed to the more sophisticated demands of tourists. In the past, Wellness services were primarily offered uniformly as a brand for all types of health services (Smith and Puczkó, 2009). The maintenance of competitiveness for the providers requires a distinct development of customer directed Wellness services. These developments led to the complexity of the concept. Moreover, Kelly and Smith (2006) remark that it is unlikely that tourists are interested in all forms of Wellness. Wellness refers to a balance between body, mind, and spirit in order to maintain and promote health (Corbin and Pangrazi, 2001). In contrast Smith and Puczkó, (2009) suggested that health tourism can be structured as follows (Figure 2).

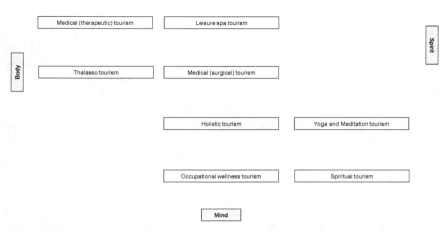

Figure 2: Integration of health tourism types into the Body-Mind-Spirit Spectrum (Smith and Puczkó, 2009)

The body-mind-spirit spectrum of health tourism reveals a one-sided focus on behavioural aspects or individual treatments. According to Smith and Puczkó (2009) guests call on Wellness services in a direct or indirect way. Direct services means taking an active role (e.g. training in a gym), whereas indirect means taking a passive role within a treatment (e.g. sitting in a Jacuzzi). Smith and Puczkó (2009) also suggest alternative use of the terms 'softcore' and 'hardcore' to describe the range of demands on health tourism. 'Softcore' signifies a spontaneous way of participation, whereas 'hardcore' is intentional behaviour. This distinction suggests the need to take a closer look at the differences between health tourism and its consumer groups.

Consumers in Health Tourism

The health tourism concept advocates many different demand segments. However, it is not possible to discuss all relevant differentiations. Berg (2008) favours a classic segmentation, which is grounded on the difference between primary prevention, secondary prevention and rehabilitation.[4]

---

[4] Berg (2008) additionally offers a fourth category: the demand of care. Considering the fact that the main focus of this article lies on the primary and secondary prevention, this fourth category is not relevant.

Primary prevention-oriented demand
Demand seems to relate to the avoidance of illnesses and infirmity. The customer is proactive and willing to pay for health services that will delay or avoid this outcome. In Germany there is little link between health services and Wellness programmes. For example, statutory health insurances are not willing to bear the costs. In this context health tourists are preventive and responsible demanders. They bear the costs for Wellness treatments on their own, instead of relying on the restrictive primary health care system[5]. In other words, health tourists tend to demand services from the secondary health care market, which have to be paid for privately in order to ensure a healthy life style.

Secondary Prevention
These consumers demand services which should prevent or delay illness. In the majority of cases medical treatment is necessary and there is a need to distinguish between the degrees of severity. In cases of low severity, the customer is often able to accomplish the necessary treatment himself, whereas cases with a higher severity have to involve a doctor so that the consumer becomes a patient. In this situation customers appear as statistics on the statutory health insurance scheme and they are limited in their decision-making. Many in this group try complementary medicine treatments.

Rehabilitative Customers
In this case demand is directly placed on medical treatment prescribed by a doctor. The patient's state of health should be at a pre-illness level as far as possible. With reference to Berg (2008) the typical customers in this category are mainly patients with sports or accidental injuries. Moreover, the insurers primarily pay the costs of treatment.

Lanz Kaufmann (2002) provides a useful and more appropriate supplement concerning this segmentation, based on health rather than disease. She distinguishes between passive and active Wellness consumers on the one hand and consumers of rehabilitation on the other, whereby the last group is similar to secondary prevention in Berg's segmentation. The main difference between active and passive customers lies in the type of treatment. While the passive guest prefers non-active treatments such as steam baths, jacuzzi or stress management, the active guest is interested in exercise and recreational services.

---

[5] In Germany the primary health care market is based on a solitary financed health care system, which mainly consists of insured customers (patients), health care providers (e.g. doctors, hospitals) and the statutory health insurances.

The Lack of Sustainability in Health Tourism Concepts

According to the different concepts, types and consumer groups in health tourism, one key element is missing: the consideration of health as a sustainable or even holistic approach. The concentration on behavioural interventions and mainly physical treatments is one-sided. The analysis of the current models in the previous sections, reveals a success in sport and spa activities as long as it is the primary preventive consumers who access these resources. All these quite useful activities demonstrate a lack of sustainability. To call health tourism sustainable it is not enough to include behavioural services, but rather to embed the concept into the local and regional environment. Thus, balanced and sustainable health tourism must include behavioural treatment as well as the protection and promotion of the region.

Responsibility towards the local destination (e.g. conditions of employment, pollution) has to be addressed, as well as the sensitivity of tourists to understand that the consumption of individual health treatments in a foreign region also requires a respectful treatment of local people, organisations and traditions. Different organisations often list 'health' as one of the most important human rights: "Our greatest concern must always rest with disadvantaged and vulnerable groups. These groups are often hidden, living in remote rural areas or shantytowns and having little political voice" (World Health Organization, 2007, p. 1). From the perspective of sustainability, the health tourism industry and its customers should identify their responsibility for a destination's circumstances, people, organisations and traditions. Some research studies have already evaluated the attitude of health tourists concerning this topic. The study of Bristow, Yang and Lu (2011) analyses the role of sustainable accomplishments in health tourism. The study examined the relevance of health tourism in Costa Rica.[6] The authors gathered different information about health tourists' attitudes towards the sustainability of health tourism practices with reference to GSTC (2008). In particular, respondents ranked the importance of criteria used to maximize social and economic advantages to the local community and minimize negative effects. Ninety-two individuals completed the survey. The assessment of the importance of sustainable tourism was examined by embedding nine criteria from the Partnership of GSTC into a questionnaire based on a five-point Likert scale ranging.

---

[6] Costa Rica is a popular destination among ecotourists.

The following items were evaluated as the most important:

- "The international or national legal protection of employees is respected, and employees are paid a living wage" (average score 3.72),
- "The company has implemented a policy against commercial exploitation, particularly of children and adolescents, including sexual exploitation" (average score 3.67),
- "The activities of the company do not jeopardize the provision of basic services, such as water, energy, or sanitation, to neighbouring communities" (average score 3.63).

The study results indicate that beside other criteria e.g. cost sensitive health tourists, there is also a need to take care of local workers and the environmental and ecological framework conditions at health destinations. The development of health tourism should include sustainable parameters, which currently, would be an innovative and competitive strategy. Referring to the German market, there is still a lack of research, especially considering the types of treatments and destinations health tourists choose.

The Case Study: Winterberg, Germany

The combination of health tourism and sustainability can be successful, especially in order to prepare for future challenges in the tourism market. A few destinations already recognise this opportunity and have modified their tourist concepts. One of them is Winterberg, a town with nearly 14.500 inhabitants in the low mountain range region of Sauerland, Germany.

The vacation product of Winterberg is still dominated by winter sports activities, but has gradually changed into a comprehensive and even more health-oriented approach. This low mountain range in Germany increasingly suffers from a lack of snow in winter. To compensate for this deficit Winterberg has developed strategic measures with the objective being to ensure independence from the winter season. These strategies also contain the intention to develop climate protective activities in combination with health and Wellness services. In terms of the last category Winterberg has invested monies in the development of suitable health facilities (Ferienwelt Winterberg, 2010).

One notable project is the Oversum - Vital Resort Winterberg. The development and planning of this project took approximately ten years and the resort will open in spring 2012. It will consist of 31,000 square meters divided into a building space area and an outside surface including different health-care services with the following facilities: recreational pools, a wellness and spa area, a medical practice, tourist information, and an event hall together with a four-star hotel with gastronomy. The philosophy of Oversum is also based on two sustainable elements: generation- and season-spanning. The wide range of health, sports and fitness facilities on offer guarantees independence from the winter sports season. Facilities can be used for the whole year. The heterogeneous service roster responds to different types of generations, so the project also includes a social context (n. a., 2010).

Besides the implementation of prospective projects in health tourism like Oversum, Winterberg is also dedicated to the environment of the region. The overall goal is to become a climate neutral winter sports destination. To ensure that this objective is achieved, several measures are, and have been, accomplished (Prinz, 2009):

- alternative use of skiing lifts in the summer season,
- enhancement of efficiency in snowmaking areas by reducing the water used
- including a solar installation of 5000 square metres for the snowmaking procedure.

Winterberg demonstrates a useful and sustainable strategy in terms of combining health tourism with essential elements of sustainability. By achieving this strategy the destination will succeed in implementing a holistic health tourist approach, connecting healthy treatments with a healthy environment.

Conclusions

Health tourism is an important part of the tourism industry. Significant changes in society have taken place, such as increased ageing of the population and underfunded health care systems, which do not meet demand, seeming to engender the growth of health tourists. Health tourism is mainly characterised by a concentration on individual treatments together with physical and mental attributes. Questions relating to sustainability are rarely dealt with and often only play a minor role. In conventional tourism a different attitude appears to be embraced, where aspects of sustainability are not only discussed as important parts of the product but are becoming essential.

The services offered during health trips are often supplemented by outdoor sporting activities and other types of exercise. This is a useful strategy because physical activity is a necessary element, especially in primary or secondary preventive treatment. Against the background of climate change, the health tourism industry should focus on a holistic development of their products, which have to include sustainable measures. With reference to outdoor sporting activities this would mean that protective measures need to be developed whereby local traditions and ecological conditions are protected. Both approaches would seem compatible as: *a healthy person also needs a healthy environment*.

References

Aderhold, P. (2000), "Der deutsche Fernreisemarkt", in Landgrebe, S. (Ed.), *Internationaler Tourismus*, Oldenbourg, München, Wien, (pp. 235-252).
Becker, C., Job, H. and Witzel, A. (1996), *Tourismus und nachhaltige Entwicklung. Grundlagen und Ansätze für den mitteleuropäischen Raum*. Darmstadt: Wissenschaftliche Buchgesellschaft.
Berg, W. (2008), *Gesundheitstourismus und Wellnesstourismus,* Oldenbourg,,München..
Bieger, T. (2007), *Management von Destinationen* (7th ed.), Oldenbourg München..
Bristow, R., Yang, W.T. and Lu, M.T. (2010), "An application of the global sustainable tourism criteria in health tourism", in C.E. Watts Jr. and C. LeBlanc Fisher (Eds.), *Proceedings of the 2009 Northeastern Recreation Research Symposium*, Newtown Square, PA: U.S. Department of Agriculture, Forest Service, Northern Research Station, available at: http://www.nrs.fs.fed.us/pubs/gtr/gtr_nrs-p66.pdf#page=104 (acessed 22 October 2010), p. 97-104.
Bristow R., Yang W., and Lu M. (2011), "Sustainable medical tourism in Costa Rica", *Tourism Review*, Vol. 66, No. 1/2, pp. 107-117.
Butler, R.W. (1999), "Sustainable tourism: A state-of-the-art review". *Tourism Geographies, Vol. 1* No. 1, pp. 7-25.
Carrera, P. and Bridges, J. (2006), "Globalization and healthcare: understanding health and medical tourism", *Expert Review of Pharmacoeconomics and Outcomes Research, Vol. 6* No. 4, pp. 447-454.
Corbin, C.B. and Pangrazi, R.P. (2001), "Toward a uniform definition of wellness: A commentary", *President's Council on Physical Fitness and Sports Research Digest, Vol. 3* No. 15, pp. 1-8.
Deutscher Tourismus Verband (2005), *Zahlen, Daten, Fakten 2004. Tourismus in Deutschland,* Eigenverlag, Bonn.
Dunn, H.L. (1959), "High-level wellness for man and society", *American Journal of Public Health and the Nation's Health, Vol. 49 No.* 6, pp. 786-792.
Europarc Federation (2002), *The European Charter for Sustainable Tourism in Protected Areas* (Updated Version of October 2002), Eigenverlag, Grafenau.
Ferienwelt Winterberg (2010), "Gesundheitseinrichtungen", available at: http://www.winterberg.de/tourismus/de/aktiv-und-entspannen/vital-und-gesund/gesundheitseinrichtungen/index.php?navanchor=1010154 (accessed 22 October 2010).

Foundation for the Rights of the Future Generations (2006), *Nachhaltigkeitsdefinitionen von Wissenschaftlern*, availbale at: http://www.generationengerechtigkeit. de/images/stories/Publikationen/nachh.pdf (accessed 12 September 2010).
Foundation Kathy Beys (2004), "Nachhaltigkeit", available at: http://www.nachhaltigkeit. aachener-stiftung.de/artikel/nachha.ltigkeit_1308.htm (accessed 12 September 2010).
García-Altés, A. (2005), "The development of health tourism services", *Annals of Tourism Research, Vol. 32*, pp. 262-266.
Haber, W. (1994), "Nachhaltige Entwicklung – aus ökologischer Sicht", *Zeitschrift für angewandte Umweltforschung, Vol. 7* No. 1, pp. 9-25.
Hall, C.M. and Jenkins, J. (1995), *Tourism and Public Policy*, Routledge London.
Hinch, T. and Higham, J. (2004), *Sport Tourism Development* (Aspects of Tourism, 13). Channel View Publications, Clevedon.
Holden, A. (2008), *Environment and Tourism* (2nd ed.), Routledge, London.
Hurrelmann, K. (2010), *Gesundheitssoziologie* (7th ed.), Juventa, Weinheim.
Krippendorf, J. (1975), *Die Landschaftsfresser. Tourismus und Erholungslandschaft – Verderben oder Segen?* (2nd ed.), Hallwag Bern, Stuttgart.
Krippendorf, J. (1982), "Towards new tourism policies: The importance of environmental and sociocultural factors", *Tourism Management, Vol. 3* No. 3, pp. 135-148.
Lanz Kaufmann, E. (2002), Wellness-Tourismus: Entscheidungsgrundlagen für Investitionen und Qualitätsverbesserungen, *Berner Studien zu Freizeit und Tourismus (2nd ed.)*, p. 38, Universität Bern, Bern.
Lee, C.G. (2009), "Health care and tourism: Evidence from Singapore", *Tourism Management, Vol. 31* No. 4, pp. 486-488.
Meadows, D.H., Meadows, D.L., Randers, J. and Behrens, W.W. (1972), *The Limits to Growth*, Potomac Associates, New American Library, Washington, D.C.
Miller, G. (2001), "The development of indicators for sustainable tourism: results of a Delphi survey of tourism researchers", *Tourism Management, Vol. 22* No. 4, pp. 351-362.
N. N. (2010), "Oversum - Vital Resort Winterberg" *EuroAmusment Professional, Vol. 6* No. 5, p. 56.
Pearce, D.G. (1995), *Tourism Today: A Geographical Analysis*, Longman, London.
Prinz, N. (2009), "Climate Change – A Challenge for Low Mountain Range Regions characterized by Winter Sport Tourism. The example of Winterberg", *International Symposium "Strategies for Adapting to Climate Change in the Regions of Europe", October 27 to 29, 2009*, available at: http://www.regional-climate.eu/fileadmin/ download/Symposium_2009/Workshop_1/5P_Prinz_Beckmann_WS1.pdf (accessed 22 October 2010).
Secretariat of the Convention on Biological Diversity (Ed.) (2004), "Guidelines on Biodiversity and Tourism development", *CBD Guidelines*, Secretariat of the Convention on Biological Diversity, Montreal.
Smith, M. and Kelly, C. (2006), "Wellness Tourism", *Tourism Recreation Research*, Vol. 31 No. 1, pp. 1-4.
Smith, M. and Puczkó, L. (2009), *Health and Wellness Tourism*, Elsevier, Burlington, MA.

The Global Sustainable Tourism Criteria (GSTC) (2009), *Global Sustainable Tourism Criteria.* available at http://www.sustainabletourismcriteria.org/index.php?option=com_content&task=view&id=13&Itemid=47 (accsessed 18 October 2010).

Trittin, J. (2004), "Vorwort in Bundesministerium für Umwelt, Naturschutz und Reaktorsicherheit (Ed.), *Natur bewegt – Natursport in Deutschland.* Bundesministerium für Umwelt, Naturschutz und Reaktorsicherheit, Berlin, p. 3.

Vorlaufer, K. (1996), *Tourismus in Entwicklungsländern: Möglichkeiten und Grenzen einer nachhaltigen Entwicklung durch Fremdenverkehr*, Wissenschaftliche Buchgesellschaft Darmstadt.

Weaver, D. (2007), *Sustainable tourism: theory and practice*, Butterworth Heinemann Oxford.

Wall, G. (1996), "Is ecotourism sustainable?", *Environmental Management, Vol.* 2 No. 3-4, pp. 207-216.

Wheeler, B. (1993), "Sustaining the ego", *Journal of Sustainable Tourism, Vol. 1* No. 2, pp. 121-129.

World Commission on Environment and Development (WCED) (1987). *Our Common Future.* Oxford University Press, New York.

World Health Organization (WHO) (1946), *Constitution*, WHO Press, Geneva.

World Health Organization (WHO) (2007), *Working for Health: An introduction to the World Health Organization,* WHO Press, Geneva.

World Tourism Organization (WTO) (1993), *Sustainable Tourism Development: Guide for Local Planners,* WTO, Madrid.

World Tourism Organization (WTO) (2010), *UNWTO Tourism Barometer,* August 2010, available at: http://www.unwto.org/facts/eng/pdf/barometer/UNWTO_Barom10_update_august_en_excerpt.pdf (accessed 20 September 2010).

Sustainability and Eco-health tourism

Robert S. Bristow

Introduction

Over the millennia, travel to foreign lands to soak in mineral waters has been popular for the privileged (Bookman and Bookman, 2007; Connell, 2011; Mitman, 2003; Reisman, 2010; Towner, 1996; TRAM, 2006). Long sought for their medicinal values, mineral springs have attracted visitors for thousands of years. And access to these resources has been possible through advances in transportation and a growing middle class that fuelled further interest in the experience of the holiday to escape the urban environment (Gilbert, 1949). The travel continues today as evidenced by the popularity of the historic mineral waters found at Saratoga Springs in the USA, Bath, England and Baden-Baden, Germany

Yet today these tourists are seeking not only a bath and massage, but may also want cosmetic surgery or a knee replacement (Goodrich and Goodrich, 1987; Goodrich, 1993a; Hall, 1992; Hall, 2003). Fed by the interest to improve oneself, be pampered, or address some health concern, health travel is likely to continue in the future. Lunt and others (n.d.) found four consequences for the emergence of the international health market: large numbers of people travelling for treatment, the shift of tourists from more developed nations to less developed ones, the rise of information via the Internet, and public and private infrastructure development to promote tourism.

Health Tourism is the umbrella term for all tourist aspects of health, wellness and medical care (Smith and Puczkó, 2009). For example, Hall (1992) notes that health tourism may be appropriately viewed on a continuum from a sun and fun vacation to the need to seek a major medical operation. Progressing along this continuum the number of tourists decreases (Hall, 2003).

Within this continuum Voigt and others (2011) define wellness tourism as those seeking a beauty spa, lifestyle resort or a spiritual retreat. A hectic daily life, high stress environment, the loss of traditions and a desire to simplify life has driven tourists to seek time away from home for an experience to maintain, promote health and well being (Voigt *et al.*, 2011).

The definition of health tourism is complex and multifaceted making it difficult to measure (Goodrich 1994). There are frequent interchangeable uses of health tourism with medical tourism (see Aniza *et al.,* 2009) in the literature, suggesting it is not clear when one term starts and the other ends. Even within these parameters, there is not a unified definition of treatments.

For the purpose of this dialogue, health tourism will be modelled after the work of Mueller and Kaufmann (2001). They suggest that health tourism is one element of the tourist experience and could be further defined as travel for the healthy or travel for the ill. For the former, illness prevention tourism would meet the specific wellness needs of a tourist or might embrace a comprehensive experience. For the ill traveller, medical treatment might necessitate some convalescence at a spa during the post operation recovery.

Given this broad explanation of the health tourist experience, how do we measure the impacts of health tourists versus others who may seek a brief treatment during a holiday? Do we count the trip when one family member visits a spa for a manicure while the rest of the family remain on the beach? A visit to the spa under this possibility is quite different when compared to the recovery stage of the health tourist experience (Didaskalou *et al.,* 2004). Beyond the marketing interest in lifestyle improvements to the individual, what are the consequences of this tourist's behaviour on the local cultural and natural environments? Are tourists becoming too self-indulgent by not recognising how their actions, and inactions, impact on others?

There are no clear estimates on the number of travellers seeking some sort of health benefit from their tour (Lunt *et al.,* 2010; Reisman, 2010; Voigt *et al.,* 2010). However the recent explosion in research indicates the growing interest in understanding this phenomenon (Hall 2011). While much of contemporary research is based on the popular press (e.g., Health Tourism Magazine), websites and blogs, little in the way of professional and academic study has explored the travel for health (Turner 2011). Even less is found addressing the issue of sustainability (Bristow *et al.,* 2011).

As global tourism grows and matures, it becomes a necessity to measure all impacts and costs of the experience. While the benefits of health oriented tourism is not at stake here, the purpose rather is to consider sustainable practices in the discussion. In this context, given the potential growth of sustainability, how might health tourism maximise the social and economic benefits and minimise negative impacts within the local host community? Is health tourism sustainable?

This chapter will firstly review the literature covering the current state of research together with the important theoretical approaches concerning: health sciences, health tourism and sustainable health tourism, and these topics will be supported by the use of specific examples. A discussion follows and the chapter concludes with recommendations for future research.

Background

The following literature provides a general review of contemporary health sciences, health tourism and sustainable health tourism. The multidimensional aspects of health tourism that Goodrich (1994) suggests provide the links and hopefully interdependencies that will be become evident as a course for sustainable health tourism becomes clear. If we are to assume that health tourism will grow, and all statistics point to this future, then two questions of sustainability need to be addressed. Firstly, can local people get the needed access to health care and secondly, how are the wastes from these industries being handled? This section of the paper will explore these questions.

Health Science

The health care sector is one of fastest growing in the world economy (Chanda, 2002). Global trading of health services is one major aspect of this economy. Often termed cross border health care, the concept described in this chapter is commonly known as health tourism. In order to begin the investigation into health tourism an exploration of sustainable health science needs to be established.

Health inequalities exist (Smyth 2008). Inequities through lifestyle choices, poverty, urban versus rural residence, awareness of opportunities, work responsibilities all impact on access to healthcare. Health is one of the most important rights for our global citizens. Dr. Chan, Director General of the World Health Organization notes in her opening remarks on WHO Reform in Geneva, Switzerland that:

> "What we all want to see is efforts and money translated into better health, whether the goal is health protection for the entire world, better health for as many people as possible, or better health for those in greatest need." (Chan, 2012, Reform of priority setting at WHO, paragraph 3)

In a global market the delivery of health care is imbalanced (Reisman, 2010). Even in the EU, access to cross border health care has only recently been made available to the citizens (Kanavos *et al.*, 1999). The relative numbers of health care professionals varies tremendously around the world. Typically this imbalance means quality care is only available in developed countries. But what is new in this case is the public and private promotion of quality health services at lower costs in developing nations.

There are no reliable records of the numbers of non-medical health care professionals globally, so the data on the number of physicians per 1,000 citizens in each country from the World Health Organization (2011) will be used to identify and quantify health provisions. Globally the median density of health care professionals is 1.15 physicians per 1,000. Highest in per capita coverage by physicians is San Marino with 47 doctors per 1,000 residents. It is important to note that the census was conducted in 1990 and even though the current population is about 30,000, it is clear that access to health care is high in San Marino relative to the countries in the WHO database.

Cuba (6.4 doctors per 1,000) and Greece (6 doctors per 1,000) are found next in physician density. Cuba should come as no surprise since this country has had a long and strong history of health tourism (Goodrich 1993b; Van Wilkinson 2008). Likewise Greece, long known for the medicinal properties of its mineral springs has the benefit of the climate and bioclimatic conditions (Didaskalou *et al.*, 2004). Progressing down the physician density list are two other countries, Malaysia and India, both known for health tourism. Malaysia is one of the primary destinations in Southeast Asia that has had the benefit of a deliberate marketing strategy by both the private and public sectors (Leng, 2007). And we find that the density of health care professionals in Malaysia (0.94) is comparable to Grenada and Peru (0.98, and 0.92 respectively). Further west, India's ranking of 0.60 is similar to the availability of doctors in Iraq, Morocco and Honduras (0.69, 0.62, and 0.57 respectively).

Countries found in the Global South generally have the lowest concentration of health professionals and average about 0.02 doctors per 1,000. It should be recognised that this measure of access to health care is a simplistic one, but it is a measure that can be universally compared across the globe. While this number illustrates the disparity among countries, even within a country, access to health care is spatially imbalanced.

This imbalance can be found based on the urban/rural population distribution. Arcury and others (2005) found inequitable access to health care in the rural Appalachian Mountain region of the United States; and even in urbanised environments, where the numbers of health care professionals are expected to be higher, distance from home to the regular source of health care was more important to urban residents than patients living in rural areas (Gesler and Meade, 1988).

Strains on medical treatment can be attributed to the added influx of tourism whether it is for spa treatment or medical care. Health professionals are leaving public and private hospitals to work in those that cater to foreigners due to the lure of higher wages (Lunt, 2011; NaRanong and NaRanong, 2011). It becomes evident that within a country access to health care may vary significantly. This action creates a further imbalance to health care for the local citizens which is only exacerbated should the country have a low density of health care providers to begin with. India is a prime example of this imbalance (Tattara, 2010).

Health Tourism

Contemporary health tourism has roots in the need to go to a foreign country for services unavailable or unaffordable at home. And while individuals seeking cross border health services are not tourists in the traditional sense, given that the travel experience is for non-work responsibilities, health tourists may be the first tourists to a destination. Health care is not new except for the tourism appendage that was coined by travel agents (Burkett, 2007).

Medical doctors in other countries could be considered to be early pioneers in the health tourism trade. Part of the educational experience for physicians in the 18th Century was to travel to learn from others. Tobias Smollett, noted Scottish poet and surgeon, sought climatic reprieve in France and Italy and wrote about those experiences in "Travels Through France and Italy" (Spillane, 1984).

This travel was also frequently motivated by the desire to escape the urban climate; when Tobias Smollett travelled through southern Europe he commented on climatic conditions being better than those at home (Spillane, 1984).

But what occurs now is the need to find affordable health care in a world where the industry has become a multi-trillion dollar enterprise. Others suggest that in less than two decades, in India alone, medical tourism could account for a $190 billion dollar industry (Hanson 2008). Part of the growth experienced in the health tourism industry could be tied to the use of the Internet to "shop" for information by taking much of the mystery out of foreign travel (Harvard Medical Letter, 2008; Lunt *et al.*, 2011; Johnston *et al.*, 2010; Turner, 2011). Using Butler's Tourist Area Life Cycle (1980), health tourism would be in the development stage, where exponential growth has been shown to exist for a decade or more.

Health tourism is popular today for a variety of reasons. Travellers are seeking low cost and timely medical care that may or may not be available at home (Bookman and Bookman, 2007; Hancock, 2006; Smith, 2006; Turner, 2007). For many uninsured or underinsured citizens, a low cost operation overseas is a reasonable expense, even after adding travel and lodging costs. Beyond the cost savings and not having to wait months or years for help, individuals have crossed borders to seek procedures or treatments not available at home due to laws or local customs. These include aquatic therapy and acupuncture (Chen, 2007), cosmetic surgery (Castonguay and Brown, 1993), dental surgery (Judkins 2007), faith healing (Baldoria and Osana, 2007), organ transplants (Budiani-Saberi and Delmonico, 2008), returning home, i.e., resulting from diaspora (Bustamante *et al.*, 2008), reproductive services and fertility treatment (Martin, 2009), sex change operations (Connell, 2006), unapproved medicine, (Urology Times, 2008), and other procedures. Given this varied need, demand for cross border health care is expected to continue.

This raises the question of who these tourists are and where do they travel? Bristow *et al.*, (2011) surveyed medical tourists to find out about the choice set of possible destinations and what country was eventually selected for a medical procedure. India, Costa Rica, Singapore and Thailand were the most frequently considered as a possible destination for health care. For those that travelled, India, Costa Rica, Mexico and Singapore were the most likely visited. The majority of tourists sought cosmetic or dental work on their tour. Most were experienced world travellers and despite current economic concerns, the vast majority of health tourists are likely to travel abroad for a vacation over the next 12 months.

About half of the sample are 40 years or older although a quarter of the sample were young adults (aged 18-29). Males were more frequent in numbers for the survey. The household income for the sample was moderate with the modal quantity being $25,000 to $ 49,999 US dollars. More than 75% of the group had at least a college degree. Nearly one half of the sample was employed full time. Fifty five percent of medical tourists are married. Most were born in the US, although some indicated their birthplace as Asia or Europe.

Health tourism has at least two concerns when viewed in terms of sustainability (Bristow, 2009). Firstly, there is a concern that access to medical care will be limited to wealthy foreigners who can afford to pay a price that is often higher than the local prevailing wages. While this type of "outsourcing" is an accepted component in a global economy this is about personal health care. Furthermore, since health tourism clinics are often private facilities, public services may be strained beyond operational capacity to meet the needs of the local population.

Secondly, in a world where clean drinking water is still a luxury for millions, there are concerns about the environmental risks to health care professionals and the local citizens. Tourists may not receive a quality and safe experience. For instance Lunt and others (2011) note the lack of follow up care and airborne sicknesses when people travel for health care overseas. In many developing countries health care professionals face potential risks in the form of infectious diseases and blood-borne pathogens (Sagoe-Moses, 2001). The risk is spread throughout the country because of improper disposal of medical waste. Medical waste is a world-wide problem; simply defined, medical waste includes used needles, soiled dressings, blood, chemicals, pharmaceuticals, medical devices and radioactive materials. Medical waste is one of the most hazardous of all wastes and the improper disposal of syringes, blood and other biohazards threatens local water supplies and the public health of the citizens (Da Silva *et al.,* 2005; Gatrell and Lovett, 1986). According to the World Health Organization (2007), approximately 20% of the waste generated from health care facilities is hazardous.

Costa Rica is one country that attracts 100,000 tourists a year for treatments (Fallas, 2009). Hospitals in San Jose, Costa Rica, alone produce 17 tons of waste a day of which 25% is classified as a biohazard. Included in the waste are body parts, including blood and samples, expired medicines, needles and scalpels and other hazardous materials which are meant to be disposed of in bright red plastic bags. However these bags are often disposed of in regular landfills exposing local scavengers to hazards (Rogers, 2007).

The growth of medical tourism is so dramatic in many countries that local citizens are unable to get adequate health care. American dollars or European Euros, while relatively inexpensive for westerners, are often out of reach to the indigenous population. For example Thailand has an extensive medical tourism industry, but many of the doctors prefer to work for private hospitals where they can earn a week's salary in one day compared to the wages offered at public hospitals (Hamilton, 2007). Public health care or nationalised health care provides equal access to free or low cost medical care. However the economics of health care dictates that the richer members in a society will secure better health and also have immediate access to it, especially where there is no national health care system free at the point of access. It is simply a case of supply and demand.

Sustainable Health Tourism

To meet the growing demand for health tourism, numerous facilities world-wide are expanding resources to meet the needs of tourists. Spas are being expanded at resort hotels, hospitals and clinics are springing up next to international airports. Hospitals can also seek international accreditation to ensure high quality health care.

The following organisations accredit medical providers:

- United Kingdom, the QHA Trent Accreditation is one organisation that promotes holistic world-wide medical accreditation (http://www.qha-international.co.uk/).

- Australia, The Australian Council of Health Care Standards (http://www.achs.org.au)
- The United States, The Joint Commission International (JCI) is another (http://www.jointcommissioninternational.org/).
- India has the National Accreditation Board for Hospitals & Healthcare Providers (http://www.nabh.co/)

While accreditation may assure visitors of a quality hospital visit, what precautions are there for local citizens? Smith and Puczkó (2009) have noted some of these concerns in the health tourism industry when the local untrained workforce cannot meet the specialised needs of the patients. Furthermore, they warn that the health tourism industry may draw from the local workers, leaving gaps for the rest of the tourism businesses. Since these clinics are often private facilities, public health services may be strained beyond operational capacity due to this "brain drain" (United Nations, 2009). The local disadvantaged citizens are particularly threatened since private clinics are priced out of reach (George 2009).

Early research has found that health tourists are sensitive to sustainable practices (Bristow et al., 2011). This study used the Global Sustainable Tourism Criteria (GSTC) that was formed by Rainforest Alliance, the United Nations Environment Programme (UNEP), the United Nations Foundation, and the United Nations World Tourism Organization (UNWTO) in 2008. These criteria are designed to be the minimum practices to ensure sustainability for the business as well as to protect natural and cultural resources. In addition, the 37 voluntary standards criteria are to be instruments to alleviate poverty (Global Sustainable Tourism Criteria, 2008).

The criteria were developed by sustainability experts and the tourism industry and based on more than 60 existing models of sustainable tourism certification already deployed around the world. The GSTC model is based on the desire to create baseline guidelines for businesses, both large and small, to become more sustainable and to serve as a starting point for the more specific needs of governments, NGO's and the private sector. Since deployment in late 2008, the criteria are starting to be critiqued at business level.

To assess the importance of sustainable practices in medical tourism, a survey was deployed to explore the role of health tourism in Costa Rica, a country better known as a premier ecotourist destination. The survey was designed to collect information about these tourists: the socio-economic characteristics, where they travelled, what procedures they sought and then an assessment of the GSTC practices.

With the intention of reaching a broad audience, a request to participate in the study was published in the *Tico Times*, a weekly English-language newspaper published in Costa Rica on 5 December 2008. In addition to this, email posts on relevant distribution lists, related health tourism blogs and other electronic communications were engaged. The survey was open to all who travelled abroad for a medical procedure and ninety two individuals responded to the call.

To determine the importance of the sustainable tourism criteria, respondents were asked to evaluate nine different criteria on a five point Likert scale ranging from not very important to very important, 1 to 5 respectively. The nine criteria were found in the GSTC section "Maximize social and economic benefits to the local community and minimize negative impacts."

The following responses were deemed to be significant and were ranked very highly by the participants:

- "the international or national legal protection of employees is respected, and employees are paid a living wage" was ranked most important.
- "the company has implemented a policy against commercial exploitation, particularly of children and adolescents, including sexual exploitation",
- "the company is equitable in hiring women and local minorities, including in management positions, while restraining child labor",
- and "the activities of the company do not jeopardize the provision of basic services, such as water, energy, or sanitation, to neighbouring communities"

Less important for medical tourists, although still higher than "indifferent", was when "the company offers the means for local small entrepreneurs to develop and sell sustainable products that are based on the area's nature, history, and culture." Table 1 summarises the mean responses and variability of the criteria.

How important are these considerations in your decision?	Mean	Std. Deviation
The company actively supports initiatives for social and infrastructure community development including, among others, education, medical, and sanitation.	3.42	1.28
Local residents are employed, including in management positions. Training is offered as necessary.	3.30	1.21
Local and fair-trade services and goods are purchased by the business, where available.	3.14	1.21
The company offers the means for local small entrepreneurs to develop and sell sustainable products that are based on the area's nature, history, and culture.	3.02	1.33
A code of conduct for activities in indigenous and local communities has been developed, with the consent of and in collaboration with the community.	3.14	1.18
The company has implemented a policy against commercial exploitation, particularly of children and adolescents, including sexual exploitation.	3.67	1.17
The company is equitable in hiring women and local minorities, including in management positions, while restraining child labor.	3.63	1.13
The international or national legal protection of employees is respected, and employees are paid a living wage.	3.72	1.14
The activities of the company do not jeopardize the provision of basic services, such as water, energy, or sanitation, to neighboring communities.	3.64	1.14

(Note: 5-point scale, 1 = not very important, 5 = very important; n = 92)

Table 1: Assessment of the Global Sustainable Tourism Criteria

These findings indicate a willingness of tourists to support sustainable practices in the cross border health care industry. In all cases the importance of the criteria was greater than the "indifferent" value and the standard deviations were uniformly consistent. One might conclude these tourists might be willing to pay a little more for their care given this acceptance, although the willingness to pay was not tested in the study.

Discussion

This chapter highlighted some of the consequences facing health tourism today. While not comprehensive in all the positive and negative impacts of the industry, an attempt has been made to highlight two of the more pressing issues: health care equity and bio-hazards.

Outside the scope of this paper are the environmental impacts of the travel itself, that is the carbon emissions of air travel half way around the world. Further, there is no attempt to explore the emergency nature of health care once a tourist is away from home. Since Richter (2003) recognizes the need for additional facilities to meet the health needs of tourists, those emergency events are not part of the tourist experience.

What obstacles remain? One obvious concern is the legal uncertainty regarding medical tourism. What rights do patients have? Since there is no current international legal regulation of medical tourism, what options are left to a patient who may suffer needlessly (Mirrer-Singer, 2007)? Cross border insurance is another area not explored in this paper. In the EU, recent rulings have eased the difficulty for health care across borders (Kanavos *et al.*, 1999).

Sustainable Tourism is much more than the "theme du jour". Born out of an era of green tourism or ecotourism, it has as many definitions as health tourism may have. It has been long recognised that tourism has social, economic and environmental impacts on the local community (Butler, 2000; Hall and Page, 2006; McCool *et al.*, 2001; Mathieson and Wall, 1982; Mieczkowski, 1995). What should be encouraged are sustainable management practices in tourism businesses that enhance the community by maximising benefits and minimising threats while still permitting growth. Health tourists should be responsible tourists as well.

Given this positive interest in supporting sustainable tourism, it is not too late to build sustainable practices into health tourism strategies. While the care of the client-tourist should always be first, the local population should not be at a disadvantage simply because they cannot afford the attention the foreign tourists demand.

What are the impacts between health tourism and host country? The nature of many health tourism experiences is one of seclusion where the tourist's exposure to local citizens is minimised. In a market driven industry health tourism promoters are ignoring the market discourse especially given the potential revenue from foreign visitors (Mainil *et al.*, 2011). Cuba in particular, is in a position to become a major leader in the health tourism market, especially if travel opens up with the United States just 90 miles away (Henthorne and Miller, 2003). But as these markets engage in our global economy, we cannot harm the local citizens in our desire to soak in a mineral spring. If we append the prefix eco to health tourism as suggested by Bristow (2009), can we not begin to recognise that sustainability lies in all markets, health care, tourism or otherwise?

References

Aniza, I, Aidalina, M., Nirmalini, R., Inggit, M., and Ajeng, T. (2009), "Health Tourism in Malaysia: the Strength and weaknesses", *Journal of Community Health*, Vol. 15 No. 1, pp. 7-15.

Arcury, T., Gesler, W., Preisser, J., Sherman, J., Spencer, J., and Perin, J. (2005), "The Effects of Geography and Spatial Behavior on Health Care Utilization Among the Residents of Rural Region", *HSR: Health Service Research*, Vol. 40 No. 1, pp. 135-155.

Australian Council of Health Care Standards (2012), "The Australian Council of Health Care Standards Homepage", available at: http://www.achs.org.au (accessed 25 June 2012).

Baldoria, F. and Osana, J. (2007), "Medical Tourism: A Booming Industry, Philippine Daily Inquirer", available at; http://business.inquirer.net/money/features/view/20070615-71419/Medical_tourism_%3A_A_booming_industry (accessed 1 February 2012).

Bookman, M., and Bookman, K. (2007), *Medical Tourism in Developing Countries*, Palgrave, New York.

Bristow R. (2009), "Eco-medical tourism: can it be sustainable?", in Klenosky, David B.; Fisher, Cherie LeBlanc, (Eds.) *Proceedings of the 2008 Northeastern Recreation Research Symposium* March 30 - April 1 2008; Gen. Tech. Rep. NRS-P-42. Newtown Square, PA: U.S. Department of Agriculture, Forest Service, Northern Research Station, Bolton Landing, NY. pp. 158-164.

Bristow, R., Yang, W., and Lu, M. (2011), "Sustainable medical tourism in Costa Rica", *Tourism Review*, Vol. 66 No. 1/2, pp.107 – 117.

Budiani-Saberi, D. and Delmonico (2008), "Organ Trafficking and Transplant Tourism: A Commentary on the Global Realities", *American Journal of Transplantation*, Vol. 8, pp. 925-929.

Burkett, L. (2007), "Medical Tourism: Concepts, Benefits and the American Legal Perspective. The Journal of Legal medicine, Vol. 28, pp. 223-245.

Bustamante, A., Ojeda, G., and Castaneda, X. (2008), "Willingness To Pay For Cross-Border Health Insurance Between The United States And Mexico", *Health Affairs*, Vol. 27 No. 1, pp. 169-178.

Butler, R. (1980), "The Concept of a Tourist Area Cycle of Evolution: Implications for management of Resources", *Canadian Geographer*, Vol. 24 No. 1, pp. 5-12.

Butler, R. (2000), "Tourism and the environment: a geographic perspective", *Tourism Geographies*, Vol. 2 No. 3, pp. 337-359.

Castonguay, G. and Brown, A. (1993), "Plastic Surgery Tourism proving a boon for Costa Rica's surgeons", *Canadian Medical Association Journal*, Vol. 148 No. 1, pp. 74-76.

Chan, M., 2012, "Opening Remarks on WHO Reform: Meeting of Members States on Programmes and Priority Setting", 27 February 2012, Geneva Switzerland, available at: http://www.who.int/dg/speeches/2012/reform_priorities_20120227/en/index.html (accessed 13 March 2012).

Chanda, R. (2002), *Trade in Health Services Bulletin of the World Health Organization*, Vol. 80 No. 2, pp. 158-163.

Chen, J. (2007), "Wellness Tourism: Measuring Consumers' quality of Life", in *First Hospitality and Leisure: Business Advances and Applied Research Conference*, Chen, J., Gherissi-Labben, T., and Mungill, A. (Eds.), available at: http://www.ichlar.ch/proceedgings (accessed 12 January 2012).

Connell, J. (2006), "Medical tourism: Sea Sun Sand and ... surgery", *Tourism Management*, Vol. 7 No. 6, pp. 1093-1100.

Connell, J. (2011), *Medical Tourism*, CABI International, Oxfordshire.

Da Silva, C., Hoppe, A., Ravanello, M., and Mello, N. (2005), "Medical waste management in the south of Brazil", *Waste Management*, Vol. 25, pp. 600-605.

Didaskalou, E., Nastos, P., and Matzarakis, A. (2004), "The Development Prospects for Greek Health Tourism and the Role of the Bioclimatic Regime in Greece, in Matzarakis, A., de Freitas, C. and Scott, D., *Advances in Tourism Climatology*, Freiburg, available at: http://www.mif.uni-freiburg.de/ISB/ws2/report/didaskalou.pdf (accessed 10 March 2012), pp. 149-57.

Fallas, H. (2009), "100.000 turistas vienen al año a recibir tratamiento medico", *La Nación*, available at: http://wvw.nacion.com/ln_ee/2009/marzo/13/economia1903413.html# (accessed 11 November 2011)

Gatrell, A. and Lovett, A. (1986), "The Geography of Hazardous Waste Disposal in England and Wales", *Area*, Vol. 18 No. 4, pp. 275-283.

George, B. (2009), "Medical tourism in India: A case study of Apollo Hospitals", in Smith, M and Puczkó, L. (2009), *Medical and Wellness Tourism*, Elsevier Science and Technology Books, Burlington, MA. pp. 367-372.

Gesler, W. and Meade, M. (1988), "Locational and Population Factors in Health Care-Seeking Behavior in Savanna, Georgia", *Health Services Research*, Vol. 23 No. 3, pp. 443-462.

Gilbert, E. (1949), "The Growth of Brighton", *The Geographical Journal*, Vol. 114 No. 1/3, pp. 30-52.

Global Sustainable Tourism Criteria (2011), *Global Sustainable Tourism Criteria*, available at: http://new.gstcouncil.org/ (accessed 1 December 2011).

Goodrich, J. and Goodrich, G. (1987), "Health-care tourism – an exploratory study", *Tourism Management*, Vol. 8 No. 3, pp. 217-222.

Goodrich, J. (1993a), "Health-care tourism in the Caribbean", in Gayle, D. and Goodrich, J. (Eds.), *Tourism Marketing and Management in the Caribbean*, Routledge, NY, pp. 122-128.

Goodrich, J. (1993b), "Socialist Cuba: A study of Health Tourism", *Journal of Travel Research*, Vol. 32, pp. 36-41.

Goodrich, J. (1994), "Health Tourism a new Positioning Strategy for Tourist Destination", *Journal of International Consumer Marketing*, Vol. 6. No. 3-4, pp. 227-238.

Hamilton, J. (2007), "Medical Tourism Creates Thai Doctor Shortage", available at: http://www.npr.org/templates/story/story.php?storyId=16735157 (accessed 8 December 2011).

Hall, C. (1992), "Adventure, Sport and Health Tourism", in Weiler, B. and Hall, C. (Eds.), *Special Interest Tourism*, Belhaven Press, London, pp. 141-158.

Hall, C. (2003), "Spa and Health Tourism", in Hudson, S. (Ed.), *Sport and Adventure Tourism*, Haworth Press, New York, pp. 273-292.

Hall, C. and Page, S. (2006), *The Geography of Tourism and Recreation: Environment, Place and Space*, Routledge, London.

Hall, C. (2011), "Health and medical tourism: a kill or cure for global public health", *Tourism Review*, Vol. 66 No. 1, 2, pp. 4-15.

Hancock, D. (2006), *The Complete Medical Tourist: Your guide to inexpensive dental cosmetic and medical surgery abroad*, John Blake, United Kingdom.

Hanson, F. (2008), "A revolution in Healthcare: Medicine meets the marketplace", *Public Affairs Review*, Vol. 59, pp. 4.

Harvard Medical Letter, 2008, "Virtual hitchhiker's guide to the medical universe", *Harvard Medical Letter*, Vol. 33 No. 12.

Henthorne, T. and Miller, M., (2003), "Cuban Tourism in the Caribbean Context: A Regional Impact Assessment", *Journal of Travel Research*, Vol. 42, pp. 84-93.

Johnston, R., Crooks, V., Snyder, J., Kingsbury, P. (2010), "What is known about the effects of medical tourism in destination and departure countries? A scoping review", *International Journal for Equity in Health*, Vol. 9 No. 24, available at: www.equityhealthj.com/content/9/1/24 (accessed 12 January 2012).

Joint Commission International (JCI) (2012), "Home – Joint Commission International", available at: http://www.jointcommissioninternational.org/ (accessed 25 June 2012).

Judkins, G. (2007), "Persistence of the US - Mexico Border: Expansion of medical-tourism amid Trade Liberalization", *Journal of Latin American Geography*, Vol. 6 No. 2, pp.11-32.

Kanavos, P., McKee, M., Richards, T. (1999), "Cross border health care in Europe", *BMJ*, Vol. 318, pp. 1157-1158.

Leng, C. (2007), "Medical Tourism in Malaysia: International Movement of Healthcare Consumer and the Commodification of Healthcare", *Asia Research Institute Working Paper Series*, No. 83.

Lunt, N., Smith, R., Exworthy, M., Green, S., Horsfall, D. and Mannion, R. (no date), "Medical Tourism: Treatments, Markets and Health System Implications: A Scoping Review", available at: http://www.oecd.org/dataoecd/51/11/48723982.pdf (accessed 15 Jan 2012).

Lunt, N., Machin, L., Green, S., Mannion, R. (2011), "Are there implications for quality of care for patients who participate in international medical tourism?" *Expert Rev. Pharmacoeconomics Outcomes Res.*, Vol. 11 No. 2, pp. 133-136.

McCool, S., Moisey, R. and Nickerson, N. (2001), "What should tourism sustain? The disconnect with industry perceptions of useful indicators", *Journal of Travel Research*, Vol. 40, pp. 124-131.

Mainil, T., Platenkamp, V., and Meulemans, H. (2011), "The discourse of medical tourism in the media", *Tourism Review*, Vol. 66 No. 1 and 2, pp. 31-44.
Martin, L. (2009), "Reproductive Tourism in the age of Globalization", *Globalizations*, Vol. 6 No. 2, pp. 249-263.
Mathieson, A. and Wall, G. (1982), *Tourism: Economic, Physical and Social Impacts*, Longman, London.
Mieczkowski, Z. (1995), *Environmental Issues of Tourism and Recreation*, University Press of America, Lanham, MD.
Mirrer-Singer, P. (2007), "Medical malpractice overseas: the legal uncertainty surrounding medical tourism", *Law and Contemporary Problems*, Vol. 70 No. 2, pp. 211-33.
Mitman, G. (2003), "Hay Fever Holiday: Health, Leisure, and Place in Gilded-Age America", *Bulletin of Historic Medicine*, Vol. 77, pp. 600-635.
Mueller, H. and Kaufmann, E. (2001), "Wellness Tourism: Market Analysis of a Special Health Tourism Segment and implications for the Hotel Industry", *Journal of Vacation Marketing*, Vol. 7 No. 1, pp. 5-17.
NaRanong A. and NaRanong V. (2011), "The Effects of medical tourism: Thailand's Experience", Bulletin of the World Health Organization, Vol. 89, pp. 336-344.
National Accreditation Board for Hospitals and Healthcare Providers (2012), National Accreditation Board for Hospitals and Healthcare Providers, available at: http://www.nabh.co/ (accessed 25 June 2012), QHA Trent Accreditation (2012), QHA Trent, availabele at: http://www.qha-international.co.uk/ (accessed 25 June 2012).
Reisman, D. (2010), "Health Tourism: Social Welfare Through International Trade", Edward Elgar, Cheltenham UK.
Richter, L. (2003), "International Tourism and its global Public Health Consequences", *Journal of Travel Research*, Vol. 41, pp. 340-347.
Rogers, D. (2007), "Faulty Control on Biowaste Creates a Lurking Health Danger" available at: http://www.amcostarica.com/060707.htm#32 (accessed 9 March 2012).
Sagoe-Moses, C., Pearson, R., and Jagger, J. (2001), "Risk health care workers in developing countries", *N Engl J Med.*, Vol. 345 No. 7, pp. 538-541.
Smith, G. (2006), "The Globalization of Medical Care: Can Medical Tourism Reduce Medical Care Costs June 27, 2006", available at: http://aging.senate.gov/hearing_detail.cfm?id=270728& (accessed 15 February 2008).
Smith, M. and Puczkó, L. (2009), *Medical and Wellness Tourism*, Elsevier Science and Technology Books, Burlington, MA.
Smyth, F. (2008), "Medical Geography: Understanding health inequalities", *Progress in Human Geography*, Vol. 32 No. 1, pp. 119-127.
Spillane, J. (1984), *Medical Travellers, Narratives from the seventeenth, eighteenth and nineteenth centuries*, Oxford University Press, Oxford.
Tattara, G. (2010), "Medical Tourism and Domestic Population Health", *Working Papers Department of Economics Ca' Foscari University of Venice*, available at: http://www.dse.unive.it/pubblicazioni (accessed 1 February 2012).
Towner, J. (1996), *A Historical Geography of Recreation and Tourism in the Western World 1540-1940*, John Wiley, NY.

Tourism Research and Marketing (TRAM) (2006), "Medical Tourism: A Global Analysis", TRAM, London.
Turner, L., 2007, "Medical tourism. Family medicine and international medical-related travel", *Canadian Family Physician*. Vol. 53 No. 10, pp. 1639-1641.
Turner, L. (2011), "Canadian medical tourism companies that have exited the marketplace: Content analysis of Websites used to market transnational medical travel", *Globalization and Health*, Vol. 7 No. 40, pp. 1-16.
Urology Times (2008), "Medical Tourists receive HIFU treatment abroad", *Urology Times*, Vol. 36 No. 9, pp.12.
United Nations (2009), *Medical Travel in Asia and the Pacific: Challenges and Opportunities*, United Nations Economic and Social Commission for Asia and the Pacific, Bangkok, Thailand.
Van Wilkinson, S. (2008), "Cuba's Tourism 'Boom": a curse or a blessing", *Third World Quarterly*, Vol. 29 No. 5, pp. 979-993.
Voigt, C., Laing, J., Wray, M., Brown, G., Howat, G., Weiler, B. and Trembath, R. (2010), "Health Tourism in Australia: Supply, Demand and Opportunities", *Sustainable Tourism Pty Ltd*. available at: http://www.sustainabletourismonline .com/42/growing-niche-markets/health-tourism-in-australia-supply-demand-and-opportunities (accessed 15 January 2012).
Voigt, C., Brown, G. and Howat, G. (2011), "Wellness tourist: in search of transformation", *Tourism Review*, Vol. 66 No. 1, 2, pp. 16-30.
World Health Organization (2007), "Wastes from Health-Care Activities Fact Sheet", available at: http://www.who.int/mediacentre/factsheets/fs253/en/ (accessed 15 February 2012).
World Health Organization (2011), "Global Health Observatory Data Repository: Health Workforce Aggregated Data, Density per 1000", available at: http://apps.who.int/ ghodata/# (accessed 27 February 2012).

Sustainable Tourism
"Wish you weren't here"

Thomas Meuser & Carola von Peinen

Introduction

Tourism, as one of the largest global economic sectors, plays an increasingly important role in the development of economically weaker countries and peripheral areas which do not possess raw materials or traditional industries. For these countries and destinations, tourism provides a tempting promise, as it can be quickly developed and attracting potential tourists seems a viable economic product.

Sustainable tourism is closely linked to the natural environment, is socially acceptable and is empathetic to the culture and the environment of a destination. Environmental protection, current social structures and culture can all be seen as providing an economic boom for a region. But the emphasis should be on advocating new developments that secure the needs of future generations as well as providing for the needs of the present.

The expression "sustainable" in this chapter, implies that we are discussing development that has a long term positive effect. This supports the notion that tourism clusters should advocate sustainable regional development. So, can an economic approach, similar to Cluster Theory, be linked to tourism and sustainable development, even when productivity, innovation and competitive ability are the motors of tourism development? The authors will attempt to verify this question and discover whether Cluster Theory and sustainable development are interdependent approaches. There is some support for their compatibility: productivity can be improved by lower costs. Business can be more effective if the population at the tourism destination is sharing benefits and the limitations and modifications can result in new tourism innovations. Thus, it could be shown that a *business cluster* can be compatible with the principles of sustainable tourism.

In the following chapter, aspects of Porter's Cluster Theory and the construct of sustainable tourism will be explained and the links between both approaches demonstrated.

Clusters of Sustainable Tourism

Cluster Theory and Cluster Definition
In 1990, Porter developed his work 'The Competitive Advantage of Nations', which was a new discussion about the specific competitive ability of several countries (Porter, 1990). Contrary to current opinions, global locations would become less and less important as globalization progressed. He suggested that spatial location was one of the most important aspects for international competitiveness. After a plethora of situation analyses in different countries and regions, he came to the realisation that, in defiance of the effects of worldwide trade, a great potential for competitiveness does not lie in, but outside, of companies, namely in the complete environment. Today's economic map is defined by clusters: a concentration of several industries with great economic success concentrated in one region or nation. Such agglomerations are found in every economy; especially in economically advanced countries (Porter, 1998).

The following section defines the cluster and explains the most important statements and phases of development, concerned mostly with Porter's works. Porter's article in the Harvard Business Review, develops the topic of ecology and social aspects inside clusters (Porter, 1998). Porter's text also illustrates how companies can profit from regional networking and gives a good summary of all important aspects that can be gained from these clusters.

Definition Cluster (Porter, 1998, p. 78):
"Clusters are geographic concentrations of interconnected companies and institutions in a particular field. Clusters encompass an array of linked industries and other entities important to competition. They include, for example, suppliers of specialized inputs, such as components, machinery, and services, and providers of specialized infrastructure."

So, clusters are about a geographic concentration of linked companies and institutions that work together in spatial and special sections in order to compete with other locations. Contrary to an industry, clusters are industry comprehensive and, therefore, can cross political and regional borders. Often their radius approximates to 350 km. Even regional foreign firms can be part of the cluster if they invest in the region, e.g. travel businesses within tourism. Well-known clusters, for example are the Computer Cluster in Silicon Valley, the Leatherware Cluster in North Italy or the Californian Wine Cluster (see Porter, 1998).

Clusters Improve Productivity
Productivity is improved through 3 main aspects in clusters:
1. Access to qualified personnel and special information.
2. Scale and synergy effects, based on good cooperation.
3. Motivation and comparability because of regional closeness.

Clusters Define the Direction and Increase the Tempo of Innovations
For maintaining competitiveness inside the cluster, companies always have to differentiate themselves from the others, for example by innovation and quality improvements. The following factors in the cluster can influence the innovation-ability in a positive way:

1. Consumers with high expectations of new products
2. Dynamic environment for new technologies through exchange in all levels of production
3. Regional proximity which is good for exchange of information and which increases competitive pressure

Clusters Build an Appeal for the Foundation of New Companies
It is a known fact that in a cluster, companies of different value-added-steps settle in regions with other supportive companies. Hence, companies which are searching for a location profit, will locate in regions where knowledge is available and there is the possibility of exchange with other businesses. Clusters need about 10 years to build a real USP (unique selling position). During this process, the companies and institutions change continuously. They can profit by their competitive advantage for a considerably long time, if internal or external circumstances do not lead to a market shift in consumers. The desire of a cluster is to create long term continuous economic growth and employment in that region.

The Social-Economy
The social structure of a location is an important element in Cluster Theory because the level of trust, community support and the engagement of the individual is very important for the success of a cluster (Porter, 1998). In addition the network of firms, suppliers and institutions is not enough for a cluster to be successful.

Porter's Diamond
In looking at the development of a cluster, it can be recognised that real national wealth is not handed down but gathered. So, it is not simply the natural conditions that make a region's competitiveness, but how the region evolves from these resources. This factor creation, the development of special factors, is the key to success. Successful businesses are those who are able to create competitiveness; however they are still interacting with their environment, which can also cause success or failure. Porter constructed these company internal and external aspects into 4 main factors, denoted as a diamond model (Figure 1).

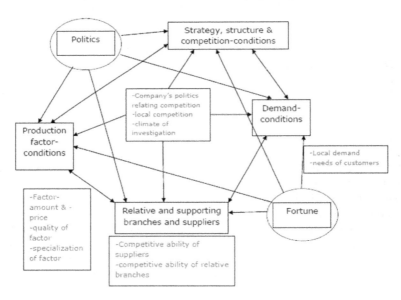

Figure 1:   Porter's Diamond (Porter, 1990, p. 223)

The Diamond model is now a core element of Porter's competition model. The result of a working, dynamic diamond is the development of special factors that are constituted for productivity and competitiveness.

Production Factor Conditions
These are the factors of regional location which are needed for production, such as human capital, material production factors, infrastructure and knowledge.

Demand Conditions
The classical Cluster Model separates local and international demand. A special role is provided for tourism, because here, the local demand depends on community and guests.

Relative and Supporting Industries and Suppliers
A further part of the diamond relates to good suppliers and other competitive industries of the environment, where the cluster may profit from cooperation and communication with them. The development of cooperation and teamwork resulting in creating a new product is especially important for tourism. The idea is to provide an attraction leading to a positive holiday experience, through consistent quality of complementary service providers (e.g. hotels, restaurants).

Strategy, Structure and Competition-Conditions
The fourth big determinant of a national competitive advantage in an industry is the context in which companies are organised and managed, and even the kind of local competitors (See the Cluster Maps for the USA and Portugal in Porter, 1998).

The Role of Fortune
Porter recognised that in a cluster, chance experiences played a role which could not be influenced by company or politics. For example, changing demands, wars abroad, or chance developments.

The Role of Politics
Competitive markets can only be created by companies, not by politics. The basic function of politics is to provide a national competitive-advantage, which has four determinants (Porter, 1990). Politics has to maintain political and economic stability in a region and to create an environment in a way that supports innovative companies, especially for tourism development (Scheyvens, 2002).

Success Factors for Cluster Building
Success of a cluster depends on many different factors. The following gives a summary of the most important:

- Strong personal relationships and engagement as key factors of success
- Cooperation and common comprehension of competitiveness
- Potential of the region and existing structures
- Interested communities which are independent of political parties or individual personalities
- Political support for pioneering companies

The success of a tourism cluster manifests itself in the level of customer satisfaction regarding the quality of service they experience. As the following picture shows, this is built by an interaction dimension, a product dimension, the quality of performance and the quality of experiences:

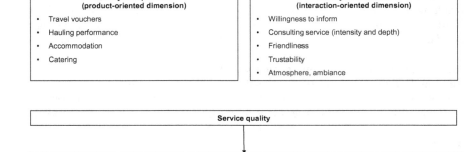

Figure 2:   Quality of Service

In order to increase the quality of performance, a positive attitude of the population and the staff is very important. Activities of the travelling industry affect nearly every area of life, and this is why a development strategy in the tourism sector always has to be involved with economic, social and environmental politics. Also, intensive staff training is an important aspect in maintaining guest satisfaction. Again to maintain a good quality experience, strong cooperation with the different service-suppliers is required.

Sustainability in the Development of Tourist Regions

Definition of Sustainable Tourism
"Sustainable tourism is probably the most important idea that has entered tourism management in the last 20 years, both as theory and as practice" (Lominé/Edmunds, 2007, p. 179). Ecotourism and community tourism account for sustainable development of many destinations. This concept is based on an idea created in 1987.

Definition 'Sustainability' (World Commission on Environment and Development, 1987, p. 4):
The 'Brundtland-Report' of 1987, defines 'sustainable development' as follows:
'We define sustainable development in simple terms as paths of progress which meet the needs and aspirations of the present generation without compromising the ability of future generations to meet their needs.'

From this article, which defines the 'generation contract', some aspects which are very important for tourism can be identified. The maintenance of ecological integrity and diversity, the fulfilling of human basic-needs, the assurance of options for future generations, reduction of unfairness and increasing of self-determination (Steinecke, 1995).

Sustainability became inevitable, especially in the course of tourist development within Eastern-Europe. This region has tried not to repeat the mistakes that were identified in Western Europe. It is asserted that many tourist destinations are found in ecologically sensitive systems and that their very popularity has a negative effect upon the destination. The example of Mallorca demonstrates that the eco-system alone, could not cope with mass tourism. For example, waste water problems, animosity from the community that could not make profits from tourism etc.

One of the problems of tourism development is that of the community and how it can be involved in tourism development directly benefiting it. The past has demonstrated that in many cases the community is forgotten, especially when there is mass tourism development. Environmental impacts are commonplace in many mass tourism destinations, illustrated by lack of water, pollution and other negative aspects. This often results in degrading the image of the region and a consequential flight of tourists. What remains are costs and problems often leading to the decay of the region. Torremolinos (southern coast of Spain), for example, was a popular holiday destination at the beginning of the '90s; today it is only mentioned as exhibiting negative images, such as ugly hotels and equally negative supporting tourist structures (for further examples see Holloway, 2009).

Definition "Sustainable Tourism" (Hunter, 1997, p. 850):

"This term has come to represent and encompass a set of principles, policy prescriptions, and management methods which chart a path for tourism development such that a destination's area environmental resource base (including natural, built, and cultural features) is protected for future development."

Sustainable development is very important in tourism because a significant number of the supplies are common goods which are especially affected by anti-social behaviour (Osterloh, 1997). Many tourist goods can be considered to be public goods but lose quality through over consumption. The goods differ in exclusiveness and rivalry for consumption, which is illustrated in the following image:

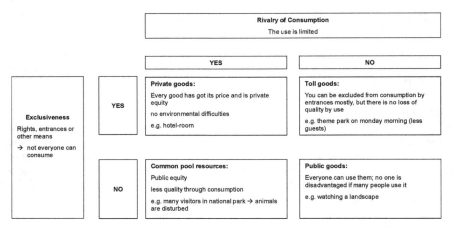

Figure 3: Typologies of Goods

This suggests that you would rather take the risk of a little impairment, rather than hope for the loyalty of others – giving the best results for both parties. This is shown by the example of a nature-park: if everyone talked quietly and stayed on the footpaths visitors could then watch a large variety of different animals (best result). But no-one knows if all the guests are going to be quiet, so people bend the rules to benefit themselves by leaving the paths and talking when they want to (sub-optimal result).

This typical negative tourist behaviour increases when tourist attractions (landscapes, special cultural goods) become overused. Furthermore, some of these resources are not always renewable (rain forest, unique plants and animals, special cultures and so on...). In economic terms we would use the expression "USP", which would justify a high price. But price as a controller of supply and

Sustainable Tourism

demand does not work because these goods are public goods (freely available). So, there is a need to develop policies preventing the travel industry from destroying its own resources, especially those goods that cannot be reproduced. This is often mentioned as a goal in current sustainable discussions, although the realisation of this might become difficult because of the great numbers of different tourist stakeholders.

Pyramid of Sustainable Tourism

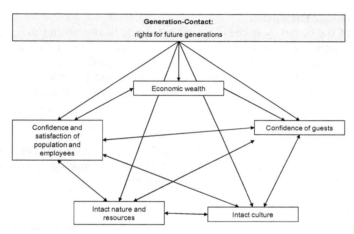

Figure 4: The Magic Pentagon-Pyramid of Sustainable Development

The basis of the pyramid is built on 5 main aspects which are all equal and which all follow the aim of the generation-contract:

- Satisfaction of the population and employee needs
- Intact nature and resources
- Intact culture
- Satisfaction of guests
- Economic welfare

These 5 basic elements contain three dimensions which build sustainable tourism:

The Ecological Dimension
Protecting landscape and the environment by businesses engaging in environmental protection will ensure long-term income generation from tourism. Therefore, not just the costs (e.g. through new developments) are important, but also the savings through advantages (like avoiding over use of resources and recycling, reducing and reusing resources).

The Economic Dimension
Growth of the economy is seen as a basis for satisfaction within the population and community because it creates jobs and increases the standard of living. It would be ideal to integrate tourism into the sustainable development of the economy. It will help to maintain income and use the potential resources of a region efficiently. This leads to independence of external markets, decreasing the risk of an economic crisis.

The Socio-Cultural Dimension
This dimension manifests itself in the satisfaction of guests and hosts, through the maintenance of culture – a very important good for tourism. It promotes the local culture but protects it from over consumption.

Sustainable Development through Tourism Clusters
In view of the above text, it is conspicuous that certain phrases come up again and again: productivity, innovations, quality, competitive advantages and the region are all central aspects to Tourism Clusters. This leads to the assumption that sustainable tourism and Cluster Theory have similar aims. Nevertheless, economically these elements are fundamental to clusters, however sustainable tourism is based on a more idealistic view of the world.

Frame-Conditions
Generally, both concepts follow a long-term orientation and have a systemic character. Both constructs, the diamond as well as the pyramid, are systems whose different aspects depend on each other. In sustainable tourism the generation contract is the most important one, in the clusters it is the competitive ability.

In both cases, future developments can be founded upon information networks with common aims, but in which any company can act absolutely independently. Political action and support are important, because they are able to influence the environmental conditions. Political stakeholders provide a special level of quality, security and environmental protection. This in turn creates a new interest for companies to invest in pioneering technologies, optimize processes and become environmentally sustainable. For both cluster development and tourism, the government has to change the framework conditions in such a way that competitive ability is supported, securing a stable, long-term economic climate.

The Natural Environment and Culture
Combining business clusters and tourism, nature and culture have a special role. On the one hand, they determine the spatial environment; on the other hand they are part of the tourist product and of the input-factors of the cluster. This means that they are resources that have to be developed and specialised, but may not be consumed completely because they build the capital of tourism. Opportunities arise, for example through landscape protection of regions, restoration of monuments or an advancement of the physical infrastructure. Thus, environmental and monument protection is related to tourism clusters, where an important condition is not to destroy the resources which are the rudiments of economic success (because this would endanger competitive ability).

The culture of an area supports the cluster approach through two dimensions: firstly through the material culture, such as buildings and cultural performances (dance, music, literature), and secondly through destination image and cultural tradition for the environment of the company to operate in. Thus cultural values and traditional structures have great influence on the competitive ability of a region. For the success of a cluster, it is really important to know and accept this value system, in order to recognise possible potential developments. This again supports the exchange of information and propagates the potential for innovation, based around the unique culture of the spatial location.

Common Aims of Clusters and Sustainable Tourism
One aim is competitive advantages through environmental awareness. Environmental and cultural protection applies pressure on companies to work more efficiently under greater restrictive conditions; So producing cost savings, together with the possibility of improving competition through differentiation of attributes.

Productivity and efficiency: Productivity and eco-efficiency are pre-conditions to reach competitive advantage and reduce the use of natural resources, thus supporting both clusters and sustainable tourism.

Economic growth: Clusters are magnets in terms of economic development: They build a dynamic action field for investors, employees, new enterprises and thus create new workplaces. Sustainable tourism also wants to create a long-term revenue foundation for the community and so make a region economically successful.

Increase quality of life of the region: If a region can develop independently, this results in a stronger ability of the population to take on new challenges. Satisfaction of the population is very important for both the development of clusters and sustainable tourism.

Protect and support uniqueness of the region: For the tourism cluster, unique selling propositions (USP) are based on the uniqueness of the natural environment together with the culture of the destination. Both approaches build on the individuality and variety of the region and have a central interest in supporting each other.

Aspects of Sustainability in Tourism Clusters
The great number of similarities between the two approaches suggests that they are compatible in a number of ways. The outcomes of sustainable tourism can even support the aims of a cluster. These consequences are shown in the figure below:

Sustainable Tourism

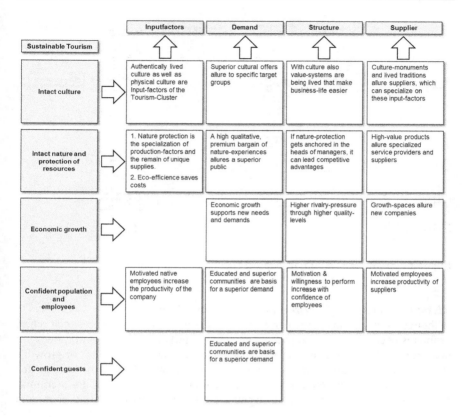

Figure 5:   Influences of Sustainable Tourism on Clusters

One assertion that can be made is that the aims of sustainable tourism can influence the development of clusters in a positive way. That is to say, a cluster can be supported by sustainable tourism and not hindered by its development.

Aspects of Clusters in the Concept of Sustainable Tourism

The concept of sustainable tourism can conversely make a profit by the development of a cluster. The natural environment and culture can be maintained through business efficiency and increasing quality. One of the aspects of Cluster Theory focuses on the needs of the community and guests because this is the derivation of any competitive ability. Figure 6 gives an overview:

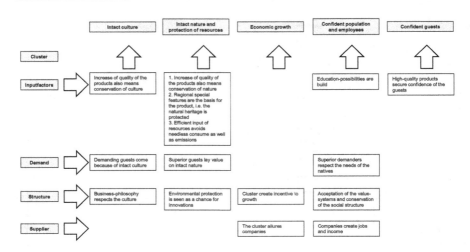

Figure 6: Influences of Clusters on Sustainable Tourism

Risks: Development of Clusters and Sustainable Tourism

Although both systems have many common features and can support each other, problems occur from time to time when controls fail or framework conditions are not optimal. The cluster is a system that can easily become a 'spiral of growth'. Without any controlling factors, it can easily produce too many tourists for specific regions. Here, the capacity of the region is very important. Furthermore, there is the danger of a growing dependence on the tourist, creating economic instability in the region.

The impacts that are produced through tourism are not always transferred to the beneficiaries, however details such as environmental damage, economic leakages and the multiplier effect also need to be considered; in essence the tourist (or the tourism industry) has only been superficially covered here. The literature suggests that the costs of tourism can be divided into three main categories (Hopfenbeck/Zimmer, 1993, p. 44):

1. Economic Costs:
Examples are traffic problems, landslide security and reforestation.

2. Social and Cultural Costs:
Such as destruction of traditional social and value systems, loss of culture, commercialisation, criminality, rise in price of land and lifestyle, as well as rural depopulation.

3. Environmental Costs:
Waste, pollution of air and water, threat to natural bio systems, destruction of landscapes.

A further problem relates to co-operation between the various companies and institutions of a region. To create a sustainable tourism development, every stakeholder and tourism actor has to work together. But often – mainly in smaller regions – certain business and social structures hinder teamwork and partnerships. These can be reflected in: political structures, alliances and associations, the fear of working with a competitor, known vs. unknown, etc. are only some of the difficulties occurring in some cluster and tourism destinations.

Model of the Future of a Sustainable Cluster
The above problems demonstrate the need for government to intervene as an arbitrator and to direct development through regulations, laws and environmental conditions. Therefore, a regional development plan has to be created, supporting the principles of sustainability and not hindering the competitive ability of the region. It is evident that political direction can influence the activities of companies and population through the following interactions (see Figure 7):

- Investments in infrastructure as well as support for competitive advantage
- Bulletin boards, associations or destination management organizations
- New laws and conditions
- Investment in education and waste management
- Investments in research and development
- Support of information and communication

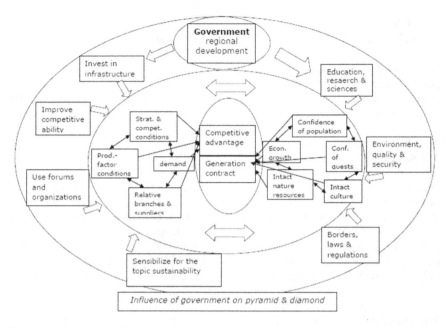

Figure 7:   Model of the Future

Conclusions

It is argued that Cluster Theory and sustainable tourism follow very similar objectives, even if there are some differences, for example the principle of sustainability is more idealistic, while the cluster follows more economic principles. It is further asserted that both theories can co-exist. In many aspects the aim of the one approach supports the other. Reaching competitive advantage and following the principles of sustainable tourism are the same and under specific conditions even dependent upon each other. The increase of business quality, the more efficient use of resources, as well as the support of innovations are basic principles of both theories.

The emergence of sustainability can be traced back almost 40 years and has accelerated in importance. In tandem with this has been the need for companies to become more environmentally responsible, especially in terms of the climate debate and the use of sustainable energy resources. Hence, the need for sustainability in tourism will increase, because today's trend identifies nature, culture and community as important elements, manifested also in the "year of eco-tourism" (WTO), in 2002.

Sustainable tourism is a long term project which can be supported by cluster development, because it produces long term organic growth of a region without endangering its individuality. Cluster Theory supports sustainable tourism, but equally can also be found to have a positive influence on developing sustainable measures in the region.

Final Thoughts

For many regions suffering from rural depopulation and underemployment, sustainable tourism is a great opportunity and can be achieved through the development of a cluster. Contrary to many views, it is not just a cluster which can influence sustainability in a positive way, but sustainable tourism can also support the development of a cluster. Thus, it can be shown that sustainable economics which respects the social needs of the population, can lead to increased income and competitive advantages. Sustainability needs to be placed on a priority agenda for the travel industry because the quality of the tourist product depends on the service quality of the employees, the friendliness of the community, together with the natural beauty and cultural authenticity of the destination.

So, *sustainable tourism* is fundamental for *successful business destinations*. Its economic potential, though, is often undervalued. In our opinion, tourism is just at the very beginning of a development that will change many facets of our economic provision, the view of the world and our way of thinking. Clusters and sustainable tourism are an essential part of a successful future.

References

Holloway, C. (2009), *The business of tourism*, 8th Ed., Pearson Education Ltd., Harlow.
Hopfenbeck, W., Zimmer, P. (1993), *Umweltorientiertes Tourismusmanagement: Strategien, Checklisten, Fallstudien*, Landsberg/Lech.
Hunter, C. (1997), "Sustainable tourism as an adaptive paradigm", in *Annals of Tourism Research*, No. 4, pp. 850-886.
Lominé, L., Edmunds, J. (2007), *Key concepts in tourism*, Pelgrave Macmillan, New York.
Müller, H. (1995),"Regionale Nachhaltigkeit – von der Idee zum Leitbild regionaler Entwicklung" in Steinecke, A. v. (Ed.), *Tourismus und nachhaltige Entwicklung – Strategien und Lösungsansätze*, Europäisches Tourismus Institut, Trier, pp. 11-18.

Osterloh, G. (1997),"Der Reisestern: Regionalisierung eines Modells zu Evaluation der Nachhaltigkeit von Reisen am Beispiel der Bundesrepublik Deutschland" in Becker C. (Ed.), *Beiträge zur nachhaltigen Regionalentwicklung mit Tourismus*, Verlag für universitäre Kommunikation, Berlin, pp. 57-76.

Porter, M. E. (1990), *The Competitive Advantage of Nations*, Free Press, New York.

Porter, M. E. (1998), "Clusters and the new economics of competition", *Harvard Business Review, Nov./Dec.*, pp. 77-90.

Scheyvens, R. (2002), *Tourism for development. Empowering Communities (Themes in Tourism)*, Pearson Education Ltd., Harlow.

Steinecke, A. 1(995), "Tourismus und nachhaltige Entwicklung: Strategien und Lösungsansätze", in Steinecke, A. (Ed.), *Tourismus und nachhaltige Entwicklung – Strategien und Lösungsansätze*, Trier, pp. 7-10.

World Commission on Environment and Develepment (Ed.) (1987), "Presentation of the report of the commission on environment and development to UNEP's 14th governing council session", Nairobi.

The Shift toward Sustainability in the Travel Trade Industry

Britt Ventriglia & Ruth Rios-Morales

"Tourism pretends to be apolitical, but it encapsulates problems of power and worth on a grand and global scale" (Mowforth et al., 2008, p. 224).

Introduction

It is an accepted maxim that the tourism industry has had both positive and negative impacts on the environment and local communities. As a result, the concept of sustainability has been embraced to regulate industry practices and respond to a growing market of concerned consumers. An increasing number of sustainable brand labels and certification organizations have emerged to evaluate the sustainable nature of products, competing with travel trade organizations and hotel companies who also provide verification of sustainable measures. It seems apparent that the concept of sustainability is now widely accepted; however there appears to be no universal understanding of exactly what sustainability encompasses; this is especially true amongst travel trade companies and adds further confusion to consumers' understanding of products.

This chapter outlines the emergence of sustainability and how it is understood and perceived within the travel trade industry. In addition it evaluates achievements and dissatisfaction related to the implementation of standards, as well as appraising demand for sustainability and customer expectation. It also suggests that without a clear universally accepted sustainability label and certification, the lack of understanding of the concept among customers will continue. It is therefore imperative to communicate a clear message of what sustainability encompasses and the benefits attained when embracing the standards. The importance of networks and the creation of partnership strategies have been advocated in sustainability research; however, the existing successful brand labels and their effect on consumer education is still limited.

The Importance and Impacts of the Travel Trade Industry

During the last century, the travel trade industry had become one of the fastest growing economic sectors in the world; both in developed and developing countries (Butcher, 2003; UNWTO, 2009). The travel trade industry is a vast and complex system composed of inter-related and inter-dependent enterprises, organizations and services; this industry constitutes one of the main expanding pillars of the economies of many countries (Bohdanowicz, 2009; Rowe *et al.*, 2002; Solnet *et al.*, 2010). Currently, the industry provides 1 in every 12.3 jobs (WTTC and Oxford Economics, 2010) and generates an economic impact reaching close to US$ 1,600 billion worldwide (WTTC, 2009). With the rapid growth and dynamic role that the hospitality and tourism industry is playing in the global economy, figures are estimated to double by 2020 (WTTC, 2009).

In addition to providing employment and economic growth, the travel trade industry also has the capacity to offer a valuable educational experience. The United Nations' World Tourism Organization (UNWTO) has declared that intercultural intelligence and personal friendships fostered through tourism and travel have demonstrated that they are a powerful force for improving international understanding, and can contribute towards cooperation among the nations of the world (UNWTO, 2009). A recent study on overseas education revealed that international education travel programs and institutions are expected to double their revenue in the next decade due to colleges and governments recruiting international students (Fischer, 2009). Related articles discuss how the big business of global **education significantly helps to keep people moving around the globe** (Brennan and Ritters, 2003). This increase shows how even with the effects of the current global economic crisis, the changes in foreign currencies, and the dangers of political instability, families and education institutions still see traveling overseas as an important part of enhancing education (Fischer, 2009).

Scholarly research suggests that the travel trade industry provides an array of positive impacts and opportunities, however it also emphasizes that if travel and tourism is not responsibly managed and monitored, it can lead to negative consequence for the environment, society and local economies (Sauvé, 1996; UNESCO, 2005; Buckley, 2009; Lane, 2009; UNWTO, 2009). Whilst the travel trade industry generates a long list of positive impacts on society, the environment and economy of countries, the negative impacts are also numerous. Table 1 summarizes the positive and negative impacts listed by a number of academic researchers.

Areas of Concern	Positive Impacts	Negative Impacts
Social & Cultural Impacts	Educational influence Local community mix Improvement of local life Better facilities, and infrastructure Job opportunities Conservation efforts on historical or cultural sites	Lack of Resources Poor sanitation could lead to heath concerns Infrastructure overuse or damage Resentment or anti-social behavior by local /visitors, resulting in poor service and perceptions Dilution of local traditions, customs, and values.
Environmental Impacts	Conservation and protection measures encouraged. Increase income and investment for upkeep and policy. Appreciation and enjoyment of flora and fauna established and promoted.	Over-development, over-population Displacement of people and wildlife Diminished or destroyed natural resources Increased rubbish, littler or waste. Greater air, noise pollution and Co2. Battle for land, industry perceived as hostile take-over of nature and society.
Economic Impacts	Employment, improvement to skilled economy Generates wealth locally, nationally, and globally New development and transport systems Foreign direct investment Increase in balance of payments, multiplier effect.	Loss to outside suppliers, leakage from local economy Labor supply problems, exploitation, seasonal work Possible over-dependencies' on industry by locals and government Inflation on local goods and services Cities and sites perceived as economic machines, capital intensive geared toward quick returns.

Table 1: Overview of the Travel Trade Industry's impacts (Blair and Hitchcock, 2001; Rowe *et al.*, 2002, Bohdanowicz, 2003; Butler, 2006; Mowforth, 2008; Moscardo, 2009; Bergin-Seers and Mair, 2009; Weaver, 2009; WTTC and Oxford Economics, 2010), compiled

The Emergence of Corporate Social Responsibility (CSR)

Although the concept of Corporate Social Responsibility has moved to the forefront in recent times, the malpractice of companies such Enron, WorldCom, and India's recent Satyam Computer Services scandal, labeled "India's Enron" by Forbes (Mohan, 2009), has marred its image. The model of Corporate Social Responsibility was introduced in the early years of this century, connected to the well-known case of the Standard Oil Co. of New Jersey. Numerous programs have been common practice for quite some time (Kotler and Lee, 2005); currently, the notion of CSR is an essential subject taught in business schools.

In addition, it has become standard practice to provide a statement of ethical standards, sustainable energy efforts and other charity or foundation program involvement via corporate websites or annual reports (Banerjee, 2006; Murphy,

2009). Numerous corporations identify themselves with business ethics, claiming responsibility towards the environment and society (Butcher, 2003), which nowadays, is seen as a very important component in the market.

Although, companies still have free reign in defining their own Corporate Social Responsibility (CRS) programs on a local level, they are embracing *the notion of being accountable towards society* (Banerjee, 2006). *"In its broadest sense, CSR takes as its premise that businesses ought to justify their existence in terms of service to the community rather than mere profit"* (Bohdanowicz and Zientara, 2009, p. 152).

The Shift Towards Sustainability

Sustainability has often been included in the context of CSR programs, however, while CSR programs have been common practice for quite some time, sustainability, with practices such as carbon emissions reporting, has only recently emerged into the mainstream (Bohdanowicz and Zientara, 2009; WTTC, 2009).

Although there is no general consensus on when the concept of sustainability was first introduced, a number of scholars concur that it appears to have originated in the late 1980s with the publication of the Brundtland Report (Elkington and Thorpe, 2007; Banerjee, 2006; Gossling *et al.*, 2009). The Brundtland Report, otherwise known as Our Common Future, was the seed for the development of sustainability into the mainstream of business, marking a new phase in global sustainability strategy.

The Brundtland Commission describes sustainable development as a process of change in which resources, directions of investments and orientation of technological development are made consistent with present and future needs (U.N. World Commission on Environment and Development, 1987). This broad definition has been cited as the root cause of several challenges and controversies over how sustainability should be operationalized and measured (Banerjee, 2006). Several authors from a variety of disciplines have also pointed out that this definition does not include the notion of human needs and wants (Redclift, 1989; Banerjee, 2006), nor does it say anything of the human relationships behind all tourism interchanges (Mowforth *et al.*, 2008).

The Dow Jones Sustainability Index website, launched in 1999, was the first global index tracking the financial performance of the leading sustainability-driven companies worldwide. This index defines corporate sustainability as follows: "Corporate Sustainability is a business approach that creates long-term shareholder value by embracing opportunities and managing risks deriving from economic, environmental and social developments. Corporate sustainability leaders achieve long-term shareholder value by gearing their strategies and management to harness the market's potential for sustainability products and services while at the same time successfully reducing and avoiding sustainability costs and risks" (Dow Jones Sustainability Indexes website, 2010).

More recently, the "triple bottom line" concept is emerging as a popular conceptualization of sustainability and is receiving significant attention within organizations and business communities (Bohdanowicz, 2003) and explicitly with business managers (Brown et al., 2006). The triple bottom line (3BL) represents an organization's social, environmental and economic bottom line (Elkington, 1998). 3BL also known as "people, planet, profit" or "the three pillars", are terms made famous by John Elkington in the early 1990s, co-founder and chair of *SustainAbility,* a sustainable business consultancy (Elkington and Thorpe, 2007).

The dispute over the application and interpretation of sustainability implies that even the definition itself can be problematic (Hall and Gossling, 2009). Sustainability is a word describing a vast, diverse, and complex system with many subdivisions and meanings (Gossling et al., 2009) and it has been suggested that sustainability must be put into context with the industry and organization (Jonker and Witte, 2006; Mootee, 2009). However, a realistic approach to the definition of sustainability can be determined as "meeting the needs of the present without compromising the ability of the future generations to meet their own needs" (WCED, 1987, p. 43).

The Progression of Sustainability in the Tourism and Hospitality Industry

Interest in sustainability has recently grown in all sectors, including the tourism industry. Some say we are witnessing a significant social and cultural shift in terms of consumption, in particular in the hospitality and tourism industry (Williams, 2002). The travel trade industry has become more committed to reforming itself and tourists towards more sustainable practices (Gossling et al., 2009). "…the travel and tourism industry has a vested interest in protecting the natural and cultural resources which are the core of its business…[therefore, the industry]…must contribute to the conservation, production and restoration of the earth's ecosystem, environmental protection,…this should constitute an integral part of the tourism development process…tourism development should recognize and support the identity of culture and interest of indigenous peoples" (United Nations: Agenda 21, 1992, p. 7)

As sustainable awareness grows and consumers become increasingly conscious of their impact, travelers are seeking low impact travel destinations which they can enjoy and also be informed of their eco-footprint (Bergin-Seers and Mair, 2009). A so called "Green Tourist" has emerged in the mainstream and has been recognized as driving change in both developed and developing countries, more significantly in the leisure tourism market (Bergin-Seers and Mair, 2009). Green consumers have been described by "their avoidance of products that have negative impacts." These products can be related to health, environment, use of large amounts of resources, unnecessary waste, animal cruelty, or by having adverse affects on other countries or cultures (Bergin-Seers and Mair, 2009; Moscardo, 2009). Although this shift in consumer behavior, in the last few years, has been significant (Weaver, 2009; York, 2009), the green tourist is still a niche market in its infancy of development (HBR Green, 2008; Hall, 2009).

Over the years, sustainable tourism has been related to green travel, ethical tourism, responsible tourism, ecotourism, and even low-impact travel (Williams, 2002). Table 2, visualizes the diffusion process of sustainably as a preventive *measure and summarizes the progression of sustainability in the tourism and hospitality industry according to Hall and Gosling.*

In Table 2 it is observed that consumer behavior, demand and supply of sustainable products, are conceptually intertwined (Hall and Gossling, 2009); and *policy measures are aligned with consumer demand on each side of the Table.* As in the case of tourism services, when production and consumption are simultaneous, the exchanges are ongoing, and a need for positive and negative feedback is essential for progress (Hall and Gossling, 2009).

The Shift toward Sustainability in the Travel Trade Industry

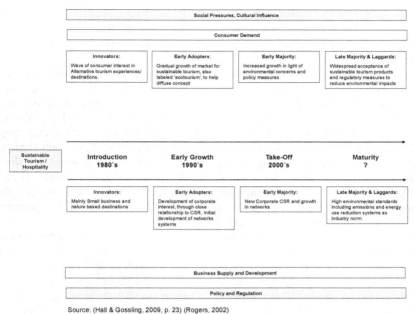

Source: (Hall & Gossling, 2009, p. 23) (Rogers, 2002)

Table 2: Summarized Progression of Sustainability in Tourism and Hospitality (Hall and Gossling, 2009, p. 23; Rogers, 2002)

The Role of the Media and Policy Change toward Sustainability

Moss (2007, p. 67) writes that the key role of government is to coordinate expectations in a favorable direction through expansionary fiscal policy; "Managing expectations may be the most important function of macroeconomic policy, both monetary and fiscal". The World Travel and Tourism Council (2009) states on its website that sustainable industries have grown because governments realize they have real economic and social value and have begun to create the necessary infrastructures to accommodate this development.

In recent years, media and advertising companies have shown a propensity towards tabling ethical practices. From the influential Oscar winning film, "The Inconvenient Truth" (Gore, 2006), to children's books, such as "If the world ran out of B's" (Shireman and Shireman, 2002), consumers are becoming more aware of climate change and sustainability issues (Elkington and Thorpe, 2007). The role of the media and policy measures has been crucial in the development and execution of the sustainability concept. Related research demonstrates that the role of the **media** and social marketing play a pivotal role in shaping public perceptions on social conditions (Tims *et al.,* 1989; Kim and Choi, 2007; Peeters *et al.,* 2009).

The concept of social marketing, using marketing techniques and principles to encourage behavioral change or advance a social cause (Kotler and Lee, 2005; Lane, 2009; Weaver, 2009) has been linked to sustainability. Research also indicates that the media's role in sustainable development and sustainable tourism is central (Lane, 2009). Since social marketing aims at influencing large audiences (Peeters *et al.,* 2009), governments and marketers have been charged with a massive task, especially in the hospitality and tourism industry where issues of pleasure, freedom and status are involved in the decision process (Lane, 2009; Williams, 2002). Jim Butcher (2003) emphasizes how powerful the elements of adventure, escape, and good-old fashioned fun are on personal motivation, a topic not commonly explored by academics.

Tourism industry associations and government agencies have attempted to recognize and reward good practices and performance through awards, eco-labels, and sustainable certification programs (Buckley, 2009; Hartlieb and Jones, 2009). Such incentives indeed stimulate and dispel the apprehension among corporate hotels that sustainability might portray an image of sacrifice conflicting with the products of comfort or luxury which is a major and important selling point for many hotels (Bohdanowicz, 2003; Butcher, 2003; Williams, 2002). "It is particularly important in tourism that a new behavior gives pleasure and be fashionable – it should be remembered that tourism is both a form of escapism and fashion pursuit" (Peeters *et al.,* 2009, p. 249).

The Supply and Demand for Sustainability

Studies on the topic of sustainability have revealed a relationship between supply and demand (Hall and Gossling, 2009) and that there is an understanding of the demand expectations of customers (Sammer and Wüstenhagen, 2005). Although many private tourism enterprises have started to adopt and implement a range of practical environment management measures and social responsibility schemes to reduce their immediate impacts, market research shows that sustainable consumer demand is in its infancy (Bohdanowicz, 2009; Dubois and Ceron, 2009).

The few successful leaders in sustainable hospitality and the tourism industry are currently dominated by independent and non-affiliated hotels (Johnson, 2009) typically small and medium sized organizations (Weaver, 2009;

Leslie, 2009); though, it has been argued that in recent years, large scale hotel companies have made a considerable effort to improve the quality of life in local communities and the well-being of their employees. This shift has been found to be true in the Marriott, Accor and Hilton Hotels (Holcomb *et al.*, 2007). Other major players in the industry have also taken steps to integrate sustainability into their hotels; reducing emissions (HSMAI, 2009), and incorporating better waste management systems (Tzschentke *et al.*, 2004; Peeters *et al.*, 2009; Environmental Leader, 2008). Studies have concluded that international hotel companies are an essential element in the development of host communities (Bohdanowicz and Zientara, 2009; Tzschentke *et al.*, 2004), though little academic research has been collected on their measurable results or challenges. In addition, hoteliers have also come to realize that they can market their environmental policies and initiatives to a growing market of green consumers (Bohdanowicz, 2009; Sammer and Wüstenhagen, 2005).

The National Business Travel Association (NBTA) reported in 2009 that any large scale changes in the hotel industry will have to come from consumer demand. Bohdanowicz (2003) found that a lack of information on the benefits and practices of sustainability is causing a lack of demand from consumers in Europe. Others found that since consumers are not insisting on these practices, hotels are not going to invest in changing their policies and procedures (Johnson, 2009). More reviews unveiled that European hoteliers rely heavily on the chain hotels to influence changes in policy, similar to the United States, where hotels do take environmental practices seriously if consumers request them (Johnson, 2009).

Future predictions for the industry included an increase in demand for green or sustainable products (Bergin-Seers and Mair, 2009). Despite the variance and controversy of definition over sustainability, most academics agree that sustainability should be considered in terms of the long-term survival and profitability (Elkington, 1998) of the industry and companies; specially, where shareholders (Hall and Gossling, 2009) and the organizational strategy for future outcomes incorporates sustainability (Gossling *et al.*, 2009).

Exploring the Mystification of the Sustainability Concept

Although the word sustainability is widely used, there is still confusion not only among customers but also managers in the tourism and hospitality industry on what the word sustainability encompasses. In an attempt to discover and understand sustainability the authors carried out a study that explored the perception of sustainability within the hospitality industry and correlated this with other industries. The study assessed the reasons behind policy implementation, the potential benefits among pioneering hotels and reviewed current challenges facing implementation. The aim was to identify sustainability insights and opportunities for decision makers in industry leadership. Data were collected through questionnaires and interviews among managers working in the tourism, hospitality and other industries. Our findings revealed the following:

a. Understanding Sustainability: out of the 78 participants, only 11 percent had full understanding of the word sustainability, while 5 percent had a confused understanding of the sustainability concept (see Figure 1).

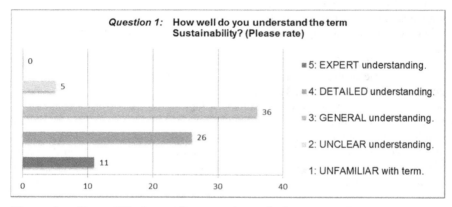

Figure. 1: Rate of Understanding – total sample frequency of response visualized. Survey conducted by the authors of this chapter during 2010

Further results among the general sustainability questions revealed only 71 percent of the participants currently use, and are exposed to, sustainable initiatives in the work place. Moreover, results filtered by segment showed that 85 percent of hospitality organizations surveyed have implemented sustainable practices in their place of business, compared to only 57 percent in the other industries.

b. Reasons behind Implementation: in Table 3 below, we can observe responses from the hospitality segment and other industries. It is important to note these results only included participants who said 'Yes' to using sustainability. The question asked participants to choose the top-5 reasons behind the implementation of their organization's sustainability programs, from a set of choice options. The choice options for this question were based on an extensive literature review, where common reasons for implementing sustainability, CSR, and change in an organization were listed.

Hospitality segment	Other Industries
1st Personal Values and Beliefs	1st Market Needs /Anticipating Consumer Demand
2nd Market Needs /Anticipating Consumer Demand	2nd Corporate Social Responsibility Goals
3rd Corporate Social Responsibility Goals	3rd Natural Resources Concern
4th Natural Resources Concern	4th Personal Values and Beliefs
5th Competitive Advantage	4th Competitive Advantage
-	4th Return/Profit/Cost-Savings

Source: Survey conducted by the authors of this chapter during 2010.

Table 3: Ranking the Top-5 reasons behind implementation. Survey conducted by the authors of this chapter during 2010

The Hospitality segment, showed 'personal values and beliefs', as the top reason for implementation of sustainability into their business, followed by 'market needs/anticipating consumer demand', 'natural resource concern', 'CSR goals', and 'competitive advantage', making up the top 5 reasons among the industry. While other industries' choices for the top five (5) 'reasons' behind the implementation of sustainability were 'market needs/anticipating consumer demand', followed by 'CSR goals', and 'natural resource concern'. Of all the eighteen (18) choice options listed, both segments revealed the same choices in the top-5, however, 'return/profit/cost-savings' was included as a top-reason.

c. Benefits of Implementation: data collected also evaluated the relationship between possible benefits, in addition to the reason behind implementation. The highest listed benefit by the hospitality segment is 'guest/client satisfaction' followed by 'press and marketability', 'competitive advantage', whereas 'cost savings/profits' and 'tax relief' received the lowest ranking (see Figure 2).

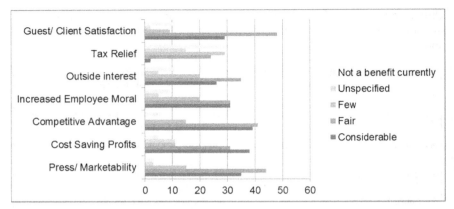

Figure 2: Hospitality Segment: 'Benefits' from Implementation, by frequency. Survey conducted by the authors of this chapter during 2010

In comparison to the Hospitality segment, other industries' respondents have considered 'press and marketability' as the most important benefit of implementing a sustainability program, followed by other benefits such as 'outside interest', 'competitive advantage', 'increased employee moral', and 'guest/client satisfaction'. It is also important to note that, again, 'tax relief' and 'cost savings/profits' received the lowest ranking, with 'tax relief' listed as not a current benefit (see Figure 3).

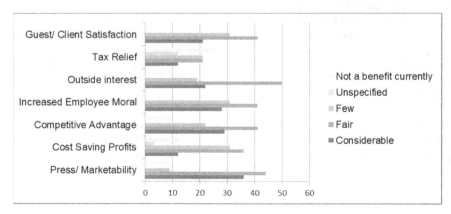

Figure 3: Other Industries: 'Benefits' from implementation, by frequency. Survey conducted by the authors of this chapter during 2010

d. Challenges of Implementation: the last objective in this study was to briefly explore and evaluate some of the challenges of implementation. Our findings have disclosed a number of challenges listed by both segments, hospitality and other industries (see Table 4). As can be seen there are positive similarities between both segments; these are discussed further in our next section where analysis and correlations will be used for an explanation of what has been found.

Hospitality Segment: Frequently listed challenges
• Costs
• Resistance to change, cultural mix, and total stakeholder Buy-in
• Lack of or limited techology
• Traning, communication and education
• Lack of benchmarket standards or consistency
• Market demand or preception
• Understanding of real benefits
• Not seen as aprioirty
• Finding partners who share your standards
• Lack of government support
Other Industry Frequently listed challenges
• Total stakeholder buy-in
• Qualifying/quantifying the cost-benefit analysis or ROI periods of technological investments versus other shorter term options prior to action/results.
• Cost away from core activities, not a priority
• Monitoring and consistency, benchmarkets /trusted measurements.
• Understanding options, confusion with choices of initiatives
• Maintaining the momentum of initiatives
• The education of staff and monitoring of staff to carry out the program consistently, A coherent understanding of everyone.
• Lack of tax / legal framework to enable the right decisions to also be the most profitable ones. "It doesn't yet 'pay' to care."

Table 4: Frequently Listed Challenges by Segment. Survey conducted by the authors of this chapter during 2010

The Preventative Cycle Model

The above findings suggest that there is a universal misconception of the idea of sustainability. The inability to universally define the term has an impact on understanding the benefits and implementing sustainability programs in all industries. From the study and the literature in this area it is possible to devise a new model (Figure 4 below) known as the Preventive Cycle model. The model illustrates continual association among variables throughout the preventative cycle. This continual and interactive association is indicated by the arrows going both ways. The model exposes the main challenges and deficiencies in different areas preventing the effective implementation of sustainability. Main Challenges come from Government and are related to costs and a dearth of benchmarks, while Social Challenges are related to lack of understanding. Challenges at the same time are linked to the absence of clear benefits and values, together with a paucity of reason and skepticism. This results in a poor implementation, together with verified results not being communicated to customers, which is a major challenge to a universally accepted concept of sustainability.

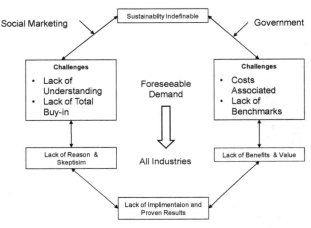

Figure 4: Preventive Cycle describing the current state of sustainability

This cycle could help to better explain the slow development of sustainability and how we are still trapped or stuck in the early adaptors phase of Hall and Gosslings (2009) adaptive Bell Curve Model. It also gives insights into the importance of implementation and measurable results, as that element of the model affects other important factors.

Moving Forward

In our attempt to bridge the gap between previous research, suggesting correlations between understanding the sustainability concept and the challenges of implementation, we suggest the implementation of three key elements for further development.

Understanding Sustainability: the term sustainability, or what it means to be sustainable, has become a common word; the concept needs a simple, consistent, brand identity that can reignite with consumers (Williams, 2002; Grove et al., 1996). Although sustainability has roots in the concept of CSR programs, the concept is largely mistaken and considered only as an ethical issue (Jonker and Witte, 2006). Again, the concept of sustainability seems to be merely related with the concept of *caring for the environment*. Sustainability is a concept that relates to the responsibility taken today for future generations related to: ecological balance, social justice, cultural identity and self-reliance (Brown *et al.*, 2006; Gill and Dickinson, 2008; Henriques, 2007; Jonker and Witte, 2006; Sauvé, 1996; United Nations: Agenda 21, 1992).

Valuing Sustainability by both consumers and businesses: sustainability research has currently uncovered an inability among programs to be able to transmit the value and real benefits for consumers and business, especially in the short-term (Peeters *et al.*, 2009). However, there are only a few acceptable models of sustainability where perception and value creation for organizations have been included (Hall and Gossling, 2009)

Involvement of all Stakeholders: research has found that organizations' ability to integrate various adaptations to their environment improves their survival rate (Sutton, 2001; Hall and Gossling, 2009). Likewise the incorporation of different stakeholders in the implementation of a sustainable program is important. The active support and cooperation of all stakeholders involved in the hospitality industry will make the implementation of sustainable practices more successful (Brown, Dillard and Marshall, 2006).

Concluding Remarks

The travel trade industry has demonstrated positive and negative impacts on the environment and local communities; consequently, the concept of sustainability has emerged to re-establish a new way of moving forward and to provide for a growing market of concerned consumers. This chapter depicts the different phases of development that the industry is going through in its process of embracing sustainability. Numerous academic papers, reports and business articles have been reviewed to cover this topic, from which has been identified the necessity of understanding the principles of the sustainability concept among industrial managers and customers. In order to further evaluate misconceptions about sustainability and find the elements missing in the process of its implementation, the authors conducted a study based on the survey method of research. Our study has found the need to adopt a universal and clear concept of sustainability. From the evaluation of our findings the research identified elements that are hindering a successful implementation of a sustainability program; from this evaluation emerges a model that illustrates the Preventative Cycle which indicates the different elements preventing the implementation of sustainable programs. Although sustainability has been a widely used term in recent times, the sustainability concept seems to struggle with being defined and successfully implemented among all industries. However, by understanding, valuing its benefits and involving all stakeholders in the implementation of sustainability, the potential to agree on a universally accepted definition is possible.

References

Banerjee, S. B. (2006), "Corporate Citizenship, Social Responsiblity and Sustainablity: Corporate Colonialism for the New Millenium", in Jonker, J. and Marco, d. W., *The Challenge of Organizing and implementing corporate Social Responsibility*. Palgrave Macmillan, New York, NY, pp. 31-47.

Bergin-Seers, S. and Mair, J. (2009), "Emerging Gree Tourist in Australia: Their Behaviours and Attitudes", *Tourism and Hospitality Research*, Vol. 9 No. 2, pp. 109-119.

Blair, A. M. and Hitchcock, D. (2001), *Environment and Business*, Routledge, London, UK.

Bohdanowicz, P. (2003), *Attitudes Towards Sustainability In Chain Hotels – Results Of A European Survey*, Royal Institute of Technology, Department of Energy Technology, Stockholm, Sweden.

Bohdanowicz, P. (2009), "Theory and Practice of Environmental Managment and Monitoring in Hotel Chains", in Gossling, S, Hall, M. and Weaver, D. (Eds.) *Sustainable Tourism Futures*, Vol. 1 No. 2, pp. 102-130.

Bohdanowicz, P. and Zientara, P. (2009), " Hotel Companies' Contribution to Improving the Quality of Life of Local Communities and the Well-being of theri Empolyees" *Tourism and Hospitality Research*, Vol. *9* No. 2, pp. 147-158.

Brennan, C. and Ritters, K. (2003), "Consumer Education in the UK: New Developments in Policy and Implementation", *International Journal of Consumer Studies*, Vol. 27 No. 3, pp. 223-224.

Brown, D., Dillard, J. and Marshall, S. (2006), "TRIPLE BOTTOM LINE: A BUSINESS METAPHOR FOR A SOCIAL CONSTRUCT", *School of Business Administration, Portland State University*.

Buckley, R. (2009), "Large-Scale Links between Tourism Enterprises and Sustainable Development", in Leslie, D., *Tourism Enterprises and Sustainable Development*, Routledge, New York. pp. 55-62.

Butcher, J. (2003), *The Moralisation of Tourism-Sun,Sand...and Saving the World?* (1st ed.), imprint of Taylor & Francis Group, Routledge, New York, USA.

Butler, R. W. (2006), *The Tourism Area Life Cycle: Conceptual and Theoretical Issues* (Vol. 2), Channel View Publications, Clevedon, UK.

Dow Jones Sustainability Indexes website (2010), available at: http://www.sustainability-index.com/07_htmle/sustainability/corpsustainability.html (accessesed 1 May 2012).

Dubois, G. and Ceron, J. P. (2009), "Carbon Labelling and Restruckturing Travel Systems", in Gössling, C. M. Stefan, *Sustainable Tourism Futures: Perspectives on Systems, Restructuring and Innovation*, Routledge, New York, pp. 222-239.

Elkington, J. (1998), *Cannibals with Forks: The Triple Bottom Line of 21st Century Business*, New Society Publishers, Stone Creek, Canada.

Elkington, J. and Thorpe, J. (2007), "Chinadialogue: Climate's elephant in the room" (1987 - 2009 SustainAbility Ltd.), available at: http://www.sustainability.com/researchandadvocacy/columns_article.asp?id=997 (accessed November 2009).

Environmental Leader (2008), Marriott, Hilton,Other Hotels Going Green. *Environmental Leader: Energy and Environmental News for Business*, available at: http://www.environmentalleader.com/2008/01/25/marriott-hiltonother-hotels-going-green/ (accessed 25 January 2008).

Fischer, K. (2009), "Internationally, the Business of Education Is Booming", *Chronicle of Higher Education*, Vol. 35 No. 38, pp. A1-A32.

Gill, D. L. and Dickinson, S. J. (2008), "Communicating sustainablity: A web content analysis of North American, Asian and European firms", *Journal of Communication Management*, Vol. 12 No. 3, pp. 243-262.

Gore, A. (2006), *An Inconvenient Truth: The Planetary Emergency of Global Warming and What We Can Do About It*, Rodale Inc, New York.

Gossling, S., Hall, C. M. and Weaver, D. B. (2009), "Sustainable Tourism Futures", In Gossling, S., Hall, C. M. and Weaver, D. B., *Sustainable Tourism Futures: Prespectives on Systems, Restructuring and Innovations*, Routledge, New York, pp. 1-15.

Grove, S. J., Fisk, R. P., et al. (1996), "Going green in the service sector: Social responsibility issues, implications and implementation", *European Journal of Marketing* Vol. 30 No. 5, pp. 56 - 66.

Hall, C. M. (2009), "Tourism Firm Innovation and Sustainability", in Hall, C. M., Gossling, S., *Sustainable Tourism Futures: Perspectives on Systems, Restructuring and Innovations*, Routledge, New York, pp. 282-297.

Hall, C. M. and Gossling, S. (2009), "Global Environmental Change and Tourism Enterprise", in Leslie, D., *Tourism Enterprises and Sustainable Development*, Routledge, New York, pp. 17-33.

Hartlieb, S. and Jones, B. (2009) "Humanising Business through Ethical Labelling", *Journal of Business Ethics*, pp. 583-600.

Hartlieb, S. and Jones, B. (2009), "Humanising Business Through Ethical Labelling: Progress and Paradoxes in the UK", *Journal of Business Ethics*, pp. 583-600.

HBR Green (2008, January 23), "Don't Bother with the 'Green' Consumer", *HBR GREEN: A Discussion about Leadership and the Environment*, available at: http://www.hbrgreen.org/2008/01/dont_bother_with_the_green_con.html (2 May 2010).

Henriques, A. (2007), *Corporate Truth: The Limits to Transparency*, Earthscan, London, UK..

Holcomb, J. L., Upchurch, R. S. and Okumus, F. (2007), "Corporate social responsibility: what are top hotel companies reporting?", *International Journal of Contemporary Hospitality Management*, Vol. 19 No. 6, pp. 461-475.

HSMAI (2009, August), "U.S. Corporate travel decline", *Hotel Sales and Marketing Association International (HSMAI) Newsdesk*, available at: http://hsmai-europe.com/category/travel/ (accessed December 2009)

Jonker, J. and Witte, M. d. (2006), *The Clallenge of Organizing and Implementing Corporate Social Responsibility*, Palgrave Macmillan, New York, NY.

Kim, S. and Choi, C. (2007), "Habits, Self-Control and Social Conventions: The Role of Global Media and Corporations", *Journal of Business Ethics*, Vol. 76 No. 2, pp. 147-154.

Kotler, P. and Lee, N. (2005), *Corporate Social Responsiblity: Doing the Most Good for Your Company and Your Cause* (Vol. 1), John Wiley and Sons, Inc., Hoboken, New Jersey, USA.

Lane, B. (2009), "Thirty Years of Sustainable Tourism: Drivers, Progress, Problems -and the Future", in Gössling, C. M. Stefan, *Sustainable Tourism Futures: Perspectives on Systems, Restructuring and Innovations*, Routledge, New York, pp. 20-31.

Leslie, D. (2009), "Environmental Performance and Tourism Enterprises in the UK", in Leslie, D., *Tourism Enterprises and Sustainable Development*, Routledge, New York, pp. 209-227.

Mohan, T. T. (2009, January 8), Auditors go AWOL at Satyam. *Forbes.com*.

Mootee, I. (2009, October 29), "The Sustainability Challenge Is Complex. Is Ecolabeling The Answer Or Just Another Greenwashing Tool?", Innovation Playground, avaliable at: http://mootee.typepad.com/innovation_playground/business-strategy/ (accessed 2009).

Moscardo, G. (2009), "Trouism and Qualtiy of life: Towards a More Critical Approach", *Tourism and Hospitality Research*, Vol. 9 No.2), pp. 159-170.

Moss, D. A. (2007), *A Concise Guide to Macro Economics* (1 Ed.), Harvard Bussiness School Publishing, Boston, Massachusetts.

Mowforth, M., Charlton, C. and Munt, I. (2008), "Global Politics, Power and Play: the macro level of responsibility", in Mowforth, M., Charlton, C. and Munt, I., *Toursim and Responsibility*, Routledge, Oxon, UK, pp. 10-52.

Mowforth, M., Charlton, C. and Munt, I. (2008) "Power and Responsibility in Tourism: Know Your Place", in M. Mowforth, C. Charlton, and I. Munt, *Tourism and Responsibilty* Routledge, Oxon, UK, pp. 224-230.

Mowforth, M., Charlton, C. and Munt, I. (2008), "Urban Tourism: the heart of darkness?", in Mowforth, M., Charlton, C. and Munt I., *Tourism and Responsibility*, Routledge, Oxon, Uk, pp. 171-194.

Murphy, R. (2009). US asks for corporate transparency, 2005-2009 Tax Research UK, available at: http://www.taxresearch.org.uk/Blog/2009/06/18/us-asks-for-corporate-transparency/ (accessed 18 June 2012).

Peeters, P., Gossling, S. and Lane, B. (2009), "Moving Towards Low-Carbon Tourism", in Leslie, D., *Tourism Enterprises and Sustainable Development*, Routledge, New York, pp. 241-256.

Redclift, M. (1989), "The environmental consequences of Latin America's agricultural development: Some thoughts on the Brundtland Commission report", *World Development*, Vol. 17 No. 3, pp. 365-377.

Rogers, E. M. (2002), "Diffusion of preventive innovations", *Addictive Behaviors*, Vol. 27 No. 6, p. 989.

Rowe, A., Smith, J. D. and Borein, F. (2002), *Travel and Tourism*, Cambridge University Press, Cambridge, UK.

Sammer, K. and Wüstenhagen, R. (2005), "The Influence of Eco-Labelling on Consumer Behaviour – Results of a Discrete Choice Analysis", *Business Strategy and the Environment*.

Sauvé, L. (1996), "Environmental Education and Sustainable Development: A Further Appraisal", *Canadian Journal of Environmental Education (CJEE)*, Vol. 1 No. 1, pp. 7-34.

Shireman, B. and Shireman, S. (2002), *If the World Ran Out of B's*, Beyond Worlds Publishing Inc. Hillsbro, Oregon.

Solnet, D. J., Paulsen, N. and Cooper, C. (2010), "Decline and turnaround: a literature review and proposed research agenda for the hotel sector", *Current Issues in Tourism*, Vol. 13 No. 2, pp. 139-159.

Sutton, R. I. (2001), "The Weird Rules of Creativity", in Tushman, M. L. and Anderson, P. *Managing Strategic Innovation and Change*, Harvard Business School Publishing, Oxford, pp. 267-275.

Tims, A. R., Fan, D. P. and Freemam, J. R. (1989), "The Cultivation of Consumer Confidence: A Longitudinal Analysis of News Media Influence on Consumer Sentiment", *Advances in Consumer Research*, Vol. 16 No. 1, pp. 758-770.

Tzschentke, N., Kirk, D. and Lynch, P. A. (2004), "Reasons for going green in serviced accommodation establishments", *International Journal of Contemporary Hospitality Management*, Vol. 6 No. 2, pp. 116-124.

U.N. World Commission on Environment and Development. (1987, August 4), "Our Common Future: Transmitted to the General Assembly as an Annex to document A/42/427 - Development and International Co-operation: Environment", *UN Documents*, available at: http://www.un-documents.net/a42-427.htm (2 May 2010).

UNESCO (2005), "The Precautionary Principle: World Commission on the Ethics of Scientific Knowledge and Technology", *UNESCO, Scientific and Cultural Organization*, United Nations Educational, Paris.

United Nations: Agenda 21 (1992), "UN Department of Economic and Social Affaris: Division for Sustainable Development", *United Nations: Earth Summit*, 3-14 June 1992, available at: http://www.un.org/esa/dsd/agenda21/res_agenda21_40.shtml (accessed 8 November 2009).

UNWTO (2009) "Tourism – an Economic and Social Phenomenon", *World Tourism Organization*, available at: http://www.unwto.org/aboutwto/why/en/why.php?op=1 (accessed 01 October 2012).

Weaver, D. B. (2009), "Reflections on Sustainable Tourism and Paradigm Change", in Gössling, C. M. Stefan, *Sustainable Tourism Futures*, Routledge, New York, pp. 33-40.

Williams, A. (2002), *Understandting the Hospitality Consumer*, Butterworth-Heinemann, Oxford, UK.

World Commission on Environment and Development (WCED) (1987**), "Report of the World Commission on Environment and Development: Our Common**

Future", Transmitted to the General Assembly as an Annex to document A/42/427 - Development and International Co-operation: Environment.

WTTC and Oxford Economics (2010), *World Travel and Tourism Council: Travel and Tourism Economic Impact Report*, World Travel & Tourism Council, London, UK.

WTTC (2009), *World Travel & Tourism Council: TOURISM IMPACT DATA AND FORECASTS*. World Travel & Tourism Council, London, UK.

York, J. G. (2009). "Pragmatic Sustainability: Translating Environmental Ethics into Competitive Advantage", *Journal of Business Ethics,* Vol. 85, pp. 97-109.

Developing Sustainable Competitive Advantage in the Tourism Industry: a financial conceptual model[1]

Henri Kuokkanen & Ruth Rios-Morales

"We hear only those questions for which we are in a position to find answers."
(Friedrich Nietzsche)

Introduction

Sustainability is one of the most common axioms used in the field of tourism (WTO, 2004). Although the international tourism literature identifies that the business world widely accepts the concepts of sustainability and Corporate Social Responsibility (CSR), research that links social and financial performance is limited. This chapter attempts to respond to this neglected area by structuring a model that can explain how businesses operating within the field of tourism could gain a competitive advantage through CSR and improve their financial performance. The purpose of this chapter is also to review studies on the topic of Corporate Social Responsibility (CSR) and to go through a few key points which are fundamental to the link between financial and social performance of companies.

CSR's Theoretical Background

Corporate Social Responsibility has been the subject of numerous studies and research on this area has been widened significantly in recent years. Nevertheless, we consider that a natural next step from the examination of CSR as theory and whether it could be applied in order to gain competitive advantage, are the studies trying to find a link between the social and financial performance of a company. A plethora of studies of this type have been made (e.g. Cochran and Wood, 1984; Waddock and Graves, 1997; Griffin and Mahon, 197; Roberts and Dowling, 2002; Goll and Rasheed, 2002) and these have further been

---

[1] This chapter is adapted from Kuokkanen and Rios-Morales (2009)

researched through meta-analyses of the results of individual studies (Margolis and Walsh, 2003; Orlitzky et al., 2003; Wu, 2006). Finding the correlation between Corporate Social Responsibility and financial performance and measures of performance are key to this study.

Orlitzky et al., (2003) emphasize the importance of the correlation found between Corporate Social Performance (CSP) and Corporate Financial Performance (CFP) and discuss the meaning of reputation for companies. They use their findings in order to – simultaneously – disagree and agree with Friedman (1970); disagree in the aspect of CSP activities being controversial to the concept of shareholder value and agree with his comments related to minimizing the role of governments. Thus, they are willing to make conclusions fully based on the results and hail the role of CSP as a tool for financial performance. Margolis and Walsh (2003) on the other hand take a much more pessimistic view and question the basis of CSP and the occasions in which this is beneficial to society as a whole. Despite the scientifically appealing results it is good to stop and ask about the limitations of these studies before rushing into a new one, even if responsible tourism as a field has not been so far extensively studied (Kuokkanen and Rios-Morales, 2009).

Margolis and Walsh (2003) went through 127 studies of this field in their meta-analysis and listed the measures used in them. There were plenty of different methods in measuring CSP but the most common ones were rankings of Fortune Magazine, KLD Social Index and CEP (currently known as Social Economy Europe), as well as mutual fund screens and company disclosures. For CFP the differences were less obvious, with most studies using either market or accounting performance, or both, for measurement. The initial results coincide with the results of another important study in the same area: both Margolis and Walsh (2003) and Orlitzky et al. (2003) found that there is a clear positive correlation between CSP and CFP and very little evidence of a negative impact of CSP. However, there is a lack of objective measure for social performance.

A multitude of different indices, rankings and ratings are being used for this purpose, but a question remains: which one of them really measures the positive impact that a corporation can have on its stakeholders? This lack of real measurement can severely impair the results obtained. Some of these measures are very likely to be relevant, but as Porter and Kramer (2006) point out, the popularity of the topic has led into what they call "the Ratings Game", a confusion caused by all the different providers of responsibility data. An example of this is provided by Waddock et al., (2002); they list examples of both rankings of corporate reputation as well as responsibility related standards – both of these lists contain more than 10 different items. Hamann (2007) continues this discussion by pointing out that the motives for assessing the social performance of a company and the instruments conducting the assessment should be carefully evaluated and questioned before taking the results. The need for clear definition and measurement of what responsibility means is evident; whether this can be done on a general level or on a company basis so far remains unclear.

Peloza and Papania (2008) emphasize the need to consider which stakeholders are in a position to reward or punish the corporation financially through their actions. According to their study this could be an important factor in explaining the correlation between CSP and CFP. The idea does have a certain appeal and poses the question of how should financial performance be measured. The method of using market valuation fully or partly for this purpose as explained earlier is controversial, as the stakeholders benefiting or suffering from the activities of a company may not have any means to affect its market valuation. As Bird et al. (2007) note, management might be misguided in their activities if they blindly follow market valuation as a guideline to which activities to pursue.

Being able to create a "CSR-brand" in tourism could be an effective way to increase sales and profit. Fuller et al. (2007) argue that leading companies can deliver products exceeding expectations and thus achieve market leadership while maintaining profitability. Jamrozy (2007) discusses marketing of sustainable tourism and suggests that the area could change profoundly. In his study of the hospitality industry, Tepeci (1999) emphasizes the importance of brand loyalty, which means keeping customers once they have been attracted, in running a profitable operation. Some efforts have been made in researching sustainable branding. Woodland (2007) studied this in the South Downs of the UK and suggested that the approach could boost business in the region. However, apart from local experiments, responsibility branding remains a largely untapped opportunity in tourism and could prove to be the next winning proposition.

Terminology Related to CSR within the Tourism Industry

The initiatives for responsible business have made their mark within the tourism business sector and there exists somewhat overlapping terminology describing them. The most important terms used are sustainable tourism, ecotourism, green tourism, environmentally friendly tourism, nature-conserving tourism and responsible tourism. The purpose of this section is to explain these concepts and discuss their differences, strengths and weaknesses.

Sustainable Tourism

The most common definition used on sustainable tourism is the one established by World Tourism Organization (WTO). The current definition (WTO, 2004) concentrates on three main points on what sustainable tourism should include, and these points include optimizing the use of resources to preserve the environment, respecting the local communities and sharing the benefits of tourism with all stakeholders. In addition, they also emphasize the satisfaction of tourists – a somewhat self-evident but highly important point when NGO's and businesses meet. This view of including all the stakeholders was also strongly promoted by Byrd *et al.,* (2008).

A recent new initiative on making the definition of sustainable tourism more practical, is the "Global Sustainable Tourism Criteria" launched in late 2008 by the Partnership for Global Sustainable Tourism Criteria (GSTC). Their mission is to build

> "a set of baseline criteria organized around the four pillars of sustainable tourism: effective sustainability planning; maximizing social and economic benefits to the local community; reduction of negative impacts to cultural heritage; and reduction of negative impacts to environmental heritage" (GSTC, 2008: "About the Partnership").

The target for this criterion is to serve as a guideline for businesses, consumers, media and other users for recognizing sustainable practices in tourism. However, the concept of sustainable tourism has been harshly criticized. For instance, McKercher (1993) points out that the combination of sustainability with tourism – due to the nature of tourism as an activity – is not feasible. On a more conceptual level Sharpley (2000) agrees with McKercher's view and concludes that sustainable tourism is not real. He argues that while many of the principles related to this area are important and tourism can be an important factor, tourism should be developed further

> "without hiding behind the politically acceptable yet – in the context of tourism – inappropriate banner of sustainable development" (Sharpley, 2000, p. 15).

Despite this fundamental type of critique, "sustainable" tourism – however defined – exists – and is also closely related to the debate about "green-washing", making unjustified claims about the environmental friendliness of a business (Kuokkanen and Rios-Morales, 2009). Lansing and De Vries (2007) studied this controversy by looking at the arguments of parties who claim sustainable tourism to be a real ethical alternative, against the parties who claim it to be a marketing ploy, and concluded that at the time there did not seem to be enough evidence to use sustainability as a basis of marketing. In another critique to the concept of sustainable tourism, Liu (2003) suggested several weak points in the research of the area but, as the growth of tourism in the long-term is likely, called for less idealistic and more practical studies in order to avoid the risk of research becoming irrelevant to the real world; this clearly advocates the positive opportunities that can be provided by the academics.

Interestingly enough the further development and use of standards in order to clearly define what is meant by sustainability in tourism is called for by several authors. Lansing and De Vries (2007) and Liu (2000) both find this important. McCool et al. (2001) defined some possible indicators for sustainable tourism in Montana, but at the same time emphasized the importance of first clarifying what is meant by sustainability before trying to measure it. Finally, Sharpley (2000) raises the question of whether sustainable tourism refers to the qualities linked with sustainable development or actually the sustainability of the industry itself. The definition of sustainable tourism itself remains controversial as pointed out by a mapping of different definitions for sustainable tourism made by Dolnicar (2006). Despite all the controversy, the "real world" development with the launch of GSTC seems to go hand in hand with what researchers are suggesting.

Ecotourism

Another important term linked with sustainable tourism is ecotourism, a term closely related to other phrases such as nature-conserving tourists and environmentally friendly tourists. The meaning of this concept requires a brief discussion.

The term ecotourism was first introduced by Ceballos-Lascurain (1996), as well as by Ballantine and Eagles (1994); both studies suggest that ecotourism means enjoying undisturbed nature. Although most studies accept the above definition of the term, there is no universal consensus on its meaning (Dolnicar, 2006). However, this definition clearly differentiates ecotourism from sustainable tourism as nature itself becomes the product around which tourism is built. Another difference between these two definitions is that ecotourism is largely demand-oriented, while sustainable tourism appears to be the opposite and driven by supply (Dolnicar, 2006). The aspect of conservation has also been strongly incorporated in the term (thus the term nature-based tourism), and ecotourism could be claimed to be a subdivision of sustainable tourism (Kuokkanen and Rios-Morales, 2009).

The use of the term ecotourism has also been heavily criticized. The credibility of ecotourism is challenged, and it has been pointed out that often this term is used for marketing related reasons (Liu, 2003). Criticism also indicates that there is no firm knowledge on who these environmentally friendly tourists actually are and whether their ecological footprint is any smaller than that of the average tourist, thus deserving the word "eco-" (Dolnicar *et al.*, 2008). Sharpley (2006) also agrees on the lack of "ecotourists" as individuals by challenging whether the increased demand for ecotourism actually means increased amounts of ecologically friendly tourists. In the view of Sharpley (2006), it is not feasible to separate this subgroup from mainstream tourism.

Measuring Sustainable Tourism

The economic contribution of tourism has particularly been recognized in developing countries (UNCTAD, 2006). Studies have revealed the contribution of tourism to a country's economy through job generation (Frechtling, 1994) and tax revenue (Burchell and Listokin, 1978). Tourism also brings foreign currency to a host country (UNCTAD, 2006). In addition, tourism has been acknowledged for its input towards political empowerment of local communities (Honey, 1999). However, the lack of concrete evidence through measuring sustainable tourism prevents tourism operators from using this statement further in their business. Moreover, Clavier-Cortes *et al.* (2007) concluded in their case study made in Spain that no link between environmental strategies and profit could be established. This study was, however, concentrating only on the natural environment and none of the other aspects of sustainability.

Currently, the most notable effort to create a set of indicators for sustainable tourism can be ISO 14001, and there is evidence that hotels are adopting these standards (Bambrook, 2008). However, general standards such as ISO can never fully meet the specific business needs of different tour operators. Furthermore, the risk of having several competing ratings, as discussed in the CSR section, exists. CSR reporting in the tourism industry, especially in hotels, has been studied by Holcomb *et al.* (2007), who claim that at the time of the study the tourism industry was still lagging behind in CSR; for example, charitable donations were still the most common form of CSR. Further proof was provided by Ashley and Haysom (2006), who studied the popularity of philanthropy related to tourism in South Africa. The obvious appeal of this approach is the easy measurement of funds donated. Holcomb *et al.* (2005) also drew attention not only to the tourism industry lagging behind in CSR but also on the minimal research in the field.

A practical approach to indicators was made by McCool *et al.* (2001), who first raised questions about the goals of sustainable tourism and then used the answers to evaluate different indicators. This remains, however, a supply-oriented approach and does not discuss the demand side of responsibility in tourism. Skinner *et al.* (2004) studied the possibility of initiating a Sustainable Tourism Stewardship Council based on the model of certification organisations. This initiative was again based on creating a one-size-fits-all set of principles that could be difficult to implement in the tourism industry, with all its small operators. So far, the practical result of this study was the launch of Sustainable Tourism Certification Network of the Americas, but no standards have been created (Rainforest Alliance, 2009).

Developing a Sustainable Competitive Advantage with Financial Gains through Responsible Tourism

The purpose of this section is to discuss, in theory, how businesses operating in the field of tourism could gain a competitive advantage through CSR with the goal of improving their financial performance. This theoretical discussion can be used as a basis for detailed analysis, including tests with the appropriate set(s) of data. The first step is a set of assumptions about the mechanism of how responsibility could lead to improved financial performance. In practice, this means determining the requirements and defining the major hurdles stopping businesses from pursuing this strategy.

Studies made by consultancies confirm that companies believe in the demand for CSR when conducting their business (Vogel, 2005). Therefore this study makes the assumption that some of the customers also in the field of tourism would be willing to choose a responsible provider of holiday activities, provided they perceive the responsibility offered meaningful. This preference would result in an increased demand for these businesses, but only when the supply meets the demand for responsibility. In terms of business, this would mean a competitive advantage through responsibility and thus improved financial performance.

In this section, financial performance is defined solely as increased sales and profitability. This is different from many studies on CSR which also consider share price movements as a measure of financial performance (Orlitzky *et al.*, 2003). The reason for the exclusion of share price, is that as the driver for responsibility in business is obtaining a competitive advantage in the eyes of existing and potential customers, an effective strategy will result in more sales. Share price increase should be regarded merely as a result of this improvement in performance (or an anticipation of it) but not a direct result of implementing responsibility. Thus, in order to study the effects of CSR on performance, only the customer-induced change in financial performance should be measured (Kuokkanen and Rios-Morales, 2009).

Transferring a perceived demand for responsibility into a purchase criteria and an actual decision can be challenging. One reason, particularly in the area of tourism, is the different ways of defining responsibility and sustainability. Therefore, here we will use the term responsible tourism as a balanced and fair approach towards all stakeholders. Furthermore, the model also follows the instrumental school of thought about CSR, believing that the prime purpose for a company to conduct business in a responsible manner is to improve profitability. By selecting this method the number of companies for which the model is applicable will increase to any for-profit organization. Companies that could have mixed motivations behind responsibility, for example some combination of profit and general "good citizenship", are not excluded as long as profitability is one of the drivers. Additional philanthropic goals of the company will not contradict this approach either. Therefore the widest possible range of companies is available without any need for subjective evaluations on their underlying motives.

Competitive Advantage through Responsible Tourism: a Financial Conceptual Model

The focus of this section is to build up a framework to gain competitive advantage. This section uses the term "responsible tourism" instead of using any of the terms presented in the previous sections of this chapter. Responsible tourism will include tourism operators' behaviour towards the environment as well as all other stakeholders of the business, from employees to suppliers and from local communities to investors and the government. All of these relationships, when handled responsibly, should be balanced and mutually beneficial. Defining responsibility this way liberates research from concentrating too much on the environmental impact of the business and enlarges the potential customer base from eco/environmentally aware individuals to anyone interested in the well-being of society as a whole. As this chapter takes a customer-oriented approach to the demand of responsibility in tourism, this framework provides a good starting point for formulating a general theory on the topic and later gathering data in order to test it.

To avoid misunderstanding, the following section will focus on financial performance indicators that can be affected by a potential customer of a tourism business. Revenue and net income of a company should be the only financial measures considered when making a customer-oriented study. The purchase decision – negative or positive – is the moment when each individual can "vote with their feet"; a customer can choose to support or reject the CSR activities taken by the company. For example, a market valuation-based measurement does not reflect the customers' immediate decisions, but the anticipation of the decisions by the financial market participants.

Considering the below assumptions we constructed a model that can explain how businesses operating within the tourism sector could gain a competitive advantage through CSR, improving their financial performance.

Assumption 1: There is dislocation in the market for products and services that promote responsible tourism.
Assumption 2: Operators in the field of tourism were able to meet their customers' real demand for responsibility, as opposed to offering a supply of what they perceive as responsibility, consequently enjoying a competitive advantage.
Assumption 3: Successful indicators used to measure responsibility in tourism have to be industry specific, understandable, concrete and meaningful for the customer.
Assumption 4: A CSR-brand operator in tourism can achieve a competitive advantage which translates into higher-than-average growth in revenue and profits.

$$SRT = (SR + ST) \quad (1)$$
$$\text{Assume: } SR = DR \text{ and } ST = DT \quad (2)$$
$$CA = SRT + RBrd \quad \Leftrightarrow \quad (3)$$
$$CA = (SR + ST) + RBrd \quad \Leftrightarrow \quad (4)$$
$$CA = (DR + DT) + RBrd \quad \Leftrightarrow \quad (5)$$
$$DR + DT + RBrd = \Delta \text{ Sales/Profits} \quad (6)$$

Where:
SRT:　　　　　supply for 'real' responsible tourism
SR:　　　　　supply for responsible aspects
ST:　　　　　supply for tourism
DR:　　　　　demand for responsible aspects
DT:　　　　　demand for tourism
PE:　　　　　product/services that meet those expectations
CA:　　　　　competitive advantage
RBrd:　　　　responsible 'brand', based on the supply
Δ Sales/Profits:　increase of sales/profits

Supply for 'real' responsible tourism must be based on two pillars: customers' expectations of responsibility and the creation of products/services that meet those expectations. By responding to demand for responsibility, tourism providers can gain a competitive advantage for their businesses. The product or service offered must carry a "responsible brand". By attracting this demand, improvement of financial performance measured by revenue and income should occur. These two measures include the effect of customer choice (revenue) and the cost of being responsible (income). This model separates the demand for responsibility from the general demand for the service in order to emphasise the importance of meeting both demands; however, responsibility must be an integral part of the service and not a label to be added afterwards.

Practical Examples of Businesses Exploring Responsibility as a Way to Boost Competitiveness

Tourism operators and other related businesses, following the global trend of responsibility, attempt to benefit and obtain a competitive advantage through expressing interest in sustainable and responsible actions. The level and credibility of these actions varies significantly, but operators are showing a clear tendency towards responsibility. The next section will take a closer look at selected examples within the tour operator business while evaluating how well these companies fit in the model presented previously.

Two travel agencies, Travelocity and Thomas Cook, both have their own green or sustainable travel initiatives (Travelocity, 2011; Thomas Cook, 2009). Both of the companies express an interest in carbon offsetting – quite a natural approach in tourism. However, some differences emerge in the other aspects that the companies emphasize. Thomas Cook takes a general approach to sustainability, discussing the meaning of responsibility and presenting recommendations on how to travel sustainably and how to guarantee animal welfare. Furthermore, it offers the opportunity to donate money to good causes. Meanwhile, Travelocity focuses on offering green hotels and travel alternatives and organises 'voluntourism' trips. During such trips the travelers can participate in volunteering activities. Similarly, Virgin Holidays (2011) offers information on responsible tourism on their website, concentrating on charitable actions but not touching carbon offsets. Thus the typical activities that these travel agencies emphasise correspond with the general supply of responsibility: environment and charity.

While all the companies clearly take an interest in sustainability, there are some differences in how in-depth the user perceives this interest. However, none of the companies will properly fit the competitive advantage model presented earlier because they are not pushing to create a business advantage through their actions. The first two companies have dedicated portals for sustainable and green tourism, which communicates serious interest in the topic, but finding these portals through the main website is difficult. Thus the potential customers must already be familiar with the existence of the portal; they seem to be targeted at customers who are already looking for such an aspect, not at attracting new customers. Virgin Atlantic does not offer a separate website for green travel but presents arguments on responsible travel under a section of the main website, and again this part of the site can only be found when actively looked for. While these travel agencies take a clear interest in sustainability, it seems that the full potential in terms of competitive advantage is yet to be developed. For a greater impact the aspect of sustainability could be taken into consideration when customers search for holidays, for example, or when results matching their searches are displayed.

In order to acquire competitive advantage the model presented earlier requires the creation of a CSR-brand – a combination of responsible actions with solid evidence. Furthermore, the actions (supply) must meet the demand of the customers. Companies must undertake more research to define this demand. Current responsible actions often tend to be based on existing sustainable practices, and customers may not find these actions interesting enough for them to influence purchase decisions. Creating a true, demand-based CSR-brand is a serious challenge and understandably, many businesses hesitate to take this step; unjustified claims of responsibility could lead to a loss of business. The evidence the operators provide for their sustainability becomes crucial for credibility. Third-party, non-profit eco-certification programs, such as the kind offered by Sustainable Travel International (2009), may provide a solution for this part of the equation, but the fundamental question of customer demand for responsibility must first be answered. Once this is known, the work to create a true CSR-brand can start.

Conclusions

Evidence suggests that the "sustainable" or "responsible" tourism offered today does not attract demand due to the dislocation between supply and demand. We argue the underlying reason being that tourism operators and service providers have little or limited knowledge of the real demand for responsibility. Providers select their responsible actions without studying the demand. Thus the demand for the existing offer of responsibility remains weak. Our model highlights the need of tourism operators to respond to their customers' expectations; meeting this demand is a key to a competitive advantage. We also argue that businesses would need to develop "responsible brands" supported by a tailored set of indicators in order to create this competitive advantage. The new demand from customers seeking responsibility will improve financial performance through increased volume and revenue.

References

Ashley, C. and Haysom, G. (2006), "From philanthropy to a different way of doing business: strategies and challenges in integrating pro-poor approaches into tourism business", *Development Southern Africa*, Vol. 23 No. 2, pp. 265-280.
Bambrook, D., Horrigan, D. and Murphy, J. (2008), *ISO 14001 with Metrics for Sustainable Tourism*, EuroCHRIE 2008 Congress, Dubai, United Arab Emirates.
Bird, R., Hall, A. D., Momenté, F. and Reggiani, F. (2007), "What Corporate Social Responsibility Activities are Valued by the Market?", *Journal of Business Ethics*, Vol. 76, pp. 186-206.
Byrd, E. T., Cárdenas, D. A. and Greenwood, J. B. (2008), "Factors of stakeholder understanding of tourism: The case of Eastern North Carolina", *Tourism and Hospitality Research*, Vol. 8 No. 3, pp. 192-204.
Burchell R.W. and Listokin D. (1978), *The fiscal impact handbook*, Center for Urban Policy Research, New Brunswick, N.J.
Clavier-Cortés, E., Molina-Azorin, J. F., Pereira-Moliner, J. and Lopez-Gamero, M. D. (2007), "Environmental Strategies and Their Impact on Hotel Performance" *Journal of Sustainable Tourism*, Vol. 15 No. 6, pp. 663-679.
Ceballos-Lascurain, H. (1996), "Tourism, ecotourism and protected areas", Switzerland: Gland, IUCN (World Conservation Union).
Cochran, P. L. and Wood, R. A. (1984), "Corporate Social Responsibility and Financial Performance", *Academy of Management Journal*, Vol. 27 No. 1, pp. 42-56.
Dolnicar, S. (2006), "Nature-Conserving Tourists: The Need for a Broader Perspective", *Anatolia: An International Journal of Tourism and Hospitality Research*, Vol. 17 No. 2, pp. 235-255.
Dolnicar, S., Crouch, G. I. and Long, P. (2008), "Environment-friendly Tourists: What Do We Really Know About Them?", *Journal of Sustainable Tourism*, Vol. 16 No. 2, pp. 197-210.
Eagles, P.F.J and Ballantine, J. L. (1994), "Defining Canadian Ecotourists", *Journal of Sustainable Tourism*, Vol. 2 No. 4, pp. 210-215.
Frechtling D. C. (1994), "Assessing the economic impacts of travel and tourism – Introduction to travel economic impact estimation" in Ritchie, J.R. Brent and Goeldner, Charles R. (Eds.), *Travel, Tourism and Hospitality Research (2nd ed)*, John Wiley and Sons Inc., New York..
Friedman, M. (1970), *The Social Responsibility of Business Is to Increase its Profits*, New York Times Magazine, 13 September 1970 (reprint from 1962), pp. 122-126.

Fuller, D., Hanlan, J. and Wilde, S. (2007), "The Identification and Implementation of Key Competitive Factors for Tourism Based Firms", *International Journal of Hospitality & Tourism Administration*, Vol. 8 No. 3, pp. 73- 90.

Goll, I. and Rasheed, A. A. (2002), "The Effect of Environment on the Relationship between Social Responsibility and Performance", *Academy of Management Proceedings*.

Griffin, J. J. and Mahon, J. F. (1997), "The Corporate Social Performance and Corporate Financial Performance Debate: Twenty-Five Years of Incomparable Research", *Business and Society*, Vol. 36 No.1, pp. 5-31.

GSTC (2008) "About the Partnership", available at; http://www.sustainabletourismcriteria.org/ (accessed 18 January 2009).

Hamann, R. (2007), "Is Corporate Citizenship Making a Difference?", *Journal of Corporate Citizenship*, Vol. 28, p. 29.

Holcomb, J. L., Upchurch, R. S. and Okumus, F. (2007), "Corporate social responsibility: what are top hotel companies reporting?", *International Journal of Contemporary Hospitality Management*, Vol. 19 No. 6, pp. 461-475.

Honey, M. (1999), *Ecotourism and Sustainable Development: Who Owns Paradise?* Island Press, Washington, DC.

Jamrozy, U. (2007), "Marketing of tourism: a paradigm shift toward sustainability. International Journal of Culture", *Tourism and Hospitality Research*, Vol. 1 No. 2, pp. 117-130.

Kuokkanen, H. and Rios-Morales, R. (2009), *Conceptual Design of a Financial Approach to Developing Competitive Advantage through Responsible Tourism*. Paper presented at the 2nd EuroMed Annual Conference, 26-28 October, Salerno, Italy, ISSN: 1971-5293.

Lansing, P. and De Vries, P. (2007), "Sustainable Tourism: Ethical Alternative or Marketing Ploy?", *Journal of Business Ethics*, Vol. 72, pp. 77-85.

Liu, Z. (2003), "Sustainable Tourism Development: A Critique", *Journal of Sustainable Tourism*, Vol. 11 No. 6, pp. 459-475.

Margolis, J. D. and Walsh, J. P. (2003), "Misery Loves Companies: Rethinking Social Initiatives by Business", *Administrative Science Quarterly*, Vol. 48, pp. 268-305.

McCool, S. F., Moisey, R. and Nickerson, N. P. (2001), "What Should Tourism Sustain? The Disconnect with Industry Perceptions of Useful Indicators", *Journal of Travel Research*, Vol. 40, pp. 124-131.

McKercher, B. (1993), "Some fundamental truths about tourism: understanding tourism's social and environmental impacts", *Journal of Sustainable Tourism*, Vol. 1 No. 1, pp. 6-16.

Orlitzky, M., Schmidt, F. L. and Rynes, S. L. (2003), "Corporate Social and Financial Performance: A Meta-analysis", *Organization Studies*, Vol. 24 No. 3, pp. 403-441.

Peloza, J. and Papania, L. (2008), "The Missing Link between Corporate Social Responsibility and Financial Performance: Stakeholder Salience and Identification", *Corporate Reputation Review*, Vol. 11 No. 2, pp. 169-181.

Porter, Michael. E. and Kramer, Mark. R. (2006), "Strategy and Society: The Link between Competitive Advantage and Corporate Social Responsibility", *Harvard Business Review*, pp. 78-92.

Rainforest Alliance (2009), "Sustainable Tourism: Sustainable Tourism Certification Network of the Americas", available at: http://www.rainforest-alliance.org/tourism.cfm?id=network (accessed 22 February 2009).

Roberts, P. W. and Dowling, G. R. (2002), "Corporate Reputation and Sustained Superior Financial Performance", *Strategic Management Journal*, Vol. 23, pp. 1077-1093.

Sharpley, R. (2000), "Tourism and Sustainable Development : Exploring the Theoretical Divide", *Journal of Sustainable Tourism*, Vol. 8 No. 1, pp. 1-15.

Sharpley, R. (2006), "Ecotourism: A Consumption Perspective", *Journal of Ecotourism* Vol. 5 No. 1&2, pp. 7-22.

Skinner, E., Font, X. and Sanabria R. (2004), "Does Stewardship travel well? Benchmarking Accreditation and Certification", *Corporate Social Responsibility and Environmental Management*, Vol. 11, pp. 121-132.

Sustainable Travel International (2009), "Our Programs: Eco-Certification", available at: http://www.sustainabletravelinternational.org/documents/sustainabletourismcertification.html (accessed 18 June 2011).

Tepeci, M. (1999), "Increasing brand loyalty in the hospitality industry", *International Journal of Contemporary Hospitality Management*, Vol. 11 No. 5, pp. 223-229.

Thomas Cook (2009), "Sustainable Tourism", available at : http://www.thomascook.com/sustainable-tourism/ (accessed 18 June 2011).

Travelocity (2010), "Travel for good", available at: http://www.travelocity.com/TravelForGood/index.html (accessed 18 June 2011).

United Nations Conference on Trade and Development (UNCTAD) (2006), "Global Economic Trends: the Tourism Industry" available at: http://www.unctad.org/Templates/Page.asp?intItemID=4270&lang=1 (20 February 2008).

Virgin Holidays (2011), "About Virgin Holidays: Responsible Tourism", available at: http://www.virginholidays.co.uk/info/about/who_are_we/responsible.aspx (accessed 18 June 2011).

Vogel, D. (2005), "Is There a Market for Virtue? The Business Case for Corporate Social Responsibility", *California Management Review*, Vol. 47 No. 4, pp. 19-45.

Waddock, S. A. and Graves. S. B. (1997), "The Corporate Social Performance – Financial Performance Link", *Strategic Management Journal*, Vol. 18 No 4. pp. 303-319.

Waddock, S. A., Bodwell, C. and Graves. S. B. (2002), "Responsibility: The new business imperative", *Academy of Management Executive*, Vol. 16 No. 2, pp. 132-148.

Woodland, M. (2007), "Sustainability and Local Tourism Branding in England's South Downs", *Journal of Sustainable Tourism*, Vol. 1 No. 6, pp. 715-734.

WTO (2004), "Sustainable Development of Tourism, Conceptual Definition", available at: http://www.world-tourism.org/frameset/frame_sustainable.html (accessed 18 January 2009).

Wu, M-L. (2006), "Corporate Social Performance. Corporate Financial Performance. and Firm Size: A Meta-Analysis", *Journal of American Academy of Business*, Vol. 8 No. 1, pp. 163.

Managing Ecological Balance

Andy Middleton

Introduction

The global tourism industry is approaching a T-junction, with a choice of routes, leading in one direction to sustainable and long-term value creation, where restoration of ecosystems is at the core of the business model, whereas the other direction, if left uncorrected (and currently more appealing) will result in the continued decline of the oceans, earth and living systems that support life on the planet.

Read any current magazine or journal on ecotourism, green tourism and responsible tourism and it is easy to find a reassuring collection of stories from businesses congratulating themselves for improving the way they deliver tourism goods and services. Examples of these stories include hotels that have installed solar thermal panels for their swimming pool; businesses that have saved 10% of their electricity or water consumption; others that are buying local food or handicrafts and those that ask guests to have their towels changed less frequently. The UK based holidays extra website states "smart use of toiletries is a key way you can save energy at your hotel" (Clarke, 2012); In the same country, and up a notch in terms of practice, The Scarlet Hotel in Cornwall uses rainwater, harvesting it to top up their natural pool, wash cars and rinse wetsuits (The Scarlet, 2011).

Whilst these examples are positive and to an extent, all progress is to be congratulated, there is one key issue missing relating to broader topics of sustainability and ecological balance, where progress rarely gets measured or promoted. The setting of scale and speed to ensure appropriate response to the challenge ahead of us may be hard to calibrate accurately, yet it seems to be a lack of courage, not data, that prevents leaders setting a true course. Clear evidence from climate and earth science shows that the most important current action for tourism operators is to set business directions, operational targets and goals at a scale that is good enough to rebuild the capability of the systems that support life. These will go way beyond 'doing less harm' and create business models that are restorative, rebuilding biodiversity, soil, water quality, social justice and a healthy balance of atmospheric gases, to a point at which they could continue indefinitely.

Change or Be Changed

Businesses large and small are failing to recognise that the laws of evolution and natural selection apply to Homo Sapiens as much as they do to any other species; Darwin didn't talk about 'survival of the fittest', but rather 'survival of the fittingest' – stating that only species that continue to adapt and to 'fit' effectively into the ecosystems that support them will succeed in the long term. To avoid increased volatility, unpredictability and cost, businesses involved in tourism, their customers, suppliers and communities must calibrate their aspirations, operational plans and progress to a scale and speed that is congruent with planning for a good long term result. The toughest realisations may be: a) that their business models will undergo radical change – it is a question of 'jump or be pushed' as to when change happens, b) that action is needed, regardless of the scale of the change that it forces on current business models, c) the level of development required to grow a culture in which rapid prototyping, innovation and creativity are part of the behavioural and genetic code of 'the way that we do things around here'.

This chapter explores some of the consequences of 'playing outside the rules of nature' for tourism operators and their customers, and discusses case studies of organisations seeking alternative, sustainable ways of doing business. The chapter explores approaches that allow businesses to tap into insights from the world's longest-running R&D programme, life itself, and to find ways of working that delivers results for all stakeholders in the system, rather than the few players who currently think that they work outside the rules.

Restoring ecological balance requires an understanding of systems theory, speed and scale that are currently missing from most areas of the tourism industry. In part, many of the problems are derived from a lack of understanding of the inextricable links between the health of humanity and the health of the world's ecosystems –a combination of willful blindness, poor data and ignorance has seen a doubling of mankind's ecological footprint:

> "In 2007, the most recent year for which data is available, the Footprint exceeded the Earth's biocapacity — the area actually available to produce renewable resources and absorb CO_2 — by 50 per cent. Overall, humanity's Ecological Footprint has doubled since 1966. This growth in ecological overshoot is largely attributable to the carbon footprint, which has increased 11-fold since 1961 and by just over one-third since the publication of the first Living Planet Report in 1998" (WWF, 2010)

Changing Paradigms

As organisational and political leaders grapple with the day to day challenges of doing business in tough times, they are too slow recognising that something radically different needs to be done, and that, as Einstein knew, we can't solve our current challenges with the same thinking that created them.

As Allenby and Sarewitz comment

> "We've made a world we cannot control: humanity's commitment to technological change is a commitment to the creation of more uncertainty, contingency and incomprehensibility. Indeed, you are surrounded by and are at this very moment being profoundly changed by Level III [highest level of complexity] systems whose implications you cannot fathom. With input from tablet computers, camera-phones and walls of dancing video, and with much of your memory outsourced to Google and your social relations to Facebook, you now embody the accelerating charge of the Five Horsemen of converging technology – nanotechnology, biotechnology, robotics, information and communication technology, and applied cognitive science – whose cumulative potency world, we desperately need to work out how to better understand it, and how to live in it rationally, responsibly and ethically". (Allenby and Sarewtiz, 2011, p. 28)

The converging challenges of biodiversity loss, resource depletion and an economic model predicated on perpetual growth are foreseen by leaders from a population way beyond the boundaries of environmental activism. Professor Tim Lang's 'Prosperity Without Growth?' paper for the UK's Sustainable Development Commission starts with the words "Every society clings to a myth by which it lives. Ours is the myth of economic growth. For the last five decades the pursuit of growth has been the single most important policy goal across the world. The global economy is almost five times the size it was half a century ago. If it continues to grow at the same rate the economy will be 80 times that size by the year 2100". (Jackson, 2010)

Although Lang's views were dismissed by many commentators when 'Prosperity Without Growth?' was first published, ex-President Sarkozy of France established the Commission on the Measurement of Economic Performance and Social Progress, supported by Amartya Sen, Joseph Stiglitz and Jean-Paul Fitoussi, to explore different ways of approaching value and measurement at a national scale:

> "No single measure, or even a limited set of measures, can provide all the information required to assess and manage an economy. But many are asking today, why did neither the private accounting system nor the public one deliver an adequate early warning?" (Stiglitz et al., 2009, p. 5)

In the UK, the Welsh Government in 2012 launched a consultation for a new approach to the management and regulation of the environment, in which the central theme is a move to an ecosystems approach which will mean "considering and regulating the environment and its health as a whole rather than dealing with individual aspects separately. It will mean weighing up and setting priorities for the many competing demands" (Welsh Government, 2012, p. 1). Although still in consultation at time of press the intention to integrate planning and use of natural resources could be a major step forward that allows business and government to re-examine the cost base and accounting processes that they use to measure success.

Tourism operators will do well too, to keep track of what is happening in other sectors and business areas, and reflect on their ambition compared to others. In March 2011, Ian Cheshire, Chief Executive of Kingfisher, a UK-based DIY retailer with £10.4 billion revenue and 80,000 employees, went on record to say: "Infinite high resource intensive growth is simply not possible, and we are already living off our future capital. It may be gradual but most businesses will have to adjust to a very different reality" (Bristow, 2011). When multinational retailers start to talk publicly about the challenges facing their industry, a call for new thinking has clearly been made. The opportunity for tourism leaders, whose business models and livelihood is dependent on the flourishing of natural ecosystems, would do well to pay heed, and start asking the unthinkable of "what would truly sustainable tourism look like".

Operators in tourism might ignore Cheshire's statements because of the excuse 'Kingfisher isn't a business like mine', or because they don't read far outside the lines of their own specialist press, and know little of what's happening elsewhere. It is hard to find any large-scale tourism operator talking in language that chimes with Cheshire's; whilst retailers may have a higher impact on ecosystems and sustainability because of the physicality of the products they sell, they are at least starting to grapple with some of the questions that go to the heart of the business model. Tourism operators must start doing the same and find an answer to the question: "what does a tourism model look like that is built to last within a carbon and resource-constrained world, where ecosystems have to be repaired and maintained at a level of resilience capable of supporting humanity?"

To maintain and restore ecological balance and life-support systems, organisations must rapidly find ways of enabling their staff, customers and others stakeholders to ask the questions that determine the path that their workplaces, communities and the tourism industry takes, towards resilience or fragility. To make this happen, leaders and managers will have to loosen the reins of control, fire up innovation and creativity and realise that they first have to imagine what a preferred future will look like before they can start to build a pathway to reach it.

Understanding the Numbers

Managing humanity's need for food, energy, water, life saving drugs and raw materials, while minimizing adverse affects on biodiversity and ecosystem services is one of our society's biggest challenges. It is essential that we acknowledge the reality that the world's market economy is a subset of a larger system that includes the flow of natural resources and ecosystem services that sustain life on this planet. The flows of materials and value must be rebalanced so that humanity's life support systems are first restored, and then maintained to a level that is in balance with the needs of a population of nine billion, taking into account the needs and rights of other life on the planet.

At the start of the process of change is a reminder of book keeping and financial prudence that you'd find in 'Accountancy 101', which would tell us that there is a fundamental difference between capital and revenue, and that all intelligent investors use revenue for risk and current living, and the capital for building future capacity. Failure to understand the difference between the two, and treating capital as revenue, means that we will slowly and surely 'kill the goose that lays the golden egg' and reduce our ability to produce the revenue that we need to live on.

The world's predominant business model is based on the idea that it is prudent to 'externalise' and ignore the costs that are deemed too complex to easily count; into the column of externalised costs for biodiversity would be a listing of species loss, soil loss, pollution, ocean acidification, global warming, loss of habitat, loss of provisioning capability and many other items. These factors can be viewed as our 'natural capital' and must be increased in value rather than treated as revenue. Current losses of natural capital are estimated to be of the order of $US 2.5-4.5 trillion (TEEB, 2010) every year – a cost that is extracted from nature, for free, to our detriment, and about equal to the GDP of the USA, the world's largest economy (World Bank, 2011, p. 1).

Despite a growing awareness of the importance of ecosystems and biodiversity to human welfare in some areas of business and government, loss of biodiversity and degradation of ecosystems still continues on a large scale, and few, if any organisations have any kind of vision for a biologically safe future in which ecosystems are restored to full vitality. Fundamental changes are needed in the way that biodiversity, ecosystems and their services are viewed and valued by society. A major difficulty to making progress is that even where their existence is acknowledged, ecosystem services are seen as a mixed bundle of public goods, and levels of use are therefore difficult to regulate, even when they are at, or near the point of exhaustion. Unless business leaders start to take the lead and pursue the full integration of currently externalised costs there would appear to be little hope of government taking the lead, as political mandate invariably follows personal awareness.

As one of the world's largest industrial sectors, with a heavy environmental footprint and hundreds of millions of employees and customers, tourism has a unique opportunity to make a bigger, positive impact on long-term biodiversity and sustainability than many other areas of business. With a high level of direct impact and the ability to affect the behaviour of people working in the sector as well as their customers and suppliers, the role of tourism in catalyzing change is more important than ever.

> "Travel and Tourism is predicted to generate an extra 69 million net jobs by 2021, including direct, indirect and induced employment. This will help to bring down unemployment rates across the globe, contribute to the much desired sectoral rebalancing and export-led growth transition of economies, and reduce poverty in developing economies" (WTTC, 2011, p. 4).

Within the span of half a generation, each one of these tourism dollars must start the journey towards becoming 'net positive' in terms of ecological quality, and at worst, neutral i.e. creating no damage to the wider system. Each job description must be re-written to comply with ecological measures, as well as those of business and community.

The tourism sector therefore has two primary challenges regarding ecological balance:

1) Rapidly move towards elimination of the negative impacts that tourism has on the life support systems on which our species depends,
2) Use the delivery of tourism products and services to maximize the influence and knowledge exchange on sustainable practice that it has with customers, employees and suppliers.

Environmental Economist, Professor Herman Daly from the University of Maryland, describes the Earth as a whole as being approximately a 'steady state', (UKSDC, 2008, p. 1) with neither the surface nor the mass of the earth growing or shrinking. The in-flow of radiant energy or materials from space is to all intents and purposes equal to the outflow, with any variations being negligible. Within a steady state system, much change can and does happen, as is the case on this blue marble planet of ours. The concern most ardently raised by Daly is the relative growth of the economy relative to the condition of the total system, and more specifically, to the ecosphere – the fragile space on our planet on which human life is possible. The closer the economy approaches the scale of the whole earth, the more it will have to conform to the physical behaviour mode of the earth. That behaviour mode is a steady state—a system that permits qualitative development but not aggregate quantitative growth that uses either resources that are themselves limited, or resources that are toxic and damage the system.

Daly contends that "Economists have focused too much on the economy's circulatory system and have neglected to study its digestive tract. Throughput growth means pushing more of the same food through an ever larger digestive tract; development means eating better food and digesting it more thoroughly" (UKSDC, 2008, p. 1). Within a steady state system, the only organisms that survive in the long term will adhere to the rules of that system – by addressing the challenges identified by Kingfisher's Ian Cheshire in the opening paragraphs of this chapter, and recognising that different does not mean the same as 'bad'.

An increasing number of organisations including the UK's Sustainable Development Commission, in their paper 'Prosperity Without Growth?' and the New Economics Foundation, in their work on wellbeing, are questioning the existing measurement and growth paradigms. They offer insights into the potential design of alternative models that can deliver economic wellbeing as well as social and ecological security. The author of this chapter contends that the 'triple bottom line' (TBL) approach to sustainable business management is now less relevant than design-led approaches to sustainability that, if applied correctly, eliminate issues at the design phase of projects rather than after problems have developed. It is also contended that appreciation must be given to the scale of ambition and development needed to create approaches that, if applied globally, would be sufficient to create long-term sustainability. Delivery of this requires an understanding that social and economic outcomes are in the long term wholly dependent on the healthy condition of our environment, and that the converse is not true. As an industrial sector, tourism risks falling behind the leaders in other sectors who are making commitments that put tourism in the shade.

Definitions

An important starting point in defining ecological balance is in the acknowledgement of the services that benefit people and are obtained from ecosystems (Millennium Ecosystem Assessment, 2005). These benefits are seen in four key services:

- Provisioning: goods obtained directly from ecosystems (e.g. food, medicine, timber, fibre, biofuel)
- Regulating: benefits obtained from the regulation of natural processes (e.g. water filtration, waste decomposition, climate regulation, crop pollination, regulation of some human diseases)
- Supporting: regulation of basic ecological functions and processes that are necessary for the provision of all other ecosystem services (e.g. nutrient cycling, photosynthesis, soil formation)
- Cultural: psychological and emotional benefits gained from human relations with ecosystems (e.g. enriching recreational, aesthetic and spiritual experiences)

There is considerably more discussion in academic journals on the meaning of sustainable tourism and ecological balance than on definition of the goals and milestones that would be reached if progress were successful. Meaning is easy to discuss, although people will disagree with you, you'll never be wrong. Action, time lines, dates and numbers though are different, requiring a level of insight and commitment that is too often absent, when leaders are asked 'what's next' in terms of ecosystems and sustainability. Definitions are still, of course, important as they capture and steer the meaning of the words and phrases that we use to describe our challenges and the responses we make to them.

The United Nations Environment Programme states that:

> "Sustainability principles refer to the environmental, economic, and socio-cultural aspects of tourism development, and a suitable balance must be established between these three dimensions to guarantee its long-term sustainability". (UNEP, 2010a)

The WTO promotes a definition of sustainable tourism that would:

> "Make optimal use of environmental resources that constitute a key element in tourism development, maintaining essential ecological processes and helping to conserve natural heritage and biodiversity.
> Respect the socio-cultural authenticity of host communities, conserve their built and living cultural heritage and traditional values, and contribute to inter-cultural understanding and tolerance.
> Ensure viable, long-term economic operations, providing socio-economic benefits to all stakeholders that are fairly distributed, including stable employment and income-

earning opportunities and social services to host communities, and contributing to poverty alleviation." (Dickinson et al., 2010, p. 44)

Although their statements are truthful, the current UNEP approach avoids effective recognition of the rapidly declining condition of mankind's life support systems – the earth's biodiversity and geodiversity – and stops short of stating that sustainable tourism is a subset of sustainable ecosystems and natural environment.

The Organisation for Economic Cooperation & Development, OECD, defines ecological balance as: "the equilibrium between, and harmonious coexistence of, organisms and their environment". (OECD, 2007, p. 227). Despite the implicit understanding of systems' interconnectedness in the OECD's definition, there is scant evidence that OECD's members are taking ecological balance into account in their decision making process.

At the University of Guelph in Ontario, Canada, Crop Ecology students were set a question that gives 'Managing Ecological Balance' a more personal perspective than the dry definitions of academic papers. When thinking how you might answer the question, remember that the costs that you are being asked to consider would, if paid, be picked up by the people and businesses who buy the farmer's products. The question states:

> "You are an Illinois corn farmer, sitting at your kitchen table, staring in disbelief at a letter to you from the Governor of Louisiana. It is a bill for $253,476.15 as your share of the cost of cleaning up the 20,000 square kilometer – and growing – hypoxic [inadequate oxygen supply for normal cell functioning] zone at the mouth of the Mississippi. US Geological Survey studies have conclusively demonstrated the dominant role of nitrogen and phosphorus runoff from corn land in the Mississippi watershed in causing this problem. Your assignment is to frame a polite response, indicating the various strategies you have implemented to retain nutrients on-farm and avoid paying the bill". (Clark, 2010, p. 3)

In 2011, a major new study, the first European Nitrogen Assessment (ENA), found that nitrogen pollution is costing each person in Europe between £130 and £650 (€150 – €740) a year. The study, carried out by 200 experts from 21 countries and 89 organizations, estimated that the annual cost of damage caused by nitrogen across Europe is £60 - £280 billion (€70 - €320 billion), more than double the extra income gained from using nitrogen fertilizers in European agriculture (Centre for Ecology & Hydrology, 2011, p. 9)

To date, few commercial models are taking into account the necessary reconciliation of the damage caused by these two elements alone to natural ecosystems. Paying for nitrogen damage would raise food costs by between £320 and £1600 per year, per household (CEH, 2011, p. 10); it is doubtful that luxuries such as tourism, let alone staples, would be affordable for all at these rates. It makes more sense to fix the system and remove the damage that we are causing than it does to pay the price, now or in the longer term.

The publication of the TEEB Report into the Economics of Ecosystems and Biodiversity in 2009 started an in-depth analysis of the impacts of ecosystem and biodiversity loss. TEEB seeks to "initiate the process of analyzing the global economic benefit of biological diversity, the costs of the loss of biodiversity and the failure to take protective measures versus the costs of effective conservation" (UNEP, 2010b, p. 18). Any valuation study should be fully aware of the 'cost' side of the equation, as focusing only on benefits ignores important societal costs such as missed opportunities of alternative uses; the TEEB approach also allows for a more extensive range of societal values to be considered; "to improve incentive structures and institutions, different stakeholders – i.e. the beneficiaries of ecosystem services, those who are providing the services, those involved in or affected by the use, and the actors involved at different levels of decision-making – should be clearly identified, and decision making processes need to be transparent" (Fisher *et al.*, 2010, p. 3).

For anyone reading this from a business perspective, imagine the response that you would have if each of the threatened species were a critical product line. 70% of the key products on which your business is based are under threat. How long would it take you to react?

WWF's online research defines ecological balance as "a state of dynamic equilibrium within a community of organisms in which genetic, species and ecosystem diversity remain relatively stable, subject to gradual changes through natural succession." and "A stable balance in the numbers of each species in an ecosystem." (WWF Global, 2012, online)

Paul Hawken, author of 'The Ecology of Commerce', one of the earliest books to directly address the junction of business and sustainability is clear about the need to understand the scale of challenge ahead of us. In "Blessed Unrest" he states "consider that the population today is 1000 times greater than it was 7000 years ago. Additionally, people use 100 to 1000 times more resources than their ancestors did. In sum, the earth today withstands at least 10,000 times the impact it did in 5000 BCE. In other words we have the same impact in five minutes that our ancestors did in a year" (Hawken, 2007, p. 33). Gossling comments that "an average holiday in the Seychelles corresponds to 17-37% of the annual footprint of a citizen of an industrialised country..." (Gossling *et al.*, 2002, p. 8). Any concept of sustainable tourism must thus take into account the full impact of the experience; flying to the Seychelles to stay in an eco-lodge cannot be considered sustainable.

Reframing the context

In a digitally connected, increasingly transparent world, tourism operators have to be aware that they need to adhere to the standards and codes of practice set down for their industry, or accept the consequences. High levels of attention to health and hygiene standards, employee working conditions, safety and food provenance are important for most hoteliers, restaurateurs and leisure providers, and essential for larger operators where investor confidence, brand and reputational risk are also important.

Sustainable Tourism has a pragmatic view. "Tourism will never be completely sustainable as every industry has impacts, but it can work towards becoming more sustainable." (Sustainabletourism, 2012,). Whilst there are truisms in the likelihood of achieving "complete sustainability", low impact, localised, closed loop (with zero net waste), powered by renewables would be a much more compelling goal to head towards than the token offerings from some organisations.

> "The 600m-year fossil record shows a pattern of continuous evolution and extinction. But naturalists now think that extinction rates are at least 100 times greater than the natural "background" rate because of pollution, habitat destruction, hunting, agriculture, global warming and population growth" (Radford, 2004, p. 1).
> "The Lemuria Resort, a new five-star hotel with 240 beds and 410 employees, is spread over an area of 110 ha (this includes a golf course). Statistically, this amounts to more than 4580 m2 per bed (or ca. 2290 m2 excluding the golf course). The energy-requirements of the hotel are confidential, but seem remarkable: Priscilla Shi Shun, Guest Relation Supervisor, indicates that the resort 'uses more energy than the entire rest of the island" (Gossling *et al.,* 2002, p. 208) with its 6500 inhabitants and its more than 1500 beds in hotels and guesthouses. "Other resource requirements are also substantial: the entire hotel is, for its large wooden parts, built with tropical wood (teak) from Indonesia. The furniture is made in Bali, finished in Mauritius, and afterwards transported to the Seychelles. There is a beauty parlour, an air-conditioned gym and a sauna with a small chilled pool. The apartments are equipped with a TV set, air conditioner, hair dryer, fan, fridge, safe, electric mosquito-coils, and stereo. Bathrooms include shower, toilet, tub and bidet" (Gossling *et al.,* 2002, p. 199).

It is not just natural ecosystems that are threatened – recent reports from areas as far removed as the Amazon and the Andaman islands have shown how the privacy and rights of no society are safe from the intrusion of tourism. In 2011, Amazonian Indians in the village of Nazareth described the way that villagers had voted to ban tourism completely because of the unwelcome impact of visiting 'outsiders'. The locals are not happy and feel, "What we earn here is very little. Tourists come here, they buy a few things, a few artisan goods, and they go. It is the travel agencies that make the good money. Nazareth resident Grimaldo Ramos feels that some tourists cannot distinguish between the wildlife and the Amazon's residents, snapping photos of indigenous families as if they were another animal" (Muse, 2011, p. 30).

In the Andaman islands, the Jarawa people have become an uncomfortable, crassly exploited tourist attraction, reported Gethin Chamberlin in early 2012:

> "Every day hundreds of tourist cars line up on the Andaman Trunk Road, which winds through the reserve. Signs at the entrance warn them of the rules; no pictures, no contact, nothing to disturb the tribe members. Most are already struggling to come to grips with the diseases of the outside world that have beset them since they started to make forays out of the jungle 14 years ago.
>
> But, on the day the Observer visited, when the gates opened the cameras immediately started clicking. Tourists threw bananas and biscuits to the tribes people at the roadside, as they would to animals in a safari park" (Chamberlain, 2012, p. 30).

It seems that until we can create a clear picture of what tourism would look like effectively embedded as part of nature and humanity, rather than as a cancer on it, change may be hard to reach. Tough questions need to be asked of the organisations that are complicit, yet turn a blind eye to bad practice, particularly the hotels and airlines who provide the infrastructure for irresponsible tourism. They're not the proponents, but they're not advocates for positive outcomes either. Leaders of infrastructure organisations could do well to ask themselves Rabbi Hillel's three questions: "If I am not for myself, who will be? If I am only for myself, who am I? If not now, when?"

Tourism Leader Actions

Although there are many examples of small tourism operators breaking new ground, it is hard to find examples in the tourism industry that match the lead taken by other consumer-driven industries. The resilience of the sector and its 'license to trade' will depend on its ability to respond to the rules of nature as well as of the marketplace.

In 2010, Ecuador became the first country to set a concrete Ecological Footprint target. The country has included the goal in its National Plan that, by 2013, its Ecological Footprint will be within its biocapacity, a trend that it will maintain going forward. "Ecuador wants to be a leading country [in] officially using the Ecological Footprint as a resource accounting tool for policy and decision-making" Ecuador Environment Advisor Dania Quirola Suárez said in a roundtable side-event with Global Footprint Network at the Copenhagen climate talks (Global Footprint Network, 2010).

Jennifer Mitchell, Global Footprint Network Director of Strategic Initiatives commented

> "This step shows that Ecuador's leaders understand the true value of their country's natural wealth and its importance in providing a high quality of life for its citizens...they recognize that ultimately, managing biocapacity will enable them to provide for their people's long-term well-being much more effectively than simply liquidating those resources" (Global Footprint Network, 2010).

The Global Sustainable Tourism Council (GSTC) have developed the Global Sustainable Tourism Criteria – a comprehensive listing, yet appearing to lack recognition of the limits that are ultimately imposed on business by nature, and the real nature of response that is needed. The purchase of disposable and consumable goods is measured, and the business actively seeks ways to reduce their use. Energy consumption should be measured, sources indicated, and measures to decrease overall consumption should be adopted, while encouraging the use of renewable energy.

Tourism Concern describe themselves as a 'non industry based' organisation and have a vision of "a world free from exploitation in which all parties involved in tourism benefit equally and in which relationships between industry, tourists and host communities are based on trust and respect" (Tourism Concern, 2012).

Whilst organisations such as Tourism Concern's mission statements i.e. to ensure that tourism always benefits local people are compelling, campaigning messages that only address components of the system without reference to the bigger picture, risk encouraging action that falls short of what is really needed to make change.

Ecotourism may thus be sustainable on the local level (in the sense that it puts a minimum threat to local ecosystems through the conversion of lands, trampling, collection of species, etc.), but it may in most cases not be sustainable from a global point of view (Gossling et al, 2002, p.200). Bearing in mind the scale of known challenges to the future resilience of business and communities, it is up to leaders, customers, shareholders to ask better questions of the accommodation and tourism providers, and inspire them with stories of success, rather than tales of fear and despair.

Travel group Thomas Cooke Plc is one of the world's largest leisure travel businesses, with sales of £8.9 billion and 22.5 million customers (Thomas Cooke, 2010). The Company has a clearly stated position on sustainable tourism, saying that it "is simply about making a positive difference to the people and environment of destinations we travel to by respecting local cultures and the natural environment". The Company lists activities including: buying local, giving fair economic returns to local families; recognising that water and energy are precious resources that we need to use carefully; helping to protect endangered wildlife; protecting and enhancing favourite destinations for the future enjoyment of visitors and the people who live there; taking responsibility for our actions while enjoying ourselves"(Thomas Cooke 2011). Whilst all of these activities do play an important role, they fall short of the scale or speed of response needed for transformation to a sustainable future.

The recently opened Asheston Eco Barns in West Wales, UK, are a good example of the benefits that accrue to businesses making appropriate scales of investment into the future. Jeff and Karen Loo's conversion of a disused range of old farm barns into five 5 star self-catering cottages uses eco-friendly materials, with energy provision from a combination of solar thermal hot water supply, wood burning stoves that burn timber from the farm, a ground source heat pump powered by on-site generated renewable electricity, clay paints and recycled stone for outside areas, and antique furniture for bedrooms. They strongly connect their high occupancy levels, good letting rates and high levels of positive PR to the level of commitment that they have demonstrated to looking after all stakeholders, from both tourism and natural worlds.

The TYF Group are an innovative adventure, learning and consulting business based in St David's, Pembrokeshire, UK. They were one of the first businesses in the world to become carbon neutral and were early members of 1% for the Planet. In the world of sports, they co-created the world freestyle kayak series and pioneered the development of coasteering, a new sport that combines ocean swimming, cliff traversing, scrambling and jumping in some of the most inaccessible parts of the coast. Their commitment to setting the highest level of environmental standards has repaid itself many times through new contracts and relationships that directly relate to the commitment they made.

Whilst the examples of both industry leaders such as Tui's Johan Lundgren's recognition of sustainability as a critical challenge (Tui Travel Plc), any travel activity that adds to the scale of ecological impact of long distance flying must be questioned within the broader question of what 'good enough' and ecological justice might look like. Newcomers such as Asheston Eco Barns, with their ultra-low impact are setting a truer direction, that if followed, would allow for multiple holiday trips that don't strain the planet's resources – provided of course, that in-country travel was low carbon too.

Learning from other sectors

The challenge for the tourism industry is to respond to the real challenge of sustainability, basing actions not on incremental improvements and 'less bad' practices, but moving instead towards a transformational approach, rigorous enough to restore habitat and ecosystems whilst reducing carbon in line with scientific advice. The examples below highlight aspects of this:

Proctor and Gamble serve 4.2 billion customers in 180 countries and have the ability to move markets when they change the way they do business; there's a growing realisation that business models and pressures are changing and that there's a need to step up the pace of change – a change at P&G that's strongly endorsed by Chief Executive Bob McDonald: "Last year, we announced a new long-term environmental sustainability vision to guide our efforts. This vision is challenging and far-reaching: 100% renewable energy to power all our plants, 100% renewable or recycled materials for our products and packages, zero consumer and manufacturing waste related to our products going into landfills. We don't yet have all the answers necessary to achieve this vision, but we are committed to making disciplined, step-by-step progress through a series of ten-year goals" (Procter & Gamble, 2011, p. 2).

Consumer products company Unilever have equally ambitious goals for 2020, setting out to help 1 billion people take action to improve their health and well-being and source 100% of their agricultural raw materials sustainably. Commentators from a wide range of stakeholders have talked of the significance of strong and visionary leadership on this topic from Unilever Chief Executive Pol Polman: "We will decouple our growth from our environmental impact, achieving absolute reductions across the product lifecycle. Our goal is to halve the environmental footprint of the making and use of our products" (Unilever, 2010, p. 2).

UK retailer Marks & Spencer were early movers at taking sustainability seriously, and have recognised the benefits that come from making real commitment to doing business in a different way. Their initial investment of £200m generated £50m of savings in addition to the significant progress that they made on carbon reduction, resource use and ecosystem impact (Barry, 2011, interview). Richard Gillies, Director of Sustainability at M&S is convinced of the benefit that this approach will bring in the future "backed by a strong business case, Plan A is at the heart of the exciting new growth plans for M&S, both in the UK and internationally" (Gillies, 2011, p. 2).

InterfaceFLOR is the world's leading manufacturer of modular carpet, and has made major commitments to making an impact on the way that it manufactures and recycles its products: "If we're successful, we'll spend the rest of our days harvesting yester-year's carpets and other petrochemically derived products, and recycling them into new materials; and converting sunlight into energy; with zero scrap going to the landfill and zero emissions into the ecosystem. And we'll be doing well ... very well ... by doing good. That's the vision" (Business Green, 2011).

River Simple is a designer and manufacturer of hydrogen-electric hybrid vehicles, with their first car currently in pre-production. They take their environmental commitment seriously: "The reduction of impact is insufficient as a goal; whilst we know that we will not achieve it soon, we want to ensure that everything that we do is a step towards the elimination of the environmental impact of personal transport" (Spowers, 2011).

Learning from Nature

UK-based consultancy BCI: Biomimcry for Creative Innovation have created an alternative approach to managing ecological balance that uses biomimicry – modeling design on nature's principles as the foundation for a philosophy and practice intended for the long term:

Build Resilience

It is more effective to develop resilience than correct poor decisions made with partial information of risk. Nature builds resilience by using change and disturbance as opportunities rather fearing them as threats, working with increased energy and information, rather than against it. The Guardian newspaper in the UK aims to be the world's leading content provider on sustainability, yet gives away its content for free, with no paywalls or price to pay. Nature tends to decentralise, distribute, and diversify knowledge, resources and decision-making, reducing the chance of negative impact if one part of the chain breaks. Nature also fosters diversity in shape, size, colour and capacity, optimising the likelihood of all niches in the ecosystem being effectively used.

Optimise

Optimization is the key to success for growth, rather than maximization or minimization. Nature can be seen to optimise by creating forms and shapes to fit functions, not the other way around, as human systems do. The clothing company Patagonia has worked for 30 years using organic, slow and steady growth, retaining a respect and level of success that many brands that came and went failed to capture. It is a good reminder that whilst nature uses complex chemistry, it optimises effectiveness to create complexity and diversity by using simple components and patterns.

Adapt

Learning how to be adaptive pays back better than 'staying a fixed course'. Left to its own devices, nature builds adaptability by creating feedback loops that sense and respond at all levels of the ecosystem. By developing sensors and sensing processes where they need to be, to gather this information, the ability to adapt is built in, rather than bolted on.

Anticipate and integrate cyclic processes

Cyclical approaches to resource management are at the centre of nature's design principles, ensuring that anything grown and used is turned into 'food' for another part of the ecosystem at its end of life. Whilst individual species produce waste, there is no waste at an ecosystem level, which means that scarce and valuable resources are always made re-available.

Work with Whole Systems

With reduced resources and a changing environment, it is better to be systems-based than independent. Nature works with whole systems by fostering synergies within an entire community, making the connections between energy, information and communication networks, and creates extended systems that allow it to continuously recycle wastes into resources.

Be Values-Based

In uncertain times, it is better to be based on a compass of values than a fixed destination point. Whilst it would be dangerous to project human values onto nature, we can see that nature reflects the idea of values in the way that it directs attention to what is really important to the communities in and with which its constituents live, interact, and impact. Nature also in effect measures what it values rather than valuing what it can measure, a key area in which many human-designed organisations come unstuck.

Support life

In the long run, it takes less effort and fewer resources to support life-building activities than be damaging or toxic and pick up the cost later. Nature supports life-building activity by designing all of its products to be water-based, renewable, bio-based, and biodegradable, unlike the processes used to make products for tourism and other industries. Nature also tends to leverage information and innovation rather than energy and materials – in effect because the first two are more abundant than the latter pair. It also creates support systems that care for the individuals who build entire ecosystems that in turn, care for individuals.

Taking action

On the pathway described in the first paragraphs of this chapter, organisations were offered a choice of directions, one leading to the creation of a restorative economy where resilience and the productivity of ecosystems and community was rebuilt to levels of natural health, and the other leading to long term decline of systems, species and choice.

To build capability and action, agents of change are invited to consider BCI's Five E model to connect business benefits with 'natural intelligence' and start or accelerate a journey that creates results worth creating. The first step is an invitation to explore reality, without blinkers on, to carefully study what is happening around elsewhere, what leading players are doing in other sectors, what is happening to nature and where the law is heading in raising standards. With a clearer set of data, take the second step of evaluating your position in relation to current best practice across any industry, and against nature's standards, asking yourself "if nature was able to vote, would my plans be good enough to pass selection?" The third step is to envision what 'good enough' looks like, using the Real 10 framework outlined below. Using your values as a compass, ask yourself what level of quality you would aim for if it were the standard that all others followed, with a hope for good long term outcomes.

Managing Ecological Balance   155

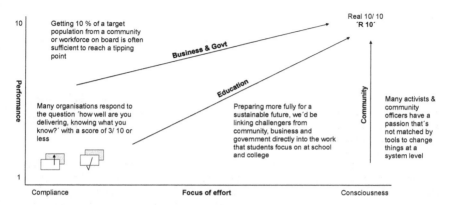

Figure 1:   R10 Change Framework

Having developed a clarity of direction and ambition, it is necessary to work out what minimum level of engagement you would need in your staff team, customers and stakeholder community to give your plans maximum chance of success. Engaging staff has the same effect as growing humus, the organic matter in soil – when a soil is rich in organic content, it is the soil that does the growing, not external inputs. Likewise, when employees are fully engaged, capability for change is optimised.

Finally, the approach to execution can be guided by nature's principles, using experimentation and reflection to gather information at the same time that action is happening. This a much more effective approach, than spending so long planning that the result, although perfect, is no longer relevant by the time anything happens.

Summary

With an education system that values compliance more than consciousness, it is no surprise that businesses have struggled to change operating models faster than they have. With better data, and a broader, deeper awareness of what excellence looks like in other sectors, and consideration of what 'good enough' looks like, the process of leaping from one step to another is one that is best approached with playfulness and hope, rather than excessive contemplation. When a few hundred organisations decide to change the rules, and show that they can win, the game changes.

References

Allenby, B. and Sarewitz, D. (2011), "We've Made a World we Cannot Control", New Scientist, 14 May 2011.

Barry, M. (2011), Personal Interview With Author.

Bristow, R. (2011), "Rethinking Business", Guardian, Guardian News and Media Limited, London, available at: http://www.guardian.co.uk/sustainable-business/ian-cheshire-bandq-kingfisher-online-q-a (accessed 18 January 2012).

Business Green (2011), "Obituary: Ray Anderson – the 'radical industrialist'", http://www.businessgreen.com/bg/feature/2100398/obituary-ray-anderson-radical-industrialist (accessed 15 Janaury 2012).

Centre for Ecology and Hydrology (2010), available at: http://www.ceh.ac.uk/news/press/european-nitrogen-assessment-pressrelease.asp (accessed 22 February 2012).

Chamberlain, G. (2012), "'They're killing Us': World's Most Endangered Tribe Cries For Help", *The Observer* 22 April 2012, Guardian News and Media Limited, London.

Clark, A. (2010), "The Future is Organic", Paper Presented to Guelph Organic Seminar Series.

Clarke, J. (2012), "Saving Energy at the Hotel", availabel at: http://www.holidayextras.co.uk/green-travel/arrival/save-energy-at-the-hotel.html (accessed 29 June 2012).

Daly, H. (2008), "A Steady State Economy", UK Sustainable Development Commission.

De Groot R., Fisher B. and Christie, M. (2010), "Integrating the Ecological and Economic Dimensions in Biodiversity and Ecosystem Service Valuation", available at: http://www.rncalliance.org/epages/rncalliance.sf/ (accessed 29 June 2012).

Dickinson J. and Lumsdon, L. (2010), "Slow Tourism", *Journal of Transport Geography*.

Gillies, R. (2011), "How We Do Business Report", Marks & Spencer Group plc.

Global Footprint Network (2010), "Ecuador Addresses its Ecological Balance Sheet", Global Footprint Network, available at: http://www.footprintnetwork.org/ (accessed 22 November 11).

Gossling, S., Borgstrom, C., Hansson, Horstmeier, O. and Saggel, S. (2002), "Ecological footprint analysis as a tool to assess tourism sustainability", *Ecological Economics*, p. 43.

Hawken, P., (2007), *Blessed Unrest*, Viking Press, New York.

Jackson, T. (2009), "Prosperity Without Growth", *Transition to a Sustainable Economy*, Sustainability Commission, London.

Millennium Ecosystem Assessment (2005), available at: http://www.millenniumassessment.org/documents/document.356.aspx.pdf (accessed 14 February 2012).

Murray, R., Caulier-Grice, J., Mulgan, J. (2010), "The Open Book of Social Innovation", The Young Foundation.

Muse, T. (2011), "Amazon Town Bans Tourists", World News, The Guardian, 25 March 2011, The Guardian, Guardian News and Media Limited, London, available at: http://www.guardian.co.uk/world/2011/mar/25/indigenous-peoples-amazon-tourism-pressures (accessed 3 July 2006).

OECD (2007), "Glossary of Statistical Terms", OECD, Paris, available at: http://stats.oecd.org/glossary/download.asp (accessed 29 June 2012).

Procter & Gamble (2011), "Sustainability Overview: Commitment to Everyday Life", P&G, available at: http://www.pg.com/en_US/downloads/sustainability/reports/PG_2011_Sustainability_Report.pdf (accessed 29 June 2012).

Radford, T. (2004), "Warning Sounded on Decline of Species", The Guardian, London, available at: http://www.guardian.co.uk/science/2004/mar/19/taxonomy.science (accessed 17 February 2012).
Spowers, H. (2011), River Simple Website, available at: http://www.riversimple.com/LatestNews.aspx (accessed 29 June 2012).
Stiglitz, J., Sen, A. and Fitoussi, J.-P. (2009), "The Measurement of Economic Performance and Social Progress Revisited", available at: http://www.stiglitz-sen-fitoussi.fr/documents/rapport_anglais.pdf (accessed 29 June 2012).
Sustainable Tourism (2012), "Vision", available at: http://www.sustainabletourism.net (accessed 12 February 2012)
TEEB (2010), "The Economics of Ecosystems and Biodiversity", Fact Sheet, December, UNEP, available at: http://www.teebweb.org/Portals/25/Documents/FACT%20 SHEET%20TEEB%20Jan2011. pdf (accessed 3 July 2012).
TEEB (2010), "The Economics of Ecosystems and Biodiversity Report for Business - Executive Summary",
The Scarlet Hotel, 2012, Initiatives, available at: http://www.scarlethotel.co.uk/environment_initiatives.asp (accessed 20 March 2012).
Thomas Cooke plc. (2010), Sustainability Report, available at: http://sustainability2010.thomascookgroup.com/approach/about.html (accessed 15 February 2012).
Thomas Cooke plc. (2011), "What is Sustainable Tourism", available at: http://www.thomascook.com/sustainable-tourism/ (accessed 11 February 2012)
Tourism Concern (2012), "Vision, Mission & Principles", available at: http://www.tourismconcern.org.uk/mission.html (accessed 14 January 2012).
Tui Travel Plc. (2010), "Sustainable Development Report: Towards a More Sustainable Future".
UKSDC (2008), "A Steady State Economy".
UNEP (2010a), "Greening Economy", Division of Technology, Industry and Economics, UNEP, Switzerland.
UNEP (2010b), "Our Planet, Natural Capital of Biodiversity", The magazine of the United Nations Environment Programme (UNEP), Nairobi, Kenya.
Unilever (2010), "Sustainable Living Plan".
Welsh Government (2012), Sustaining a Living Wales Consultation Document.
Werbach, A. (2009), "Strategy for Sustainability", A Business Manifesto, Harvard Business Press, Massachusetts.
World Bank (2011), World Development Indicators database, World Bank Group, Washington, available at: http://data.worldbank.org/data-catalog/world-development-indicators (accessed 29 June 2012).
WTTC (World Travel & Tourism Council) (2011), "Economic Impact of Travel & Tourism", WTTC, London, http://www.wttc.org/site_media/uploads/downloads/4pp_document_for_WTM_RGB.pdf (accessed 29 June 2012).
WWF (2010), "Living Planet Report", WWF, Gland, Switzerland, http://assets.wwf.ca/downloads/lpr2010.pdf (accessed 29 June 2012).
World Wildlife Fund (WWF) (2012), "Ecological Balance", available at: http://wwf.panda.org/about_our_earth/teacher_resources/webfieldtrips/ecological_b alance/ (accessed 17 February 2012).

Politics, Community Tourism and Sustainability

Mark Piekarz & Michelle Callanan

Introduction

Politics is often a misunderstood term. To 'play politics' is a pejorative phrase, referring to activities which somehow seem divorced from reality and fair decision-making. A closer examination of the concept of politics reveals the limits of such a simplistic view. Crick (2000), in his classic essay on politics, argues that the essence of politics relates to collaborative decision-making, resource allocation and compromise. It is a process of discussion, whereby in order to be properly effective, it needs people with contrary stances. When viewed in this sense, it is rare, even in authoritarian political systems that some form of politics does not operate, although clearly there are restrictions to the degree of difference tolerated. Furthermore, Crick is also keen to stress that democracy is not the same as politics, as it can at times be the enemy of politics, particularly when democratic processes become dominated by the politics of populism. This can lead to what J.S. Mill, the nineteenth century British philosopher, described as the tyranny of the majority (Mill, 1859, cited in Acton, 1972, p. 73), whereby minority views are removed from political debate and dialogue. This understanding of politics forms a critical underpinning for this chapter which explores how notions of sustainability are used to frame politics at a local or community level, in order to shape or influence tourism developments. It is important to point out however, that when one encounters tourism developments which are deemed as neither sensitive nor sustainable to local areas and communities, this is not necessarily because of politics, but rather the lack or weakness of political processes and debates.

When examining sustainability within the context of tourism and local politics, it is clear that over time, the concept has changed in definition and focus. Deeply rooted in 1970s' environmentalism, sustainability became closely associated with notions of green politics and environmentalism, where to be 'sustainable' was deemed as being more harmonious with the natural environment. From the 1980s, sustainability discussions shifted towards strengthening community lives and their social capital, yet also tried to ensure a sound economic base. The often cited 'triple bottom line' approach (striving for environmental, social and economic balance in communities) framed sustainability within the context of *inter*-generational and *intra*-generational equity of communities. In other instances, there are examples where sustainability refers to communities which can exist and live beyond tourism, having the capacity to survive capricious tourism demand. Here, the emphasis is on sustaining a balance between alternative types of economic activities other than tourism based work, which may not necessarily mean that the developments will be sustainable in an environmental sense. Whatever the position taken, arguments of sustainability can be powerful weapons in the armoury of local political discourse; they can add emotional charge, gravitas and legitimacy to arguments about tourism, whether justifying, opposing or simply changing tourism developments or projects. Clearly then, politics is endemic within the sustainability debate, having gained popularity in political rhetoric, often cited in many international conferences. Whilst the term has been criticised as being malleable by Newton and Freyfogle (cited in Paddock and Sears 2005) in terms of its ability to develop concrete practices, others, such as Sarewitz (2001) and Padock *et al.* (2005), dismiss this complaint about sustainability, as they argue its strengths lie with its adaptability to multiple situations, environments and populations.

Set against this background, there are a number of reasons why the themes of tourism and sustainability are examined at a local political level. Within the context of development politics, minority groups are often presented as local communities, or indigenous people, where their perceived needs become the centre of many political debates. Yet these groups are often treated as homogenous in nature, with similar needs and goals. As Mayo (1994, p. 48), cited in Shaw (2006) observes:

> "It is not just that the term [communities] has been used ambiguously, it has been contested, fought over and appropriated for different uses and interests to justify different politics, policies and practices."

Within this context, the arguments of sustainability are often endemic in local political discourse when used to justify a particular position to tourism policies or developments.

Secondly, it can be at the local level where decisions on tourism projects are taken, centred on issues of resource allocation and levels of community participation, with the strength of local political systems tested at this stage. Finally, building on from the previous theme, there can be a great deal of advocacy for notions of community participation and empowerment in tourism developments, often presented as 'community-tourism' or 'community-empowered tourism' or 'tourism empowering communities'. All these highlighted themes will be reflected upon within this chapter.

To help frame the discussion in this chapter, a systems theory approach is adopted, using a simple model to understand local political systems and how notions of sustainability can shape and influence tourism development outcomes. It is important to note that, as with all models, a contextualisation to local conditions is required on application, as the interaction of all the different elements fundamentally affects the outcomes. Throughout the discussion, various case studies will be used to illustrate the key points.

A framework for Analysis

According to the World Commission on Environment and Development (WCED) in 'Our Common Future' (1987), sustainable tourism development requires a political system that:

> "...secures effective citizen participation in decision making....The law alone cannot enforce the common interest. It principally needs community knowledge and support, which entails greater public participation in the decisions which affect the environment. This is best secured by decentralising the management of resources upon which local communities depend, and giving these communities an effective say over the use of the resources. It will also require promoting citizens' initiatives, empowering people's organisations, and strengthening local democracy." (WCED, 1987, pp. 17-18)

This is of interest as much for the age of the report, as for the variety of themes which it highlights, including the desired local political system for effective resource allocation and management and for the empowerment of local communities. This statement also identifies some important themes with which to help structure the discussion about tourism, sustainability and politics. If politics is about discourse and shaping the allocation or governance of resources, then this would suggest an inherent dynamism, whereby to talk about notions of political stability can be something of a misnomer. The political environment (local, national and global) should be characterised by the interaction of many forces of change, whether anticipated or not.

Accordingly, it can be useful to utilise some basic concepts from complexity theory and systems theory from which to develop a model and to convey the inherent dynamism in political systems. In Figure 1 the local political system is represented, whereby a variety of factors are highlighted which can interact and subsequently shape the development of tourism. What should be appreciated is that tourism itself becomes one of the forces which impacts on politics: basically, tourism can be both shaped by local politics, and, in the process, shape local politics itself. Into this mix goes the issue of sustainability and how it is used by different groups to rationalise their arguments and shape the final outcomes. Tourism is represented as the key input into the system, which will demand space in both a physical land-use sense, and in a less tangible social dimension, such as in terms of local cultural lives and everyday living. As such, as it vies for resources, it will inevitably produce tensions and contests between the different groups competing for chattels, ranging from developers, local residents, tourists or local and central governments.

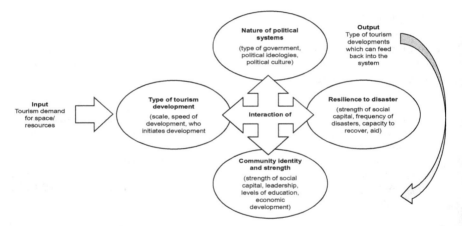

Figure 1:   The Local Political System Factors Shaping Tourism Outcomes

To understand the system, it can be helpful to consider four broad categories of factors (represented in Figure 1) shaping tourism outcomes, which are:

- **The nature and construction of the political system and its institutions** (levels of government, independence of key institutions, type of government, political ideologies, degree of freedom etc.)
- **The ability of different interest groups to articulate and represent their arguments** (level of economic and social development, openness of the system, basis of community identification, political culture, social capital etc.)

Politics, Community Tourism and Sustainability 163

- **The nature of tourism** (stages of the tourism development life cycle, nature of the developers, degree of community participation, extent of cultural clash etc.)
- **Vulnerability of the environment to crisis** (natural disasters, political upheavals, economic problems and social/human disasters etc.)

These areas form the basis for structuring the discussion in the rest of this chapter. A variety of case studies will be used to illustrate how issues of sustainability have been used to frame local political discourse and tourism developments. Not surprisingly, a constant theme that emerges within the forthcoming discussion is the ambiguous nature of sustainability.

Nature of the Political System

In essence, the nature of the political system can play a critical role in how local communities can shape patterns of tourism. The idea of the political system refers to the degree that the system is open and free with mechanisms for local people to shape outcomes, such as electing local politicians, or having opportunities to influence land-use plans and developments. In theory, if a country has open and free democratic processes, then the expectation would be that this can create more opportunities for local communities to shape tourism developments which are more sustainable. This is certainly evident in Fossen and Lafferty's (2001) study, where land and environmental issues have been a strong driver and focus for local Hawaiian politics and identity, such as the Save Our Surf (SOS) group, which they say can be regarded as one of the most effective local environmental groups in the USA. Here it is noticeable that there are both the political institutions and mechanisms for democracy and community involvement, complemented by a political culture and ability of local communities to articulate their views. As such, land-use regulations are very stringent, with some arguing that they are stifling progress, making the process for approving tourism projects time consuming and potentially discouraging entrepreneurial activity. This ultimately may mean that some communities, whilst being environmentally sustainable, may not be economically sustainable. Furthermore, having such a strong, regulatory system may still not be enough to ensure that developments will deliver sustainable outcomes.

Whilst in democratic political systems one would expect to see stronger community representation and sustainable projects, this does not necessarily mean community tourism does not exist in authoritarian political systems. For example, in China, with its single party rule, Yiping (2004) explains how there are examples of community tourism, but which, it must be emphasised, is not quite the same as saying they are effective examples. The development which has taken place on Hainan Island, China's only tropical province in the South China Sea, adopted a community tourism approach that, on paper, was supposed to lead to more sustainable tourism development. The reality was more complex; the developers took an authoritarian approach to various community projects designed to soften the impact of huge and rapid tourism developments. One example was the building of the Buddhist Cultural Park, which developers assumed the community would be grateful for. However they were surprised when it in fact created tensions, as it emerged that the local community would not be responsible for managing it. There were also various examples of negative environmental impacts, such as using foreign plants not suitable for the area, together with Western style hotel and golf resorts near sacred Buddhists sites. Yiping (2004) highlighted that part of the problem was the lack of effective community participation and consultation.

The political system in China is such that the single party dominance of government means it can fail as an effective arbitrator between community and developer's interests; developments possibly are an extension of government policy. The speed of the development also meant that there was little time for local community groups to form and articulate their views in a timely manner. Even if communities had had time to form as a cohesive group, the nature of the political system would have continued to place restrictions on community actions. Furthermore, whilst compensation was given to local people and jobs created, the peasant workers, many of whom had worked on the land for generations, found themselves dislocated from their local community, often finding that they had neither the skills nor the desire to work in the new urban environments, resulting in them having to eke out a living elsewhere. It is also a system which can lend itself to corruption, with innumerable barriers to effective community participation, such as not being able to elect key officials to represent communities.

Another interesting example which shows some of the complexities and paradoxes of community tourism and sustainability, can be found in Zimbabwe. Meadowcroft (2004) argues that in relation to society's capacity to manage the environment, it is significantly increased by an extension of deliberative democratic practices in environmental and natural resource policy. Such practices seek to deepen the understanding of collective problems and focus on constructing a shared vision. The CAMPFIRE Project in Zimbabwe has been used as an interesting example of these deliberative democratic processes in operation. It was set up in 1989 as a means of local governance over local resources. Up until then, wildlife had often been viewed by many locals as pests, destroying many farms and putting local lives at risk. Understandably, locals took action by killing this threatening wildlife, but their actions put pressure on certain wildlife species with numbers dropping dramatically (Meadowcroft, 2004).

During this time, President Mugabe introduced many land reforms in Zimbabwe with the CAMPFIRE programme established to empower locals through a deliberative democratic process. It received support from international organisations such as WWF and USAID, on the sustainable use of their resources using ecotourism and trophy hunting. Many benefits were initially accrued by locals including employment (guides, lodges etc.) infrastructural developments, share of wild meat, and cash dividends, albeit sporadic and inconsistent in lean times. However, over the years as the project has grown in scale, locals have become peripheral to decision-making powers and to accruing benefits. This concern is highlighted by Average and Ephraim (2010), who conducted a study on the Mahenye Campfire Project (Zimbabwe). They concluded that the rural district councils have taken too much control over the projects, reaping more and more of the benefits, at the expense of the local people. This example illustrates a familiar pattern and problem which can occur with sustainable community projects: success can bring growth; growth can bring bureaucracy; bureaucracy can bring distance; distance can bring emotional detachment from projects; detachment can help legitimise self-benefit and even corruption. The problems in the wider political environment in Zimbabwe have only helped to further erode the effectiveness of these community projects. The inference which can be taken from this is that the most sustainable projects tend to be those that are small and community-run, but they will also be dependent on wider economic and political conditions.

Ability of Local Groups to Articulate Interests

Having a political system where there are opportunities for influencing the decision-making process is not sufficient in itself for securing the involvement of local groups. Such systems may include opportunities for involvement and influence, but if groups do not have the knowledge or the ability to access these points and articulate their opinions, then they can count for very little. Not surprisingly in developed countries it is often the better educated, middle class groups who are the most effective at communicating their viewpoints and mobilising opinion to help support their stance. In contrast, groups in poorer communities are often more isolated, and can find it difficult to develop a collective vision and coordinate actions to support their viewpoints. Here some of the key elements which influence the 'ability' factors relate to the strength of the social capital, levels of education, the quality of leadership, political cultures and, of increasing importance, the ability to access technologies, such as the internet, through which ideas and actions can be shared.

To begin with, exploring the theory of political culture gives some useful initial insights into the opportunities for communities to influence tourism planning processes. Simply put, political culture refers to the shared values and beliefs that people have as to the political actions they can take and the degree of legitimacy that the political system confers on governments. In North America for example, some of the core strands of the political culture relate to ideas of freedom and democracy, and people having the right to form pressure groups which can influence political parties and national/local issues. In relation to the earlier cited example of Hawaii, Fossen *et al.* (2001) highlight how the political culture is one where democracy and pluralism help nurture a grass root political scene which is vibrant and active, where groups can use arguments of sustainability to help frame their political stance in relation to proposed developments.

Another interesting example relates to how local people in Bimini, in the Bahamas, managed to successfully prevent the development of a mega resort and casino which would have involved cutting down mangroves and causing further destruction to the Bimini Bay area. The Bahamian government agreed to halt the development, announcing that they wanted the people of Bimini to "act as the government's eyes and ears" by flagging environmental concerns relating to the Bimini Bay resort (Tourism Concern, 2009). The result has been the creation of a marine protected area. This example shows the importance of both local people believing they have a right to fight the development, along with the government accepting that their views are legitimate and need to be listened to.

The importance of culture, issues of sustainability and political processes does however have some more complex elements to it. Here, work which examines the development of national cultural identities can help give a useful insight into why notions of sustainability can become woven into national identities and thus help shape local politics. Gellner (1983) in his seminal work on nationalism, raises the important and provocative question of asking not why there are so many nationalisms in the world, but why there are so few? His basic argument is that nationalism is essentially a product of industrialisation and the modern age, because before then, there was neither the technology, nor a coherent education system whereby an effective shared culture or national identity could be communicated to all levels in society, to all parts of a country. What the process of industrialisation does is construct a national identity which destroys, borrows and synthesises a variety of cultures. Nationalism, in short is a construct which can be constantly shaped and changed, and where the opportunity exists for the construction of new cultural identities. What this suggests is that cultural identities are malleable and can be woven together utilising a variety of strands, ranging from language, history and heritage to physical landscapes. The latter point is of particular interest in this work, as one can find examples of how groups who want to differentiate themselves culturally from the core state, may develop an image of a local people who love and care for the natural environment they are rooted in. This imagery could be particularly strong in relation to indigenous groups, such as in North America (Native American Indians) and Australia (Aboriginals). As modernity has encroached on the lands which they have inhabited, the arguments of sustainable developments have been powerful with which to focus around, not least because they can be so emotive. Another interesting example of how notions of green politics and sustainability shape identity can be found in Northern Spain, where these ideas have become tied in with Basque cultural identity and claims for a separate nation state; this in turn also impacts on the marketing and development of tourism in the region.

A key point which should be appreciated is that notions of sustainability and cultural identities can be open to accusations of romanticism and not necessarily grounded in hard reality or facts. In much the same way that poets and artists reacted to industrialisation in Britain during the nineteenth century, where they would hark back to the loss of a green and pleasant land, others questioned the veracity of this romanticisation of the past. Within a similar discourse, criticism can be levelled at various contemporary community representations of themselves as they exist in their local environments. It is in this sense that, according to Singh *et al.* (2003), it is important to maintain a sense of perspective whereby an automatic corollary should not be made between a local community's interests and sustainability, and also that the 'local' should not be romanticised as it can be within tourism planning. Conflict and dissonance are common within any discussions at the local level (Millar and Aiken 1995, cited in Singh 2003). Millar *et al.* (1995) go on to say:

> "...conflict is a normal consequence of human interaction in periods of change, the product of a situation where the gain or new use by one party is felt to involve a sacrifice or change by others".

Thus, whilst local groups can construct identities which have identifiable themes related to notions of being 'green' and 'sustainable', it is vital *not* to then make the assumption that any decision or action they take is by association 'green' and 'sustainable'. One can find examples in Hawaii and China where local people acted out of simple self-interest, rather than any over-arching concern for the natural environment or others in the community. It is an issue also raised by Matarrita-Cascante *et al.* (2010) in relation to their study of the Costa Rican town, La Fortuna, which was forced to move because of a volcanic eruption. Whilst they note that generally the subsequent development of tourism in the area has been a model of good practice in terms of sustainability and community involvement, they still observe that there can be instances where people act out of self-interest and not for the wider benefit of the community or sustainable developments.

The final interesting concept to consider is the notion of social capital. This idea refers to the strength of social networks which people have and the sense of a shared community. The role of tourism as a catalyst in helping to build or destroy social capital and social cohesion is a complex one. Examples can be found where it is in opposition to new developments that community consciousness is aroused. In Argentina for example, the indigenous people of Nazareno, have rejected government sponsored tourism projects in their ancestral lands. The building of a lodge at Camp La Cruz was denounced by local communities, arguing that it was done without consultation and ignored the right of self-determination of peoples. Fossen *et al.* (2001) in their examination of tourism developments in Queensland, Australia, noted that tourism was characterised by limited regulation in the 1980s, where the local political agenda was driven by an authoritarian National Party state government, with an explicit commitment to rapid development, often in the face of considerable community opposition (Fossen *et al.*, 2001). They illustrate how in the Noosa area of Queensland, there were many examples of unplanned developments, yet interestingly in some of these developments, as the communities became established, important changes took place, which were demonstrated by the opposition of community groups to a number of new developments. Here, the community which had steadily expanded over the years was a largely urban, tertiary-educated and professional business group, who had moved there for lifestyle reasons; subsequently it did not want to see the quality of the environment eroded by further tourism expansion. In this instance, the proposed tourism developments acted as a catalyst for an awakening of community consciousness, a building of social capital and a focus for action. Whereas in the past, tourism developments in Queensland were dominated by a free market, resulting in a more undisciplined approach to tourism planning, Fossen *et al.* (2001) use the Noosa case to show how people can still shape developments in a more sustainable way, similar to more highly regulated tourism planning systems, such as in Hawaii. The critical factor to recognise in the Noosa example, however, is that there was an articulate, relatively young, middle class group, who were capable of organising, communicating and accessing the political decision making process to shape the tourism outcomes.

Nature of tourism

The type of tourism project or development which takes place is another factor which can shape local community reactions and the debate about sustainability. Simply put, building large scale hotels, second homes or developing some basic tourist facilities will vary in the impact they have on the environment and local people's consciousness. This in turn is able to provide agency to reactions and the flow of political discussion. Another important element relates to who the key actors are in initiating the developments. There is a great deal of advocacy in various academic papers for Community-Based Tourism (CBT), where it is recommended that the community takes the lead in shaping the development, as opposed to tourism developments simply being imposed on the local area without consultation. No doubt one of the reasons for this is because there are so many examples from around the world of tourism developments where there was little or no consultation with local communities resulting in further problems. For example, Kaypoe (2008) highlights the case of the Paduang women or the 'long necks', originally refugees from Burma, living in northern Thailand. Evidence suggests that they are being forced to stay in this region despite some wanting to leave, leading to criticism from the United Nations High Commission for Refugees (UNHCR). In a press report (as cited by Tourism Concern, 2008) the Paduang refugee villages have been dubbed as 'human zoos'; the reason for this being their value as tourism commodities, with their needs as a community being subsumed to the wider demands of tourism.

A further issue raised by Goodwin (2009), in a study of the 116 nominated Community-Based Tourism (CBT) initiatives around the world, found only four that were economically sustainable. Goodwin and his team identified a number of challenges facing such projects, ranging from over dependency on donors, lack of adequate markets and the ambiguous nature of the parameters of CBT. Indeed, Goodwin noted a number of initiatives which are not CBT, including the Manda Wilderness (Mozambique), Aga Khan Development Network in Pakistan (Baltit and Shigar Forts) and Chumbe Island (Tanzania), which have provided significant benefits to the locals including new opportunities for local employment and new developments enhancing community life.

Benjaminson and Svarstad (2008) provide an interesting example of how dogsledding has grown in a mountainous community in Southern Norway, whose economic base has traditionally been based on farming and hunting moose. Some of those who participate in dogsledding have gone on to set up dogsledding tourism services, but they are a group who have mostly come from outside the area causing various tensions with some local groups, particularly with some of the farmers who resent these 'outsiders' coming into the area. They argue that the 'outsiders' have had a negative impact on moose hunting which was one of the ways local farmers could supplement their relatively low incomes, as farming has become less economically viable in the area. Interestingly, both dogsledders and farmers use notions of sustainability and environmentalism to help shape their arguments. The dogsledders argue that their activity is environmentally friendly and sustainable, and draws tourists to the area; the local farmers on the other hand claim that dog sledding disrupts the traditional migratory patterns of the moose, which in turn affects the opportunities for hunting. Here the concept of viability extends to the idea of older communities and whether they have a future in terms of their traditional activities and being able to live in the area. The case also illustrates the theme of modernity impacting on established communities, where middle class people from outside the community clash with people who see their traditional economic activity (farming and hunting) becoming marginalised. The malleable nature of sustainability is further shown as both sides use it, with the local government acting as an arbitrator of interests. What is also particularly important to highlight in this case is that both groups want to lay claim to the arguments of sustainability, because 'environmentalism' plays such a strong moral position in national Norwegian politics (Benjaminson *et al.*, 2008). Consequently, it is not surprising that different interest groups try and gain the moral high ground by claiming to be both environmentally friendly and sustainable.

As discussed earlier, just because tourism is rooted within the community, does not automatically imply it is morally correct, sustainable or in a wider community's interest. Just as outside developers and governments can be ignorant of local people's needs, so too can local people be ignorant of the needs of the wider community. Fossen's *et al.* (2001) discussion of the Hawaiian tourism development at Kihei in the 1970s illustrates this, where the area was developed in order to profit from the tourism boom and many local small land holders built condominiums eventually resulting in an unplanned sprawl. One of the compounding factors inhibiting a more sensitive development was the fact that many of the local politicians had considerable investments in these tourism structures. Similarly, Yiping (2004) also gives examples of local people acting out of their own self-interest, rather than the community's needs in relation to the Hainan Island tourism development in China.

In order to deal with some of the tensions which can arise from developments, various strategies can be adopted to try and enhance the community benefits and deal with issues of sustainability. For example, in Jamaica, the government whilst keen to attract large corporations and investors, stipulate that these groups buy certain supplies from local suppliers. Although this is not community-based tourism, it is a simple example of how communities can benefit from tourism while maintaining their economic viability. Other examples can include the need for businesses from other countries to try and find local business partners in order to establish their businesses. Concomitant to this can also be the strength of land-use plans, or regional and national strategic development plans. Here certain areas of land may be designated for environmental protection, or marked for tourism expansion. Clearly, the degree to which local people are involved in the development of these plans will vary according to the political system, the people's knowledge and awareness of these processes, together with the dominant political ideals at the time the plans are produced.

Vulnerability of the Environment to Crisis Events

Tourism has been subjected to increasing turbulence and crisis events over recent years, such as terrorist attacks, natural disasters, health scares, economic recessions and political unrest. In theory, the role of local policy-makers and decision-makers should be to reduce the vulnerability of local areas to these risks and to help rebuild and rehabilitate an area post-crisis. However, the post-crisis stage, which Klein (2007) labelled as the 'politics of shock', often prompts conflicting interests over how to rebuild an area, and can lead to political elites exploiting the situation to enhance their interests. This exploitation has been coined by Klein (2007) as 'disaster capitalism'. Within this context, a destroyed area post-disaster is viewed as a 'blank canvas' to be exploited, often denying many indigenous people their right to return to their homelands and continue with their traditional livelihoods. The tsunami which hit Asia in 2005 reveals a range of examples in relation to the issue of 'disaster capitalism' and 'shock policies' (Klein, 2007) following a disaster. Klein (2007) cites a statement from the Thailand Tsunami Survivors and Supporters Group, which reveals a number of interesting themes, stating:

> "In Thailand, the conflicts in how this coastal land is used have been around a long time. But the tourism boom of the past 10-20 years has really raised the stakes. The big money that has been trying to develop the prime coastal areas has increased pressures to evict poor fishing villages from the land they occupy. Because both local and national politicians are partners in – or beneficiaries of – various schemes

to commercialize Thailand's Andaman coastline, the government's role in managing these fragile coastal environments has been deeply compromised by conflicts of interest. To these groups of businessmen-politicians, the tsunami was the answer to their prayers, since it literally wiped these coastal areas clean of the communities which had previously stood in the way of their plans for resorts, hotels, casinos and shrimp farms. To them, all these coastal areas are now open land!" (2007, p. 402)

Here the traditional communities can find it hard to resist modern developments, having a political system which is difficult to access in order to represent community interest, together with a weakened social capital and a political culture where government is not seen as a true arbitrator of interest. Nowicka (2005) also picks up on these themes, presenting the case of how the development of luxury tourism resorts has been favoured over traditional activities in Sri Lanka, noting how tourism is trumpeted by governments in the global south as a 'quick-fix means' of generating the needed foreign exchange demanded by the IMF and the World Bank. Yet in doing this, he notes that there is rarely any consultation with ordinary people whose "lives are irrevocably affected by the influx of wealthy foreigners, and little regard to the environmental, social and cultural impacts at the sharp end" (Nowicka, 2005, p. 1). Nowicka observes how in the aftermath of the tsunami, this disaster event has been used as an opportunity for developing various new luxury hotels, whilst the former local inhabitants were still housed in temporary accommodation, with the local government announcing a "200m to 1km coastal development zone that excludes locals from the beach on grounds of safety – but five-star resorts are allowed within the zone" (ibid, p. 1). Such policies attempt to reengineer a local area suffering from shock with unpopular policies that benefit local elites and external tourism developers. In effect, local communities become 'lost' or 'forgotten' with forced relocation to make way for big-brash tourism developments. Weaver (2006), citing the report, "Tsunami Response – a Human Rights Assessment", highlights how the relief agencies studied 95 towns and villages hit by the disaster and found extensive evidence of forced relocation. Cases ranged from India, Sri Lanka, Indonesia and Thailand, where locals are losing out to the development of new tourist resorts.

It should, however, be noted that the response to a disaster is not automatically one where negative, non-sustainable outcomes emerge. Tan-Mullins *et al.* (2007) illustrate how after the Tsunami in 2004 the rebuilding of communities was affected by the strength of social capital. They noticed how the linked-communities, who had a longer and deeper associated history, could have stronger social capital, meaning they could deal with the crisis better. They do however observe that the comparatively more recent settlements, such as the tourism operators, or excluded groups, such as some of the Muslim fishing villages, found it more difficult to respond to the crisis. Another more positive example of disaster responses helping to deliver seemingly sustainable outcomes is shown by Matarrita-Cascante *et al.* (2010) in their discussion of the town of La Fortuna, in Costa Rica. This town was forced to move after a volcanic eruption in 1969, but which led to the setting up of the community group ADIFORT (Asociacion de Deseraollo Intergral del La Fortuna), which has been very influential in shaping tourism developments with a strong green and sustainable emphasis.

Overall, the vulnerability of the external environment, especially to disasters and crises, can be used to justify shock policies for development in some cases. However, the response to a disaster can also reawaken community consciousness and cohesiveness. The nature of the political system and the community itself are key factors in determining the post-disaster response and development of a local area.

Conclusion

When answering the question of whether tourism helps to empower communities and lead to more sustainable projects, there is no simple yes or no answer. This may seem like a trite response to an important question, but it reflects the reality that there are cases to support each side. However the evidence suggests more weight in favour of community-based tourism, leading to outcomes which can be deemed as sustainable. The dynamic nature of political systems, results in a wide variety of factors constantly shaping outcomes. These range from the nature of the political system, the levels of education and the vulnerability of the environment to crises and disasters.

When reading the literature on the social impacts of tourism and how some of the negative effects can be dealt with, a misleading impression can be given that empowering communities automatically leads to sustainable community and tourism developments. This is both simplistic and naïve. Certainly tourism which has been shaped by communities can engender more sustainable developments, particularly if part of the community identity is based on the land and has been articulated and vocalised by community leaders. Here the levels of economic and educational development and the strength of the social capital can all be important. Yet, it is also possible to find local communities wanting to make the most from short term economic gains, which can ultimately degrade the environment, destroying their communities, resulting in the area becoming less attractive for tourism.

What this discussion illustrates is that the idea of sustainability is a contested and malleable term that changes, depending on the local political, social and economic conditions of the area. Fundamentally, it implies striving for a balance between the economic, social and physical environments of a local area, whilst operating within a dynamic environment. What many of the case studies under review have also highlighted is that the success of some community projects is dependent upon the emotional attachment of those involved to either the place or the projects themselves. Thus one can propose a 'quadruple bottom line' approach to include psychological factors, in addition to the more familiar environmental, social and economic factors. Here, the emotive appeal of the arguments of sustainability can be a vital force in arousing feelings of anger, frustration, nostalgia or pride, which can in turn be crucial in generating engagement and action with the political system. Sustainability is a social construct, not an objective reality, but it is a powerful and emotive ideal, which can form the key part of the grist of local political discourse and so shape tourism developments.

References

Acton, H.B. (Ed.) (1972), *Utilitarianism, on Liberty and Considerations on Representative Government*, Dent & Sons, London.

Average, C. and Ephraim, C. (2010), "The Decentralisation-Recentralisation confusion: An analysis of the decentralised management of common pool resources in Mayenye Campfire projects in Chipinge, Zimbabwe", *Journal of Sustainable Development in Africa*, Vol. 12 No.1.

Benjaminson, T. A. and Svarstad, H. (2008), "Understanding traditional opposition to modernization: narrative productions in a Norwegian mountain conflict", *Journal Compilations: Swedish Society for Anthropology and Geography*, pp. 49-62.

Crick, B. (2000), *In Defence of Politics*, (5th ed), Continuum, London.

Fossen, A. and Lafferty, G. (2001), "Contrasting models of land use regulation: community, government and tourism development", *Community Development Journal*, Vol. 36 No 3, pp. 198-211.

Gelner, E. (1983), "Nations and Nationalism", Blackwell, Oxford.

Goodwin, H. (2009), cited in New Study: "Community-based tourism doomed to fail", *Brave New Traveler*, April 8th.

Matarrita-Cascante, D., Brennan, M.A. and Luloff, A.E. (2010), "Community agency and sustainable tourism development"; the case of La Fortuna, Costa Rica, *Journal of Sustainable Tourism*, Vol. 18, No. 6, pp. 735-756.

Mayo, M. (1994), "Communities and Caring: The Mixed Economy of Welfare", Macmillan, London.

Meadowcroft, J. (2004), "Deliberative Democracy", in Durant, R. F., Fiorino, D. J. and O'Leary, R., (Eds.), *Environmental Governance Reconsidered*, The MIT Press, Cambridge, Massachusetts and London, UK, pp. 183-217.

Mill, J.S. (1859), *On Liberty*, Longman, Roberts and Green, London.

Millar, C. and Aiken, D. E. (1995), "Conflict resolution in aquaculture: a matter of trust", in Boghen, A.D. (Ed.), *Cold-water agriculture in Atlantic Canada,* Canadian Institute for Research on Regional Development, Moncton, Canada

Nowicka, P. (2005), "Invisible in paradise", The Guardian, Wednesday 5 October.

Padock, C. and Sears, R. R . (2005), "Conserving Concepts: in Praise of Sustainability", *Conservation Biology*, Vol. 19, No. 1, pp. 39-41.

Tan-Mullins, M., Rigg, J., Law, L. and Grundy-War, C. (2007), "Re-mapping the politics of aid: the changing structures and networks of humanitarian assistance in post-tsunami Thailand.", *Progress in Development Studies,* No. 7, pp. 327-344.

Kaypoe M. (2008), "Padaung refugees trapped from tourism", *In Focus*, Tourism Concern, Spring edition.

Klein, N. (2007), "The Shock Doctrine: The rise of Disaster Capitalism", Penguin Books, London.

Yiping, L. (2004), "Exploring community tourism in China: the Case of Nanshan cultural tourism zone", *Journal of Sustainable Tourism*, Vol. 12, No. 3, pp. 175-193.

Singh, N. (2003), "Governance for Poverty Eradication and Sustainable Development: Issues in development co-operation", *Governance in the Age of Globalisation*, pp. 471-498.

Tourism Concern (2008), "Exploitation of women: Burmese refugees trapped by tourism", available at: www.tourismconcern.org (accessed 28 March).

Tourism Concern (2009), "Victory in the Battle for Bimini", available at: www.tourismconcern.org (accessed February 2012).

Shaw, M. (2006), "Community Development & the Politics of Community", *Community Development Journal*, Vol. 43 No. 1, pp. 24-36.

Sarewitz,D. (2001), "Commentary on 'sustainability'", in Mirovitskaya N.And Ascher,W. (Ed.) *Guide to sustainable development and environmental policy*. Duke University Press, Durham, North Carolina, p. 74 I.

WCED (1987) "Our Common Future", Oxford University Press, Oxford.

Weaver, M. (2006), "Tsunami victims evicted by developers", The Guardian, Wednesday February 1st.

Media and Sustainable Tourism

Roland Schroeder & Oliver Hahn

With support of:

Eugenia Ekhardt, Christoph Grundig, Sonja Gurris, Bernadett Jung, Anna Maria Petermann, Alesja Salewski, Eva Skudlarek, Julia Swierczyna, Katharina Titz and Lisa-Marie Wilhelm

Introduction

"Climate change is already happening and represents one of the greatest environmental, social and economic threats facing the planet." (Environment Directorate-General of the European Commission, 2010). The 2010 UN Climate Change Conference in Cancún Mexico[1] has confronted politicians, media and people all around the world with that urgent and serious issue.

Reports and news about climate change and the greenhouse effect have increased over the last years. Today, *green* topics can be found on media agendas all over the globe. Thus, media have been raising awareness of climate change and placing the topic in people's mind: a global trend towards a *green* life or a lifestyle of health and sustainability can be observed. But what exactly is the role of the media? Do they react to a societal discourse or do they initiate the discourse and help establish it onto society's agenda?

The degree of correspondence between the media agenda and the public agenda tends to increase with greater exposure to the media (McCombs, 2004).

---

[1] The 2010 United Nations Climate Change Conference was held in Cancún, Mexico, from 29 November to 10 December 2010. The conference is officially referred to as the 16th session of the Conference of the Parties to the United Nations Framework Convention on Climate Change and the 6th session of the Conference of the Parties serving as the meeting of the Parties to the Kyoto Protocol.

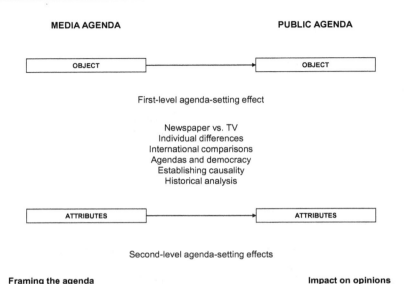

Figure 1: Topics discussed in the various chapters are displayed here as first- and second-level agenda setting effects

The diagram illustrates the familiar elements of the agenda-setting idea: the media agenda, and the public agenda, following McCombs (1997).

Our perceptions and judgments are mediated by the media, we receive information through media, we accumulate knowledge through media and we are entertained by the media (Hartmann, 2008). With the help of mass communication, people get information, recognize connections between several topics, expand their knowledge and learn with the help of the media (Maletzke, 1981). Most of what people know comes to them "second" or "third" hand from the mass media or from other people (McCombs and Shaw, 1972). Because of this strong influence, media can create a growing awareness of ecological topics; they can affect opinions and negotiations.

Roessing (2009, p. 53) suggests that this impact can be observed on three levels:

- Cognitive Effects (Knowledge, Opinions, Thoughts)
- Affective Effects (Emotions, Feelings, Reviews)
- Behavioral Effects (Negotiations, Behavior)

All these effective components are not isolated from each other. In most of the cases the effects are combined. We see reports about global warming and build up a specific knowledge about the role of carbon (Cognitive Effect); we are surprised about the global impacts (Affective Effect) and we decide to behave more ecologically (Behavioral Effects).

Nevertheless opinions are not only created by the media. The perception of opinions takes place within the direct social environment combined with the mass media (Roessing, 2009). Cohen (1963, p. 13) explained: "[The press] may not be successful much of the time in telling people what to think, but it is stunningly successful in telling its readers what to think about".

With the help of agenda setting processes the mass media, in particular journalists, decide which topics will be reported and which not. This concept is closely related with the concept of news values that help journalists with this decision. They decide which news has a direct relevance for their audience (McCombs, 2004). Another theoretical aspect to highlight pertains to a special topic, the method of framing. Entman (1993, p. 52) notes:

> "To frame is to select some aspects of a perceived reality and make them more salient in a communicating text, in such a way to promote a particular problem definition, causal interpretation, moral evaluation and/or treatment recommendation".

So media create attention for certain topics through selection, emphasis and omission. They frame specific information and facilitate classification by the recipients. Simultaneously, recipients have their own frames in which they embed information. Thus, frames could also be seen as "(…) mentally stored clusters of ideas that guide individuals' processing of information" (Entman, 1993, p. 52). For an example media reports on ecological topics such as the greenhouse effect and climate change have a negative frame. Mostly these reports also have a schoolmasterly resonance.

This illustrates that awareness influences and changes many aspects of people's lives, their way of thinking and living as well as their way of performing business. Small wonder, then, that the tourism industry is affected by this global trend. Travelling by plane and driving has a negative impact on nature; hence the tourist industry, in particular, is creating a large carbon footprint every day.

The effects of media agenda setting on public opinion can be traced back to a study on the Watergate scandal that suggested that media had a strong influence on selecting issues to evaluate political actors (Weaver *et al.,* 1975).

However, a tourism sector promoting responsible and sustainable travel behavior is slowly but steadily emerging. "Sustainable Tourism, Ecotourism, and

Environmentally Friendly Tourism" are terms describing this new travel field facing the challenge of climate change and global warming (Kaefer, 2010).

It seems to be a fact that sustainable issues concerning travelling are appearing on the media's agenda more frequently. This leads to the hypothesis that the topic of *Sustainable Tourism* has developed in the media over the past 10 years, and seems related to the time sustainability first entered the public discourse. Consequently, we may assume that the number of articles on the subject have increased continuously over this time. The purpose of this paper is to analyze the development of *Sustainable Tourism* in order to support an hypothesis. For this study the most popular travel magazine in Germany, *GEO Saison*[2] has been chosen. The articles from January 1999 until December 2009 have been analyzed using different criteria within a quantitative content analysis. The methodology is described below.

Definitions

> "Tourism in the twenty-first century will be a major vehicle for fulfilling people's aspiration for a higher quality life… tourism also has the potential to be one of the most important stimulants for global improvement in the social, cultural, economic, political and ecological dimensions of future lifestyles." (Edgell, 1990, p. 55)

The tourism sector is one of the fastest growing industries in the world. Nevertheless there are also negative effects related to this continuous growth. The current development will place great stress on preserving biologically diverse habitats and indigenous cultures, which are often used to support mass tourism. Hans-Magnus Enzensberger (1979) has stated that tourism destroys what it seeks by finding it. He stresses the fact that travelling harms the environment. No matter how it is undertaken, it causes negative external effects on nature. On the one hand Enzensberger appears to be correct, but on the other hand *Sustainable Tourism* reduces the environmental impact of travelling.

Focusing on the research question, it is important to define the scope of *Sustainable Tourism*. The following section presents definitions which the authors have taken into consideration when approaching the theme.

John Swarbrooke (1999, p. 13) defines Sustainable Tourism as "forms of tourism which meet the need of tourists, the tourism industry and host communities today without compromising the ability of future generations to

---

[2] GEO saison is a travel magazine of the German publishing house Gruner + Jahr in Hamburg. It is distributed nationally ten times a year. In June 2012, GEO saison had a paid circulation of 96,743. (IVW, 2012)

meet their own needs". Some scholars feel that trying to provide definitions of Sustainable Tourism is difficult. "This is because general definitions can give the impression of simplicity in what is a complex area. Tight definitions might also limit the range of issues to be covered under the heading of Sustainable Tourism. Definitions tend to be irrelevant, misleading, and ever changing" (Swarbrooke, 1999, p. 13). To be precise, there is no commonly accepted definition of Sustainable Tourism.

Nevertheless, for this study, we have restricted the meaning of *Sustainable Tourism* to the *Declaration of Rio de Janeiro on Environment and Development* and the recommendations of *Agenda 21*.

Here, tourism should meet certain criteria: including ethical and social justice, cultural adaptation, ecological capacity and economic reasonableness. These dimensions of sustainability are strongly related and correlate to each other. This is why they have to be covered in an integrated manner.

Figure 2:   The relationship between Sustainable Tourism and other terms referring to Swarbrooke (1999)

This diagram illustrates the relationship between *Sustainable Tourism* and other related terms, which have been identified as relevant concepts and topic areas for this study. People tend to use them as synonyms, but none of them are congruent. Moreover, there are difficulties translating these aspects of Sustainable Tourism into different languages, therefore making a clear and global understanding almost impossible.

Methodology

The first step was to gain insight into the topic through a broad Internet search. The subject matter of the study is *Sustainable Tourism* which includes specific investigations on issue-related websites, forums and encyclopedias. The market leader in German travel magazines had been defined by recent statistics of print circulation in Germany (IVW, 2012). According to the criterion of monthly publication *GEO Saison* was taken into consideration. This magazine is published by *Gruner+Jahr* , located in Hamburg and has the largest circulation in Germany. Using the press data bank of this publishing house, the team aimed at proving or disproving the assumption that *"the number of articles increased in relation to the rising relevance of the topic"*.

It is necessary to precisely define the concept of *Sustainable Tourism*. A generally accepted definition does not exist. Hence, related terms should be researched and checked for their relevance. As mentioned above, the keyword *sustainable* is often linked to other concepts such as *Soft Tourism, Eco Travel* or *Eco Tourism*. To define the concept it was necessary to identify potential keywords, so further detailed Internet research was conducted.

The results were structured and categorized during a brainstorming session. This creative technique is useful for finding out more aspects and for adopting different perspectives. In the following step, a *mind map* was generated to cluster the various possible keywords in a broad range of categories.

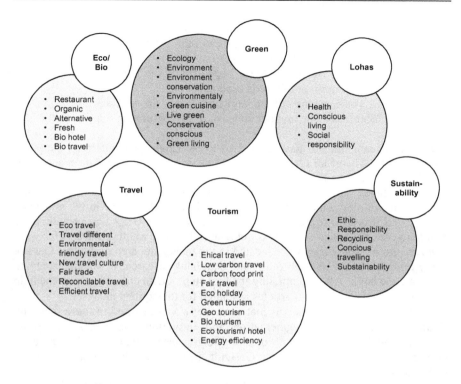

Figure 3: Keyword Cluster for Sustainable Tourism

The next step was to allocate the keywords generated into different categories: *Travel,* LOHAS (Lifestyle of Health and Sustainability), *Sustainable, Green, Organic.* Due to the high number of English language terms (also used by German native speakers) touched on in the topic areas, the keywords are listed in English and German. Thus an international comparison can be made – bearing in mind that an exact translation is sometimes difficult.

The analysis of the articles from *GEO Saison* covers a timeframe of ten years, from January 1, 1999 to December 31, 2009.

Different description categories have been applied to encode the issue development in travel journalism with regard to several criteria:

- Media: Allocation of the analyzed magazine
- Date: The article's date of publication described in the European standard format

- Title: The article's headline stated in the index
- Prominence: Categorizing the articles into different categories (reports, features, comments, columns, essays)
- Front-page story: According to the popularity of the article
- Story size: The number of words used in the article
- Keyword: The frequency of the keyword used in the article
- Picture/Text ratio: The number and size of the pictures in relation to the text

The project team did not have access to every single printout from the years 1999 to 2009. Therefore *Gruner+Jahr* publishing house granted free access to the *Gruner+Jahr* data base.

The articles' format in the data bank was not standardized, neither were any pictures shown, nor could the context and position of the article in the magazine be assigned. Because of possible layout re-launches of *GEO Saison* within the past ten years, the project team was not able to find out whether the articles were *main stories* or where they were located in the magazine. Due to the fact that not every criterion could be analyzed in the data bank research, it was necessary to adopt a code book. After completing the first step of data collection with the help of quantitative factors, 1,536 articles remained for the content analysis.

One of the main issues was that some keywords resulted in more than one finding, so that further segmentation and limitation was necessary. Some keywords with an ambivalent meaning e.g. *'green'* had a wide range of definitions. Also *'health'* (German: Gesundheit) had to be checked in the context of *Sustainable Tourism*.

A decisive search key for *'travel differently'* (German: Anders Reisen) was to search for both words in one search phrase, because in many cases they were listed as single words. This approach reduced the number of articles to a total of 322 relevant articles. Altogether, over the past ten years *Gruner+Jahr* had published 4,695 articles in the press data base.

With regard to a qualitative approach, the project team decided to manually check the articles to identify the subject of *Sustainable Tourism*. As a consequence, only articles which covered ecological and/or sustainable topics with corresponding contents would be listed. Based on the conclusion that many topics were mainly mentioned as marginal notes at the beginning of the ten year period, another classification was implemented. This new table was structured into: hotel news briefs, information about restaurants and food, travel equipment, wellness recommendations, travel agencies/tour operators. Moreover, the significance of the articles needed to be evaluated. Therefore, the table was supplemented with: the *number of keywords in text, number of keywords in title* and *number of keywords in the figure*.

Media and Sustainable Tourism

Date	Title	Keywords	In text	Title	Teaser	underline	Border: hotel advice	Border: restaurant advice	Border: wellness advice	Border: travel equipment	Links	Travel operator
01.02.1999	Oasen im Ozean	Grün	1	0	0	0	0	0	0	0	0	0
01.02.1999	So schön war Gondwana	Grün	1	0	0	1	0	0	0	0	0	0
01.02.1999	Xnisa, Xhanee und Xtsgoma	Gesundheit	0	0	0	0	0	0	0	1	0	0
01.03.1999	Goldene Palme '99 Entdeckerreisen	Ökotourismus	0	0	0	0	0	0	0	0	0	0
01.03.1999	Goldene Palme '99 Entdeckerreisen	Öko	1	0	0	0	0	0	0	0	0	0
01.03.1999	Goldene Palme '99 Grüne Palme	Ökotourismus	0	0	0	0	0	0	0	0	0	0
	Goldene Palme '99 Grüne Palme	Green	1	0	0	0	0	0	0	0	0	0
	Goldene Palme '99 Grüne Palme	Umwelt	0	0	1	0	0	0	0	0	0	0
	Goldene Palme '99 Grüne Palme	Ökologie	1	0	0	0	0	0	0	0	0	0
01.03.1999	Nett für die Natur	Umwelt	1	0	0	0	0	0	0	0	0	0
01.03.1999	Provence mit Seitensprüngen	Grün	6	0	0	0	0	0	0	0	0	0
01.03.1999	Zum Trinken zu Schade	Gesundheit	0	0	0	0	0	0	0	0	0	0
	Zum Trinken zu Schade	Umweltfreundlich	1	0	0	0	1	0	0	0	0	0
01.04.1999	Almhütten in Kärnten	Bio	0	0	0	0	2	0	0	0	0	0
01.04.1999	Als Leichtmatrose von Kapstadt nach Rotterdam	Grün	0	0	0	0	0	0	0	0	0	0
01.04.1999	Das kann doch nicht wahr sein	Green	1	0	0	0	1	0	0	0	0	0
	Das kann doch nicht wahr sein	Grün	0	0	0	0	0	0	0	0	0	0
	Das kann doch nicht wahr sein	Bio	5	0	0	0	0	0	0	0	0	0
01.05.1999	Algarve Wohnen wie Gaudi in Portugal	Ökologie	0	0	0	0	0	0	0	0	0	0
01.05.1999	Die Freiheit nehm' ich mir	Umwelt	1	0	0	0	0	0	0	0	0	0
01.05.1999	Mein Leben in der Jogginghose	Grün	1	0	0	0	0	0	0	0	0	0
01.06.1999	Rügen	Grün	0	0	0	0	0	0	0	0	0	0
	Rügen	Bio	7	0	0	0	0	0	0	0	0	0
	Rügen	Öko	0	0	0	0	0	0	0	0	0	0
01.06.1999	Sylt	Grün	1	0	0	0	0	0	0	0	0	0
01.07.1999	Ayurveda	Gesundheit	3	0	0	0	0	0	0	0	0	0

Figure 4: Extract of the spreadsheet presenting the articles, keywords and categories

Critical reflections on the methodology

A fundamental difficulty concerning the research was the lack of a generally accepted definition of *Sustainable Tourism*. The project team had to choose an alternative way of research, by using broader or related definitions combined with relevant keywords referring to the generic term.

A certain amount of subjectivity during the search of the keywords could not be excluded. The lack of a standardized definition, as well as the absence of representative surveys, led to the fact that the keywords may not have had validity. However, this disadvantage was compensated for by the different suggestions and reflections of the project members. Another critical aspect was the filter function of the *Gruner+Jahr* data base. The inaccuracy of the tool caused the team to list articles which did not contain any of the keywords – the code word could only be found within the superior section name. In addition, the arrangement of the images and the layouts of the articles could not be retraced.

Analysis and Discussion

In order to present the results visually, descriptive graphs have been chosen. This allowed the development trend of the term Sustainable *Tourism* to be tracked over time. The following graph (Figure 5) shows the number of articles dealing with *Sustainable Tourism* in the *GEO Saison* during the past ten years. The green graph displays all articles dealing with the topic, while the blue one illustrates the number of articles where the keywords referring to the topic are not used in the subcategories. The subcategories consist of hotel news briefs, information about restaurants and food, as well as travel equipment, wellness recommendations, links and contact details of travel agencies.

Assuming that the articles, excluding subcategories, are of higher relevance, the graphs are examined separately. It goes without saying that there is a strong divergence between the two graphs. This discrepancy highlights the difference between the topic's relevance in the articles with subcategories and without. Taking a closer look at the year 2008, the green and the blue graph identify the largest discrepancy during the ten years due to the high amount of keywords in the subcategories. In the following year, the keywords are reallocated from the subcategories into the main parts of the articles, which is why the graphs converge. Thus there is a higher focus on the topic.

Overall, the line of the curves is irregular. However, a slight growth is noticeable.

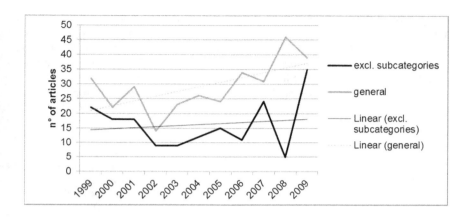

Figure 5: Number of articles concerning Sustainable Tourism from 1999 to 2009

The graph for the year 2004 demonstrates the enormous influence of the subcategories. In order to rule out falsifying the interpretation, the articles were examined separately.

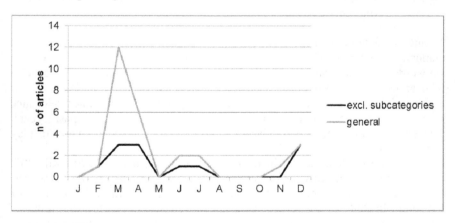

Figure 6: Comparison of articles with and without subcategories in 2004

The following graph shows the number of articles in *GEO Saison*, where the keywords were found in the text, title and/or figure.

Studying the graph (Figure 7), there is no explicit trend observable in the past ten years. However, there are some peaks that are worth noting, for example in the years 2004 and 2008. It might be possible that there is an association between the peaks and natural catastrophes or climate summits. After researching certain occurrences, no facts could be found to support this assumption.

Irrespective of the seasons, *Sustainable Tourism* is a recurrent topic.

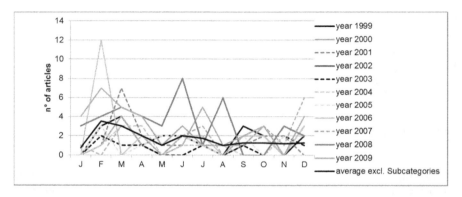

Figure 7: Number of articles with keywords in the main categories monthly (monthly overview)

Taking a qualitative observation perspective, the content of all articles was manually examined. The strategic approach was to identify the number of keywords within a certain article. The graph below shows the number of articles with at least three keywords related to the topic of *Sustainable Tourism*. An article with a greater amount of different keywords is of higher relevance regarding the development of *Sustainable Tourism* over past years. Consequently, the articles with a larger number of cross-linked keywords display a greater value.

It is asserted that there is inconsistency during the period 1999 until 2003. In 2004 there are no articles consisting of at least three keywords. However, from 2007 onwards, there is a tendency towards an increasing importance of the topic. In 2009 in particular, there are eleven articles with a minimum of three various keywords, indicating that awareness of the issue is more prominent.

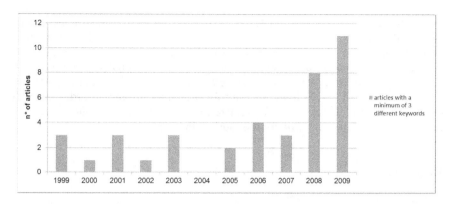

Figure 8: Number of articles with at least three keywords related to the topic

Conclusion

Surprisingly, the authors only noticed a slight increase in the number of articles on *Sustainable Tourism* in *GEO Saison*, over the past ten years. This seems contrary to the assumption that there has been a considerable rise in articles related to the research subject. Only 7% of all articles published between 1999 and 2009 have a direct connection to the topic area of *Sustainable Tourism*. Out of 68 related keywords, only 37 appeared in all the articles. Equally, 31 keywords did not match the search criteria and were not applied in the articles. This means a total of 46% irrelevant keywords. This approach was necessary to avoid the problem that keywords might have been overlooked.

The qualitative analysis demonstrates that the subject moved increasingly into a central focus – that is from subcategories to the main part of the articles. This development seems to be logical, because the media agenda is linked to people's awareness of relevant topics. However, the relatively small number of articles in a leading travel magazine is still difficult to explain.

If *Sustainable Tourism* wants to be a topic within the media agenda and consequently, the public agenda, it has to work with active agenda setting strategies to create an awareness of ecological traveling. This is important because there is huge market potential in this sector. According to a study of the market research institute *AC Nielsen*, in collaboration with *KarmaKonsum.de* (2008) 30% of the German population is living a sustainable lifestyle. In particular, the demographic group of LOHAS (Lifestyle of Health and Sustainability) can be seen as a target group with high potential. Consumers within the LOHAS segment continue to be early adopters, influencing friends and family. They are less price sensitive than the average traveler and show more brand loyalty. Both their social structure and internalized values form the basis for making them an attractive consumer target for the sustainable tourism sector. In this context a strategic media plan is necessary to place reports and articles in the media, which are relevant for the target group/s in order to create awareness of ecological travel. To realize this potential, *Sustainable Travelling* has to become a relevant issue for the tourism industry.

References

AC Nielsen/ Karma Konsum (2008), "Was LOHAS wirklich kaufen," available at: http://www.lohas-blog.de/2008/05/31/neue-lohas-studie-von-acnielsen-und-karmakonsum/ (accessed 23 September 2012).
Cohen, B. C. (1963), *The press and foreign policy*, Princeton University Press, Princeton.
Edgell, Sr., David, L. (1990), "International Tourism Policy", Van Nostrand Reinhold, New York, NY.
Entman, R. M. (1993), "Framing: Toward Clarification of a Fractured Paradigm", *Journal of Communication*, Vol. 43, pp. 51–58.
Environment Directorate-General of the European Commission (2010), European Commission, 2. June 2010, available at: http://ec.europa.eu/environment/climat/home_en.htm (accessed 06 June 2010).
Enzensberger, H.-M. (1979), Bundesamt für Naturschutz, available at: http://www.bfn.de/0323_iyesanft.html (accessed 12 May 2010).
Hartmann, F. (2008), *Medien und Kommunikation*, Facultas Verlag, Wien.
IVW - Informationsgemeinschaft zur Feststellung der Verbreitung von Werbeträgern e.V (2012), Heftauflagen, Publikumszeitschriften, available at: http://www.ivw.eu/index.php (accessed 05 September 2012).
Kaefer, F. (2010), Blog on Sustainability, CSR and Climate Change, 23. January 2010, available at: http://blog.floriankaefer.com/sustainable-transport-travel-tourism/ (accessed 06 June 2010).
Maletzke, G. (1981), *Medienwirkungsforschung. Grundlagen, Möglichkeiten, Grenzen*, Niemeyer, Tübingen.
McCombs, M. and Shaw, D. L. (1972), "The agenda setting function of mass media", *Public Opinion Quarterly*, Vol. 36, pp. 176-187.
McCombs, M. (1997), *Communication and Democracy*. Lawrence Erlbaum Associates, Mahwah, New Jersey, NJ.
McCombs, M. (2004), *Setting the Agenda: Mass media and public opinion*, Polity Press, Cambridge.
Roessing, T. (2009), *Öffentliche Meinung- die Erforschung der Schweigespirale*, Nomos, Baden-Baden.

Swarbrooke, J. (1999), *Sustainable Tourism Management*, CABI Publishing, Wallingford, UK.

Weaver, D., McCombs, M. and Spellman, C. (1975), "Watergate and the media: A case study of agenda-setting", *American Politics Quarterly*, Vol. 3, pp. 458–472.

Education and Copernicus

Ian Jenkins

Introduction

Changing 'hearts and minds' is at the core of any successful movement. Even though this sounds perspicacious the practice of changing attitudes is not easy. For some 1,500 years it was accepted wisdom that the world was the centre of the universe and challenges to this viewpoint seemed folly (Magee, 2010; Mulder, 2010). However, changing hearts and minds during the medieval period did occur and it became accepted that the sun was at the centre of the universe, not the earth, nor for that matter, man (Magee, 2010; Mulder, 2010). Copernicus was the man that recognised this and his evidence proved irrefutable. The resultant change reverberated around the western world, permanently changing attitudes to the authority of the Church. This analogy is a useful one for the current debate on sustainable development (SD) and it is somewhat of a paradox that the name 'Copernicus' is once again at the heart of a new debate. Certainly, tourism and business needs a seismic change to fully embrace sustainable development. This is somewhat surprising as the very essence of sustainability has been nurtured for some 25-40 years (Hall and Lew, 1998; Junyent and. Geli de Ciurana, 2008; Scott, 2011), but is only now being fully recognised.

Education and knowledge are possibly antecedents of all change. Education nourishes and shapes the next generation and also enlightens the present one. The foundations and attitudes of all future leaders are usually shaped and moulded through education; therefore in order to ensure a bright future for ensuing generations it is necessary to understand the assertion that sustainability should pervade and be at the centre of higher education. This can be supported by the Copernicus Charter which states : "Education is critical for promoting such values and improving people's capacity to address environment and development issues. Education at all levels, especially university education for the training of decision-makers and teachers, should be oriented towards sustainable development and foster environmentally aware attitudes, skills and behavior patterns, as well as a sense of ethical responsibility. Education must become environmental education in the fullest sense of the term" (CRE, 1994, p. 1)

Consequently, the statement that sustainability be permeated through all university systems in Europe, seems to be axiomatic, but also an ideal that can be viewed positively. It is purported that to challenge the notion of sustainable development is similar to 'burning one's bridges'; short term benefits for the loss of long term goals.

The development of the Copernicus Charter for universities in 1988 was a bold undertaking and it took some years to get to the stage where European Universities were taking sustainability seriously; some 326 universities had signed up to the Charter at its peak. Disappointingly, by 2005 the initiative had declined and in 2009 efforts were being made by the Copernicus Alliance to revive the initiative (Alliance Copernicus, 2010) to engender the principles of taking this Charter seriously and looking at the incorporation of SD into every facet of a university's operations and curriculum.

Copernicus stands for:
The "Cooperation Programme in Europe for Research on Nature and Industry through Coordinated University Studies" (CRE, 1994, p. 1) and as noted above this was first started by the Association of European Universities (CRE) in 1988.

In order to support this development there have been a series of declarations and important staging posts along the way (adapted from CRE, 1994) namely:

- Brundtland Report (*Our Common Future.* Report of the Brundtland
- Commission, Oxford University Press) 1987,
- Rio Conference (UNCED) in 1992
- Copernicus Charter 1994

Copernicus Project and Strategies

Copernicus was designed to foster co-operation and multi disciplinary approaches to the problems of the environment. It hoped to see universities and other relevant organisations co-operating to cultivate strategies in SD throughout a university's operations. The initiative developed a number of principles and action points which guided the development of the programmes which can be seen below.

"Principles of action"
"1. Institutional commitment
Universities shall demonstrate real commitment to the principle and practice of environmental protection and sustainable development within the academic milieu.

2. Environmental ethics
Universities shall promote among teaching staff, students and the public at large, sustainable consumption patterns and an ecological lifestyle, whilst fostering programmes to develop the capacities of the academic staff to teach environmental literacy.

3. Education of university employees
Universities shall provide education, training and encouragement to their employees on environmental issues, so that they can pursue their work in an environmentally responsible manner.

4. Programmes in environmental education
Universities shall incorporate an environmental perspective in all their work and set-up environmental education programmes involving both teachers and researchers as well as students – all of whom should be exposed to the global challenges of environment and development, irrespective of their field of study.

5. Interdisciplinary
Universities shall encourage interdisciplinary and collaborative education and research programmes related to sustainable development as part of the institution's central mission. Universities shall also seek to overcome competitive instincts between disciplines and departments.

6. Dissemination of knowledge
Universities shall support efforts to fill in the gaps in the present literature available for students, professionals, decision-makers and the general public by preparing informative didactic material, organising public lectures, and establishing training programmes. They should also be prepared to participate in environmental audits.

7. Networking
Universities shall promote interdisciplinary networks of environmental experts at the local, national, regional and international levels, with the aim of collaborating on common environmental projects in both research and education. For this, the mobility of students and scholars should be encouraged.

8. Partnerships
Universities shall take the initiative in forging partnerships with other concerned sectors of society, in order to design and implement coordinated approaches, strategies and action plans.

9. Continuing education programmes
Universities shall devise environmental educational programmes on these issues for different target groups: e.g. business, governmental agencies, non-governmental organisations, and the media.

10. Technology transfer
Universities shall contribute to educational programmes designed to transfer educationally sound and innovative technologies and advanced management methods."

(Copernicus Campus, 2007, pp. 36-37)

Sustainability and Education

The evidence from the literature further supports the assertion that education is a key motivator to change. Universities and higher education institutes are also important sources of knowledge for society which need to be melded with the local community and private sector in order to enhance all types of development, including sustainability (Trivun et al., 2008). Higher education has the aura of representing leading edge research and wisdom. This is possibly the axiom that should be applied to sustainability at universities and higher education institutions (Mitchell, 2011).

The constant discourse on sustainability, seems to place the emphasis upon the environment and supporting texts appear to uphold this image (Hall and Lew, 1998; Wu et al., 2010). A quick review of the leading precepts of Copernicus, reiterates emphasis upon the environment. It is asserted that "[t]he concept of sustainability first came to public attention with the publication of the World Conservation Strategy in March 1980" (Hall and Lew, 1998, p. 2) its main focus being upon the natural environment. Unfortunately, this pervasive emphasis tends to overlook the equally important aspect of sustainability and its relation to people. However, what is evident is that the environment is contingent upon human activities and vice-versa. It is asserted that the environment to a large extent dictates man's culture. The geography and weather of a location reflects quite clearly the cultural tenets of the location and it is axiomatic to state that climate and the environment seem to duplicate themselves in culture (WHC, 2011). Types of dwellings, the food eaten and the rituals performed, relate so much to the locale which in turn is dependent on resources and climate. Therefore it does not seem too far removed to argue that the other elements of sustainability, such as social, economic and cultural are contingent upon the element of environmental sustainability, and should be equally important. However, simply focusing on the environment is not what Copernicus is about, neither for that matter, is sustainability; the economic social and cultural needs of humans also need to be addressed. But the main principles of Copernicus appear to have an environmental focus.

Sustainability and the Copernicus Charter should be directed to all areas of a university's operations. To many the notion of active sustainability can be seen in terms of simply a recycling policy and how this is made visible to stake holders (staff and students). In one sense this is simply the 'tip of the iceberg'. Sustainability should be seen as permeating all areas of a university from its transport policies, accommodation, staff training, through to the pedagogy and research that it undertakes (Nicolow, 2010), as well as how it interacts with the community (local and global). Sustainability looked at simply from the viewpoint of the natural environment can be quite limiting and ineffective; there is a need here to expand the elements of sustainability to incorporate the other three pillars: social, economic and cultural which are so often overlooked.

Staff development is also an important component in delivering a sustainability strategy. It is implicit that staff (academic and support), delivering the programmes and policies of sustainability, must also be part of the process. There is an imperative for a comprehensive programme of staff development related to how to operate sustainable polices. It is not uncommon for conference organisers and marketing departments, to be oblivious to the aspects of sustainable resources and they consistently order marketing materials that are neither environmentally friendly nor produced from sustainable sources. The ubiquitous conference pack is a classic example, especially the conference bag. More "stuff" that delegates do not really want or need!

In addition, administrative and support staff have important parts to play in the running of a university along sustainable principles. Management of recycling, procurement of sustainable energy and transport policies for students and staff are all Copernicus issues that are mainly non-academic.

From a curriculum perspective new models and approaches to sustainability are being developed and presented and should be used with renewed effect in ensuring that sustainability permeates into graduate and undergraduate programmes and modules (Junyent and Geli de Ciurana, 2008). Junyent and Geli de Ciurana note that: "Higher education should play a critical role in assisting change towards a sustainable present and future within our society. Universities must function as places of research and learning for sustainable development, and as initiators and poles of activity in their communities and nationally. Educational theory and innovative practices frequently emerge from research programmes and academic investigation. Sustainable development needs to become a central priority in determining areas of educational research and development." (2008, p. 764). This clearly supports Copernicus's initiatives and echoes the need to place sustainability centrally within a university's spirit of education.

Methods and Philosophies within Academia.

As can be seen from the previous section the framework of SD can be managed on a number of levels within a university, namely: curriculum development, research action and projects, administration and management, buildings and resource management. These items are discussed below in the actions and priorities for universities.

There are a number of 'tool box' methods that can be used to ensure that SD is delivered by a university. The tool boxes are divided into a number of system areas such as: human resource management and resources together with policies and strategies that can be embraced by the university. The following are some areas adapted from IISD (1996) that universities should action:

1. Campus Policies (include strategic imperatives)
2. Management Systems:
   - Campus Environmental Management System
   - ISO 14000
   - Manitoba Round Table Organizational Framework for Sustainable Development
3. Sample Waste Management Practices:
   - Contracts to reduce waste
   - Recycling successes
   - Laboratories
   - Composting on campus

These policy instruments, to a certain degree are a framework for sound SD management. However, others may also be added such as new designs for sustainable buildings, energy procurement and transport planning. Certainly, the principles engaged in are ones that need to be filtered through the aspects of university life (Nicolow, 2010). Possibly the hardest is that of 'Campus Policies': when this is loosely examined the real significance is down to the individual responsibilities of all staff and students on the campus not just management (and changing attitudes is no easy task). The assertion here is for all staff, management and students at a university to take sustainable actions relating to

SD (to include social and economic aspects); this could also include not just the locality of the buildings and campus grounds, but also should take into consideration the wider notion of the community that the university finds itself within (Nicolow, 2010). Currently, a number of universities are realising that they need to consider the community at large and the impact that universities have. From the author's perspective most students are viewed as not part of the local community and rather like tourists, are there as visitors; consequently, students have the same impact as tourists. Small communities, with large student populations, are the hardest to convince of the benefits that students and the university provide for the community. There is evidence to suggest that universities in these locations are not viewed as positive assets to the community.

Possibly the most important part of the above policies relate to evaluation of success. As with most initiatives good intentions and enthusiasms are usually found at the start. The effectiveness of the SD policy is only evaluated by actually looking at attitudes and real achievements which have been made, against past benchmarks (Fonseca *et al.*, 2011; Lozano 2010). There are assessment systems to be used but perhaps the plethora of these diminishes evaluation as a common bench mark. The process of evaluation is also plagued with subjectivity and how actions which have marginal or little progress are dealt with. In some aspects this could also be at loggerheads with the main aims of the university, especially if the university is a private and profit making company where profits are the primary aim. Complementing environmental with sustainable cultural and economic goals may not fit appropriately into the strategic objectives of sustainable developments.

As has already been mentioned, simply recycling on campus is possibly not a measure of success; knowing what actually happens to the waste and how this is recycled should also be a principle of the SD policy of a university. It is also evident that success and development of measures related to SD are still being developed and debated (IISD, 1996). Nevertheless, commonly understood measures, such as volume of recycling and methods of purchase and what is purchased are the more tangible and normally understood ones (Jabbour, 2009).

Curriculum Development

The coverage of sustainability in the curriculum is currently disparate and ad-hoc. Certainly, from a business and tourism perspective this is an area that needs to be urgently included within module and course developments. An examination of tourism and business degrees will identify that courses or degrees in sustainability have a propensity to be located in the natural sciences and reflective of environmental issues, often concentrating on the natural environment (Scott, 2011). This can be seen from the continuous focus of climate change and the link with the sustainability theme (Scott, 2011). Scott (2011) clearly sees the environmental issues of climate change as critical to the sustainability debate, further supporting the theme, environment first and economic social and cultural second. From the author's experience many issues relating to sustainability are subsumed and sometimes lost within module deliveries and usually fail to have a contiguous development theme through a degree or course and for that matter a university. Wu *et al.* (2010) have also found a diversity of curriculum emphasis related to sustainability with many universities around the world reflecting this. Emphasis changes on undergraduate and graduate studies, depending on the geographical location and is reflective of the educational systems of these regions.

Perhaps the way forward is to take a far more strategic approach to delivery and start with sustainability as a core or framework theme to be found in any degree. This has been the case with some universities, especially those who have embraced the importance of sustainability. Utrecht University in the Netherlands is an example of an educational establishment attempting to permeate sustainability throughout the whole University (Van Ginkel, 1996). Nonetheless, there are arguments to suggest that other important subjects which affect the sustainable environment such as Corporate Social Responsibility (CSR), management, economics, et cetera also need to be considered. Sustainability is not a discrete subject, rather it needs to be incorporated into all disciplines and as the title of this book suggests, needs consideration within all universities. Certainly, within hospitality and tourism pedagogy, sustainability can be incorporated throughout all levels and can be seen as a foundation to any of these courses.

However there is concern emanating from current research. It is becoming evident that preaching SD is not necessarily the way to convert and educate students. Curricular should foster healthy evaluation of current assertions and students and lecturers should encourage an evaluation of these 'normative values' related to SD. This will enable students to develop a vigorous and constructive view on how these principles might be actioned, as they will be the decision makers of the future (Junyent and Geli de Ciurana, 2008; Mulder, 2010).

Research Action and Projects

A key element to any university is research. If sustainability is to be the new dictum for the next decade, then sustainability must have some prominence in research strategies and projects. There are a number of ways this can be done. Certainly, policies and management actions need to be in place demonstrating that research carried out by the university is endeavouring to adhere to sustainability principles; this can be seen in a number of ways:

- Sensitivity to community and cultural values:
    o adhering to cultural norms, not changing the ambience of the location
- Appropriate types of transport for research purposes:
    o car sharing, train rather than plane, public transport,
    o mitigation of carbon foot prints
- Use of renewable resources:
    o recycled goods, paper/hemp rather than plastic materials
- Appropriate resources for the distribution of research
    o electronic rather than paper
    o electronic conferencing
- Projects designed to enhance the local community's social and cultural standing
    o employment evaluations, cultural festivals, social competencies
- Benchmarking projects for sustainable outcomes (include Corporate Social Responsibility)

(Copernicus Campus, 2007; Harris, et al., 2002; Hall and Lew, 1998; Lozano 2010; Scott, 2011)

There is also the conception of applied research based upon exploring aspects of sustainability. Certainly, for hospitality and tourism it is immense and not limited. It is suggested that if the Copernicus Charter is to be engaged with then research into sustainability should be present as themes and sub-themes throughout all research. Perhaps in view of the above discussion on sustainability, a renewed emphasis should be actioned with a focus on more research, combining the other three pillars of sustainability: social, economic and cultural. This is not to suggest the diminishing of the environment and its current emphasis upon climate change and the need for environmental sustainability (Scott, 2011).

Types of Initiatives: Environmental Policies

A number of universities have whole heartedly embraced the idea of sustainable development and these have to a large extent led the way for others to follow. In 2007 there were more than 320 universities and higher education institutions, consisting of 38 countries that had endorsed the Copernicus Charter (Copernicus Campus, 2007). This is out of an estimated 1,000 EU universities (based upon 1 university per 500,000 population) that could be part of the Copernicus Charter, within Europe.

Utrecht University in the Netherlands is an exemplar of sustainable development and has incorporated much of the Charter into its actions and philosophies of education. In 1993 the University began the process by looking at sustainable policies via a working party. It took as its working arena Agenda 21. It used a problem-orientated approach to the solution of encompassing sustainability. It is noted that:

> "This statement essentially reflects the commitment of the academic community to contribute to finding solutions to environmental and development issues by means of intensified research, effective cooperation and improved transfer of knowledge to the general public and government authorities." (Van Ginkel, 1996, p. 3)

The University's working party then reported back and the recommendations were incorporated into the 1995-1999 development plan and centred the debate on a bottom-up approach; the rationale being to make it relevant to staff and researchers. The University then developed clear principles of action dictating how the policy would work. Even pure sciences such as chemistry incorporated the principles into their curriculum for example: "First-year students of chemistry follow a course called "Chemistry and Society". It presents them with questions such as "What are the ingredients in a tin of paint? How were these ingredients processed into semi-finished products and then into a finished product? What harmful substances are released when paint is applied? What happens with the waste?" These questions help students to understand the chemical aspects of the production process. There is also attention to the control of technological development. Which parties – the consumer, the government, trade and industry – influence the activities of the manufacturer, in this case the paint factory?" (Van Ginkel, 1996, p. 3).

The idea was also to try and centralise the development of the curriculum so that there was a co-ordinated and controlled educational flow to the students' developments where, if they wanted, they could specialise in environmental subjects in their final years. Utrecht also adopted an inter-disciplinary approach to the development, reflecting the aims of the Copernicus Charter.

Other universities have followed suit and have tried to emulate the development of SD. The University of British Columbia is a good example of this. It appears to have extensive policies dealing with all aspects of sustainable development, such as energy use, climate change, waste disposal, recycling and these appear to be linked to educational aspects of both staff and students, where they engage the university community in the aspects of SD (UBC, 2011(a)). In addition it also seems to be clearly focused upon the future with the opening of a new building reflecting the ethos of what the University is trying to achieve. It notes: "When it opens [new building CIRS] in spring 2011, CIRS will be the most innovative and high performance building in North America, serving as a living laboratory to demonstrate leading-edge research and develop sustainable design practices, products, systems and policies" (UBC, 2011(b), p. 1). Clearly the concept of sustainability seems to be permeating the University and demonstrates what universities can do for SD.

These two case studies clearly illustrate that universities are able to wholly embrace sustainability tenets if the effort and motivation are there. Both these case studies are excellent examples of what can be achieved; however they are not alone and as will be demonstrated in the next section, other universities have followed their lead.

New Buildings and Sustainable Management

The most visible and tangible facet of sustainability within universities, is that of new buildings and the revivifying of old ones. This refers to the new standards of build relating to materials used and energy consumption and conservation (Intrachooto, 2002). Some national authorities are already specifying high standards of build reflecting the policies of national governments and their understanding of sustainability. Certainly, the Swiss Authorities believe that they are setting high standards for buildings and ensuring the reduction of carbon foot prints (Minergie, 2010).

As mentioned earlier, the most tangible facets of a sustainable programme can be seen through buildings and how they are managed by a university. The operation of recycling points and the visibility of sustainable information are critical to the principles of SD (Nicolow, 2010). There are clearly some sound examples of this. One good case study is that of West Michigan University, which appears to be addressing many of the sustainable aspects of building design, waste management and polices. This case study is a clear example of what can be achieved when the proper policies and positive attitudes are brought together (Nicolow, 2010).

Intracooto (2002) also suggests that university authorities should be more active in the role of sustainable builds and in developing co-operation between designers and their capacity for helping new approaches to sustainable buildings. Intrachooto notes: "Researchers have the opportunity to test their theories and demonstrate how their works can be applicable to the industries and stand a better chance for future funding. On the other hand the success of the project increases designers' knowledge, recognition and opportunity to receive future works" (2002, p. 161).

However, what can be disappointing is the perception that universities actually recycle waste but do not know what happens to it after it leaves the university. There are cases where lecturers have adroitly recycled paper and other materials only to find that they end up in landfill mixed together with non-recyclable waste; not an effective SD policy! For that reason, the emphasis should be upon management systems and acceptable processes and end points. A good example (not a university) of this traceable policy is the UK National Theatre, based in London. The Theatre sells water in plastic bottles which when used are sent to a recycling plant in the East End of London where the deposits are recycled and the bottles returned to the National Theatre (Butler, 2010). This perhaps raises issues of waste management and the need to not just assume that a university recycles effectively, simply because it has a recycling policy.

Energy is another area that needs closer scrutiny. The use of sensor light switches and energy saving bulbs is also an obvious resource that many universities participate in. Nonetheless, a more pertinent issue is: who supplies the energy and is it from a renewable source, a carbon neutral source? This again is the responsibility of management and moving from introspective verification to a more central view of the principles of sustainability. Perhaps more focus should be placed upon procurement of energy, rather than the conservation of energy per-se.

Transport policies are also an important issue and how greener forms of transport can be encouraged, from car sharing to charging for parking at the university, and to carbon offsetting depending on the overall distance travelled throughout the year by staff and students. Car parking charges are certainly commonly used in the UK (Exeter University, 2011). Perhaps, students also need to consider their transport needs and the university should incorporate this into their planning for sustainability. Students are as much a part of the carbon footprint as staff. They are richer and more demanding than previous generations of students and travel more extensively around the world, as well as having ubiquitous car ownership. Carbon footprint increases are also compounded by universities offering placements at global destinations thousands of miles from the university.

In addition, more universities are now economically dependent on attracting international students, further intensifying carbon emissions. Perhaps mitigation and contribution to off-setting is one answer, although this seems rather unfair on other nationalities, especially as these students tend to come from developing countries that have a propensity to have lower carbon emissions compared to developed countries. Is this apposite Corporate Social Responsibility by universities?

As noted earlier, another aspect of the sustainability debate might also be the use of sustainable energy, which in many cases is possibly a secondary concern for universities even though they could be considered to be generally high users of energy. The energy source could be an important element in a sustainability policy. With the energy market open to negotiations in many countries, perhaps universities need to be more vigilant in sourcing their energy from suppliers who have sustainable policies; either demonstrating mitigation or ensuring that the energy is as sustainable as possible. Universities might also consider generating their own energy from waste and renewable sources of power. This might be a cost to the university but if the Copernicus Charter is to be adhered to, should be further evidence of securing a sustainable future for the university. Surely, universities in energy rich countries should consider pursuing such policies?

Cooperative Community Integration

The linkage of universities to the community has been a consistent debate for the last 20-30 years and there is still a need to make higher education more relevant to the community in which it finds itself (Trivun *et al.*, 2008). There is also a cultural tenet to this, depending upon where the university is located. Some countries are seen as having proactive and integrated policies related to sustainability. Certainly the situation in Switzerland is one where this seems to be the case. The policy here is to ensure that universities and the HES (Haute Ecole Spécialisée) are in tune both with the society and sustainability. There are clear policy instruments affecting the curriculum and the very fabric of the university and a requirement to ensure that sustainability reverberates through the whole system. However, to what extent the university has a positive effect upon the community is somewhat debatable. Perhaps this is further exacerbated depending upon the type and cultural identity of the student residing within a university. Certainly there is evidence to show that an international university located in a European country may have very varied outcomes relating to the community and its concomitant affects on the community's sustainability. It is suggested that the cultural background of the student may well influence the cognition of sustainability policies and their relevance to those students.

Without doubt, the importance of having sustainability policies and ensuring that these are found in taught modules is an assured way of trying to educate the student in SD and hopefully will be further fostered by students once they are fully employed within their various industries.

It seems appropriate that universities should try to further their outreach to local communities by either incorporating courses that can be offered to the whole community or by students engaging in a voluntary capacity with community projects. Universities could also have mandatory community modules as part of degree programmes. Actioning these initiatives would support the spirit of the Copernicus Charter; support for local communities is a fundamental principle of sustainable policies and certainly one which Copernicus validates.

Community policies can often change the perception of a community towards a university, which is frequently viewed as an 'ivory tower'. Repeatedly there is the perception that students have mainly negative impacts upon a community, verified through unacceptable behaviour and students contributing very little to the cultural and economic wellbeing of the location (rather like mass tourists). This is a common problem as evidenced by a number of university towns, Swansea, UK, being one which has a large number of students in which the community fails to see the benefits that these students bring to the economic level or the cultural one (Davies, 2009).

However, it is clearly evident that universities can be important energisers for communities and a university's sustainable ethos could be transferred to local communities. Perhaps more could be done, in some cases, to ensure that the community knows exactly what the university's sustainable policies are and how these are being enacted within the community.

University Windows: Website & Sustainability

Websites and the use of the Web have now become commonplace and it seems self-evident that a fundamental way of demonstrating the policies of sustainability of universities to stakeholders including the community, is via a website. As will be shown from the following section, the standardisation and evidence portrayed by these sites does vary, mirroring research carried out on global curriculum developments (Wu *et al.,* 2010).

A good example of a website demonstrating the sustainability policies of those detailed in the Copernicus Charter, is that of Oxford University, UK. A verification of key elements of sustainability policies within the University, identifies many of the Copernicus Charter's key areas and reflects the idea that this University is taking the issue of sustainability seriously (Oxford University, 2011). Its fellow competitor, Cambridge University also follows suit and it is possible to identify many of the Copernicus Charter's important actions for universities (Cambridge University, 2011). This clearly is very heartening, particularly as the top UK universities seem to be addressing SD. However, what was somewhat surprising was that when searching these two websites, no reference was made to the Copernicus Charter and the sites search results revealed no connections. Perhaps this reflects the demise of the Copernicus project and its relevance to universities. Yet, as mentioned earlier many of the precepts of this Charter are being adhered to, if the information on the two websites is to be taken at face value.

In addition, website content evaluation of lower ranking UK universities, clearly demonstrates that the ideas and policies of sustainability are being incorporated with an assumption that part of their policy instruments are incorporating sustainable principles. Swansea University is one such university demonstrating a sustainability policy and it appears to incorporate many of the Copernicus' principles (Swansea University, 2011). Perhaps the next question relates to the notion of whether these policies are being implemented. This gives rise to questions of how to measure these outputs and validate the statements (Schriberg 2002). Conceivably this is the next stage of the Copernicus Charter; developing a framework for assuring validation of the policies and their operational delivery.

That said, a review of some of the Swiss university websites, actioned in 2010, did not yield such a fruitful outcome for sustainability policies. There were elements of sustainability but in terms of policy and details relating to energy and waste management, the review showed rather mixed results which were not as clearly defined as in the UK. This appears to be a pattern which is repeated with some of the Swiss tourism companies where information is scarce or non-existent (Jenkins *et al.,* 2011) and is somewhat of a paradox, as Switzerland is perceived as an environmentally sensitive country with strong policy instruments related to sustainability.

This raises a number of questions related to the policy and information that universities across Europe exhibit. Perhaps Swiss universities are delivering sustainability policies and see no need to promote this on their websites, however, websites are a good gauge as to what exactly a company or university *might* be doing.

Conclusions

It seems evident that the Copernicus Charter has to some degree lost its impetus. As noted earlier the initiative has more or less come to a halt with attempts to try and revive it on-going. However, it is also evident that the precepts which this Charter laid down have been adopted or incorporated by many universities, with the main principles and ethos continuing to permeate the university sector. Certainly, with the climate debate more or less proven, universities need to be seen to be sustainable and adhering to sustainable principles. It is evident that a coherent effort by universities is very mixed, demonstrating a diversity of responses to SD. However, this could be down to cultural overlays and national policies which differ from country to county. It is certainly pleasing to see that the top UK universities demonstrate many of the principles specified by the Copernicus Charter which seems to be a positive move for the future developments of universities and their actions within local communities. Nonetheless, what seems to be missing is a co-ordinated policy of development and measurement of outcomes; therefore the possible revival of Copernicus and its re-launch would be a very useful propellant to current SD within universities. It would be propitious to have a single body that could monitor and co-ordinate developments within universities, both from a European perspective and possibly worldwide. This would make measurement and evaluation of the effectiveness of the stated university policies much easier to assess.

References

Alliance Copernicus (2010), "Background", available at: http://www2.leuphana.de/copernicus/background/ (accessed 14 December 2010).
Butler, R. (2010), "Going Green, Ten Green bottles , Flying through the Air: a Heartening Trip to a High-tech Recovery Plant", The Economist, London, *Intelligent Life*, Vol. 3 No. 4.
Cambridge University (2011), "About the Sustainability Leadership in the Built Environment Programme", Cambridge University, Cambridge, available at: http://www.cpsl.cam.ac.uk/programmes/slp_in_the_built_environment/about_the_step_leadership_prog.aspx (accessed 10 February 2011).
Copernicus Campus (2007), "COPERNICUS-Guidelines for Sustainable Development in the European Higher Education Area", University Oldenburg.
CRE (Association of European Universities) (1994), "Copernicus Charter", Geneva, Stockholm University, Stockholm.
Davies, L. (2009), "Swansea Students' Crimes Under the Spotlight", 11 November 2009, Northcliffe Media Ltd., London, available at: http://www.thisissouthwales.co.uk/news/

Swansea-students-crimes-spotlight/article-1504007-detail/article.html (accessed 16 March 2011).
Exeter University (2011), "Car Parking", Exeter University, Exeter, available at: http://www.exeter.ac.uk/staff/stafflife/carparking/ (accessed 15 March 2011).
Fonseca, A., Macdonald, A., Dandy, E. and Valenti, P. (2011), "The state of sustainability reporting at Canadian universities International Journal of Sustainability, *Higher Education*", Vol. 12 No. 1, pp. 22-40.
Hall, M. C. and Lew, A. A. (1998), *Sustainable Tourism: A geographical Perspective*, Addison Wesley Longman, Harlow.
Harris, R,, Griffin, T., Williams, P. (2002), *Sustainable Tourism: A global Perspective*, Butterworth Heinemann, London.
IISD (International Institute of Sustainable Development) (1996), "The Shadow Curriculum: On Campus Activities", Winnipeg, Manitoba, Canada, available at: http://www.iisd.org/educate/ (accessed 15 March 2011).
Intracooto, S. (2002), "Nurturing Green Innovations for Academic Institutions", *International Journal of Sustainability in Higher Education*, Vol. 3 No. 2, pp. 155-163.
Jabbour, C. J.C. (2009), "Greening of business schools: a systemic view", *International Journal of Sustainability in Higher Education*, Vol. 11 No. 1, pp. 49-60.
Jenkins, I. S., Rios-Morales, R. M. and Cevera, R. (2011), "Professed Sustainability of Caribbean Companies: Case Study of Internet Evaluation of Company Websites as Vicarious Information Systems for Company Products", AGA, January 2011, Conference Paper.
Junyent, M. and Geli de Ciurana, A. M. (2008), "Education for sustainability in university studies: a model for Reorienting the Curriculum", *British Educational Research Journal*, Vol. 34 No. 6, pp. 763-782.
Lozano, R. (2010), "The state of sustainability reporting in universities", *International Journal of Sustainability in Higher Education,* Vol. 12 No. 1, pp. 67-78.
Magee, B. (2010), *The Story of Philosophy*, Dorling Kindersley, London.
Minergie (2010), "Planning and project, The MINERGIE®-Standard for Buildings", *Information for Architects*, Minergie, Bern, available at: http://www.minergie.ch/ (accessed 16 March 2011).
Mitchell, R. C. (2011), "Sustaining change on a Canadian Campus Preparing Brock University for a sustainability audit International", *Journal of Sustainability in Higher Education.* Vol. 12 No. 1, pp. 22-40.
Mulder, K. F. (2010), "Don't preach. Practice! Value laden statements in academic sustainability education International", *Journal of Sustainability in Higher Education,* Emerald Group Publishing Limited, Vol. 11 No. 1, pp. 74-85.
Nicolow, J. (2010), "Greening the Campus", Harnessing the LEED-EB Certification Process to improve Campus Operations and Maintenance, Environmental Design and Construction, July 2010, pp. 28-32.
Oxford University (2011), "Estates Directorate: Environmental Sustainability", Oxford University, Oxford, available at: http://www.admin.ox.ac.uk/estates/travel/ (accessed 10 February 2011).

Schriberg, M. (2002), "International assessment tool for sustainability in Higher education", *International Journal for Sustainability In Higher education*, Vol. 3 No. 3, pp. 254-268.

Scott, D. (2011), "Why sustainable tourist must address climate change", *Journal of Sustainable Tourism*, Vol. 19 No. 1, pp. 17-34.

Swansea University (2011), "Campus Sustainability Policy Statement Our approach to Sustainability", Swansea University, Swansea, available at: http://www.swansea.ac.uk/media/Media,41722,en.pdf (accessed 10 February 2011).

Trivun, V., Silajdzic, V. and Mahmutcehajic, F. (2008), "Public-Private Partnership In Achievement Of Competitiveness", *Tourism and Hospitality Management*, Vol. 14 No. 1, pp. 185-198.

UBC (University of British Columbia) (2011(a)), "Greening the Campus" ,UBC Vancouver, B.C, available at: http://sustain.ubc.ca/campus-sustainability/greening-the-campus (accessed 16/3/2011).

UBC (University of British Columbia) (2011(b)), "UBC Centre for Interactive Research on Sustainability (CIRS)," Vancouver, B.C, available at: http://sustain.ubc.ca/hubs/cirs (16 March 2011).

Van Ginkel, H. J.A. (1996), "Implementing Sustainable Development: A Case Study", Keynote Speech, Conference Paper, October 4-6, Bradford, UK.

WHC (2011), "Cultural Landscape", UNESCO, World Heritage Centre 1992-2011, United Nations, available at: http://whc.unesco.org/en/activities/ (accessed 10 March 2011).

Wu, Y.-C. J., Huangs, S., Kuol., and Wu, W.-H. (2010), "Management Education for Sustainability: A Web-Based Content Analysis," *Academy of Management Learning & Education*, Vol. 9 No. 3, pp. 520–531.

Sustaining Sustainability

David Horrigan

This book has presented different views of sustainability within different contexts: education, business, media, politics, and of course, the natural environment. As Spindler's chapter has illustrated, the concept of sustainability has evolved over time shifting its meaning within varying conditions. Currently, sustainability's meaning is being affected by the unstable global economy and the growth of the technology industry. Historically, sustainable products and services that were friendly to the environment received mixed results in the marketplace (Manna *et al.*, 2011; Radlbeck *et al.*, 2005). To help protect the environment meant a consumer needed to spend more money or sacrifice comfort and quality. However, technological advancements are currently helping to balance the costs of product manufacturing and service delivery that are positively affecting product quality and consumer price (Golovatche *et al.*, 2010). This chapter takes a market perspective towards sustainability in order to consider its shelf life in an unstable global economic environment.

The concept of sustainability for business strategy is appealing to particular segments of both industry and markets, but for sustainable practices to be sustainable, sustainable products and services need to achieve strong demand by the mass market (O'Rourke, 2005). The idea to responsibly protect the environment for future generations is initially attractive to consumers. Ask business people or consumers if they believe that protecting the environment should be considered in business strategy and practice and there will be an overwhelming positive response across many segments (Vermeir and Verbeke, 2006). The market response becomes more convoluted when people are asked what they are willing to sacrifice in order to support responsible and sustainable business behaviour that produces consumer services and products (Szmigin et al., 2008; Young et al., 2010). To further complicate the acceptance of sustainable business strategy, uncontrolled conditions such as the economy can change the willingness of businesses and consumers to adopt sustainable practices and products.

The term sustainability has natural advantages. Conceptually, most people believe in behaving responsibly, but when responsible behaviour means too many sacrifices such as personal comfort, cost, quality and value, consumers naturally reconsider their tolerance level toward their own responsible behaviour concerning the protection of the environment (James, 2006).

There is continuing debate regarding environmental science among global political structures (Allouche, 2011; Holzl, 2010; Houston, 2008). Science has been used both positively and negatively with regards to how industry and consumer behaviour is affecting the environment. Pro economic development politicians diminish the importance of responsible and sustainable business practices because of the negative effects on the global economy while pro environment politicians champion responsible industry and consumer behaviour. The one area of agreement among most constituents is that the adoption of sustainable behaviour needs to balance the needs of the many. However, defining the appropriate balance and finding sustainability consensus regarding politics, society and business is complex.

The chapters in this book introduce various perspectives of tourism and the use of sustainable business practices. As a whole, the narratives of the book outline the realities of adopting sustainability strategies and define sustainable tourism in terms of a balance between economic and environmental issues. In addition, much of the content in the chapters prove that the adoption of sustainable practices is slowly increasing and much of the demand for sustainable tourism practices is found in niche markets. Many multi-national companies within the hospitality and tourism sectors recognise the importance for sustainability strategies and are adopting sustainable practices when it is economically feasible (Manna et al., 2011).

What the authors do not proffer is a definitive formula for achieving sustainable business practices. Philanthropic arguments and the need for balance between social, economic and environmental concerns have been made, but a solid business model where there are real short and long-term economic benefits for tourism businesses' adoption of sustainable practices has not been presented. The reason for this lies in the complexity of satisfying the many constituencies that have stakes in any business practice meant to appeal to a large and influential market (James, 2006). The successful adoption of sustainable business practices by the tourism industry needs a solid business model that provides a competitive advantage within the marketplace that has the potential for generating revenue and satisfying consumers' expectations regarding price, quality and comfort. Historically, the adoption of sustainable business practices has increased capital expenditures, operational costs, and consumer prices (Choi and Ng, 2011). Significant market demand for sustainable services has been historically too low for these products and services to be considered a competitive advantage by the tourism industry (O'Rourke, 2005).

Advances in technology are beginning to positively affect business returns on investments toward sustainable products and services (Golovatchev et al., 2010). Yet there still exists a perception in the mass market that sustainable products mean higher prices at the register or products that lack acceptable levels of quality. The traditional sacrifices consumers need to make to support sustainable products and services have historically appealed to a niche travel market rather than the mass market (Radlbeck et al., 2005). In order for sustainable services to be appealing to the mass travel market, and hence be sustainable themselves, the market needs to perceive that services utilising sustainable practices provide similar quality experiences at competitive prices as the current products and services in which they engage. As the industry utilises technology to move towards a greater balance between its economic, societal and environmental concerns, the new and improved products and services being produced through sustainable practices need to be communicated to the mass travel market in order to set new market expectations. A mass market attitude change will take time, as well as a significant and strategic effort by advocates of sustainable tourism practices and services. However, because of technological advances, these advocates now have the products and services that appeal to a larger market appetite.

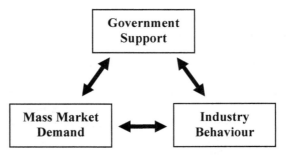

Figure 1:   Influences on Sustainability Strategies

Figure 1 suggests the cycle of influence affecting industry's decisions toward adopting sustainability practices. Market demand directly affects industry behaviour while government support is provided and affected by both the demand of the market, industry strategy and behaviour.

The market perception that sustainability means expensive or sacrifice in quality has had decades to be ingrained in consumers' minds. Utilising the knowledge and positions of this book's chapters and other material, a process for attitude change toward mass market acceptance of sustainable tourism services is outlined below. To achieve mass market attitude change toward the consumer value of sustainability, sustainability needs to be redefined, branded, communicated and continually evolved.

Redefining Sustainability

As the authors throughout this book and other scholars have suggested, defining sustainability has had historical difficulties. Definitions of sustainability have been inconsistent due to competing and varied emphases by individual scholars and professionals to forward their own independent agendas (Quental *et al.*, 2011). Whether emphasis has been the environment or societal effects or economic development, literature attempting to set parameters for independent positions has caused a divided front in the effort to achieve a mass understanding for the benefits of sustainability strategies for tourism.

A definition for sustainable strategies that appeals to the mass market as well as industry should utilise the key attributes of sustainability that has the broadest shared value across its targeted segments (Prattipati, 2010). In addition, a cohesive definition should rely on the benefits of sustainability, having the greatest advantage in affecting the mass market attitude and a desired change. Theoretically, most consumers and industry professionals believe more attention is needed in business practice to protect the environment. This understanding and belief starts to deteriorate as the investment in sustainability practices threatens industry's expected return on investment (Houston, 2008). Consumers' beliefs are also vulnerable if the expected service and product value of the mass market does not satisfy their expectations.

The mass market accepts the idea that sustainable business practices, services and products will result in a better world for future generations. The market needs to be convinced that with the advances in current technology, production and operational practices, sustainable strategies will support the delivery of quality products and services for reasonable consumer costs (Koos, 2011). The comfort and quality levels travellers expect for the price paid needs to be similar for services based on sustainability strategies as it is for non-sustainability based products and services. Hence, the value proposition written into a tourism sustainability definition needs to emphasise affordable quality and comfort based on technological advances, over the benefits to the environment that consumers already understand. This was a theme identified in Bristow's chapter on medical tourism. Environmental benefits are known and accepted and need less emphasis in today's understanding of sustainable practices which again was detailed in Jenkins' text on climate change and sustainability.

Sustainability Branding

All movements benefit from branding strategies that communicate a shared value between multiple constituencies (Harsh, 2007). Global warming emphasised the negative impacts of the industrial age on our environment. Climate change replaced global warming in political discourse in order to reach a broader audience and shift the debate from the negative effects of industry's impact on the world's climate to an acceptance that climate change is due to more than just industry's behaviour. As illustrated in Jenkins' text, the term climate change allows for broader debate on how to manage the inevitable rather than argue about whose fault it is.

Similarly, abortion rights activists utilised a "women's rights" campaign in the United States in the 1970s to reshape the political and legal debate on a woman's right to give birth or abort a pregnancy. The sustainability of the women's rights campaign was momentous. The anti-abortionists lost significant ground on the debate as the right to choose one's fate, branded Pro-Choice, appealed to more women than the idea that the State has the right to determine a woman's fate once she is pregnant. The anti-abortionists responded by branding or politically framing their right-to-life position as Pro-Life to add validity to their position and to frame the Pro-Choice stance in negative terms. The branding of both these movements allowed for each side to reach a broader audience and shape their messages in a more objective and positive manner that provided a sustainable message that consumers could clearly and simply understand (Vanderford, 1989).

Similar to the sensitive subject of abortion, the term sustainability needs to discard its negative perception, particularly in terms of being expensive to both industry and consumers, and emphasise how sustainable practices have evolved into a cost and environmentally friendly strategy that helps provide value to consumer's lives. Middleton's chapter attempts to illustrate new business models that support a more balanced perspective of sustainability and how businesses can be successful by embracing sustainable practices. The emphasis on the consumer benefit is intended to create demand within the marketplace. An increase in demand for products and services supported by sustainable practices can be utilised to put pressure on industry to invest in cost-effective sustainable production and operational processes.

As the demand for sustainable practices, products and services increases, businesses can promote a sustainability strategy to create competitive advantages as Kuokkanen and Rios-Morales suggest in their chapter. Sustainable business practices are increasing as detailed by Middleton's narrative. Much of this increase is being managed in new developments throughout the tourism cycle as more businesses recognise the need to protect the environment and technology has made many sustainable practices more affordable. The branding of sustainable products and services is not enough in today's marketplace because of the negative perception toward cost to quality ratio, so sustainability itself needs to be rebranded.

It will take time to brand sustainability in a way that is appealing to a multitude of consumer segments. Consumer attitudes and perceptions are difficult to change. To achieve attitude change or formation, it takes reinforcement through messaging as well as consumer experience with the services and products branded as supported through sustainable processes. This is particularly important for education (Viswanathan *et al.,* 2011). Jenkins' chapter on Copernicus has highlighted that the concept of sustainability varies within the higher education environment, and the current demise of Copernicus may be a presage to the diminishing importance of sustainability in many higher education establishments.

Marketing Communications Campaign

A series of communications campaigns over a significant period of time could influence how the mass market perceives the value of sustainable services and products (O'Rourke, 2005). An awareness campaign that informs consumers of today's sustainability message is needed for mass understanding – "today's sustainability is a cost and environmentally friendly strategy that provides added value to consumer's lives." As this message is reinforced and the term sustainability develops a meaningful advantage in the mass market as an economic value to consumers, then products and services that are supported through sustainable business practices could increase their market demand.

Concurrently with a consumer awareness campaign, a communications campaign is needed that targets industry trade groups and individual business owners that provides these groups with information about the new economic viability of a sustainability strategy for business practices (Erdem *et al.,* 2008). Knowledge regarding how advances in technology are making production and operational processes cost effective (without losing levels of consumer quality and services) should be a major theme in this particular communications strategy.

Examples such as Accor's new initiative, Planet 21 that is attempting to engage both employees and customers in making a commitment to reach 21 sustainable goals by the year 2015 can reinforce this message (Anonymous, 2012). The more examples of industry practice utilising sustainability strategies will strengthen the message and should result in a broader commitment within the tourism industry.

Businesses that promote sustainability through their products and services will need to attract consumers to experience sustainable offerings. This consumer experience with products and services supported by sustainability strategies is needed to reinforce and strengthen positive consumer attitudes toward the new meaning of sustainability (Chang, 2011). There will have to be a quality assurance system in place to ensure that products and services are following sustainability standards set by the trade to ensure that consumers' experiences are consistent and meet expectations.

Once the attitudes of business leaders and the mass market have significantly changed toward a more positive perception of the economic and personal value of adopting sustainable products, services and practices, then a political campaign should be developed to strengthen governments' resolve toward creating policy and laws regarding sustainability strategies for industry. With industry and consumer leverage, politicians should be more proactive toward supporting the sustainability cause. A media strategy utilising all forms of media is needed to develop an effective integrated marketing communications campaign that targets multiple constituents and audiences to maximise message penetration.

As stated above, consumers' support is critical in the sustainability movement chain. Without a mass market to adopt and demand products and services that are supported by sustainability processes, industry and governments will have less motivation towards creating and supporting sustainable business strategies (Radlbeck et al., 2005). Technological advances are making sustainability affordable and attractive. It is time for sustainability to become popular and globally accepted. A well coordinated branding and communications effort is needed to raise awareness and persuade people that sustainability is not just about personal sacrifices and environment causes. Rather, sustainability is about adding value and comfort into people's lives.

Campaign Evaluation & Evolution

A complex and integrated marketing communications strategy with multiple campaigns overlapping and targeted to multiple audiences needs to be measured for effectiveness (Dahlen et al., 2008). The progress and developments of the campaigns will also need to be assessed based on how they need to evolve. The evolution of the campaigns depends on how well they achieve their intended goals, whether they are to raise awareness, to create understanding or to change attitudes. As campaigns achieve their goals, new phases of the campaigns need to be introduced (Bruce, 2008). For example, market audiences can be segmented by governments, industry and consumers. Each of these segments can be further divided. Consumers for example can be segmented by level of motivation towards engaging in purchasing sustainable products or they can be segmented by their awareness level of the value of sustainable products and services. A continuous measurement of each campaign that is targeted towards particular audience segments is needed to establish when campaign goals are reached, in order to change the campaign to meet the audience's new need. For example, once high awareness of the new definition of sustainability is reached, a new campaign that educates consumers regarding the new consumer value of sustainable products can begin. A branding campaign may follow depending on the results of the campaign.

The ultimate goal for the sustainability campaign is to increase demand in the mass market for sustainable products and services so this demand can influence policy, laws and industry practices. Sustainability campaigns can utilise a staged approach towards reaching this goal as it will take a change in mass market attitude to understand the benefits of sustainable products and services. A process of building awareness and educating the market, regarding the benefits of sustainable products and services should be introduced, before a branding strategy is implemented to reinforce an emotional connection between the value of sustainability and the market. Finally, a campaign is delivered that persuades the market to adopt sustainable products and services.

Figure 2 illustrates the stages discussed above. To achieve a positive mass market attitude change toward the perception of sustainable products there is a need to alter the present skepticism. This can be done by reassuring the mass consumer that sustainable products/services, have similar values as their traditional products and services. This then should effect motivation for mass market consumers to purchase sustainable products.

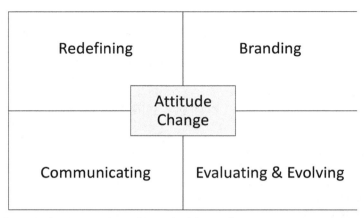

Figure 2:   Value Perception of Sustainable Products

The term sustainability has lost much of its significance due to an inconsistent use of the term, both in academic literature and professional practice. There is a need to reclaim the term in a manner that is relevant to the current global economic climate. This chapter summarises a few key points made within the other chapters of this book, and supports the authors' assertions that there is a need to develop a consistent understanding/meaning of sustainability. This requires a framework to achieve message consistency that will resonate among critical constituencies for the promotion and use of sustainable practices and products. The timing for influencing the mass market toward the adoption of more sustainable behaviour has never been better. New technologies have given the advocates of sustainable practices what they have needed – a balance between cost, value, and return on investment.

References

Allouche, J. (2011), "The sustainability and resilience of global water and food systems: Political analysis of the interplay between security, resource scarcity, political systems and global trade", *Food Policy*, Vol. 36 No. 1, pp. 3-8.

Anonymous (2012), "Accor officially launches PLANET 21". Green Lodging News. available at: http://greenlodgingnews.com/accor-officially-launches-planet-21 (accessed 01 October 2012).

Bruce, N. (2008), "Pooling and dynamic forgetting effects in multithem advertising: Tracking the advertising sales relationship with particle filters", *Marketing Science*, Vol. 27 No. 4, pp. 659-673.

Chang, C. (2011), "Feeling ambivalent about going green", *Journal of Advertising*, Vol. 40 No. 4, pp. 19-32.
Choi, S. and Ng, A. (2011), "Environmental and economic dimensions of sustainability and price effects on consumer responses", *Journal of Business Ethics*, Vol. 104 No. 2, pp. 269-282.
Dahlen, M., Rosengren, S. and Torn, F. (2008), "Advertising creativity matters", *Journal of Advertising Research*, Vol. 48 No. 3, pp. 392-403.
Erdem, T., Keane, M. and Sun, B. (2008), "A dynamic model of brand choice when price and advertising signal product quality", *Marketing Science*, Vol. 27 No. 6, pp. 1111-1125.
Golovatchev, J., Budde, O. and Kellmereit, D. (2010), "Technology and innovation radars: Effective instruments for the development of a sustainable innovation strategy and successful product launches", *International Journal of Innovation & Technology Management*, Vol. 7 No. 3, pp. 229-236.
Harsh, V. (2007), "Branding: Context, content and consequences", *Journal of Management Research*, Vol. 7 No. 1, pp. 27-39.
Holz, R. (2010), "Histoicizing sustainability: German scientific forestry in the eighteenth and nineteenth centuries", *Science as Culture*, Vol. 19 No. 4, pp. 431-460.
Houston, D. (2008), "Crisis and resilience: Cultural methodologies for environmental sustainability and justice", *Continuum: Journal of Media & Cultural Studies*, Vol. 22 No. 2, pp. 179-190.
James, H. (2006), "Sustainable agriculture and free market economics: Finding common ground in Adam Smith", *Agriculture and Human Values*, Vol. 23 No. 4, pp. 427-438.
Koos, S. (2011), "Varieties of environmental labeling, market structures, and sustainable consumption across Europe: A comparative analysis of organizational and market supply determinants of environmental-labelled goods", *Journal of Consumer Policy*, Vol. 34 No. 1, pp. 127-151.
Manna, D., Marco, G., Khalil, B. and Meier, S. (2011), "Sustainable markets: Case study of Toyota Motor sales, U.S.A., Inc.", *Journal of Business Case Studies*, Vol. 7 No. 3, pp. 63-72.
O'Rourke, D. (2005), "Market movements: Nongovernmental organization strategies to influence global production and consumption", *Journal of Industrial Ecology*, Vol. 9 No. 1/2, pp. 115-128.
Prattipati, S. (2010), "Sustainability and the role of information and communications technologies" *Business Renaissance Quarterly*, Vol. 5 No. 2, pp. 23-40.
Quental, N., Lourenco, J. and Nunes da Silva, F. (2011), "Sustainability: Characteristics and scientific roots", *Environment, Development and Sustainability*, Vol. 13 No. 2, pp. 257-276.
Radlbeck, C., Dienes, E. and Kosteas, D. (2005), "Sustainable competitiveness of aluminum building products", *Structural Survey*, Vol. 23 No. 2/3, pp. 131-138.
Szmigin, I., Carrigan, M. and McEachern, M. (2008), "Flexibility, dissonance and the conscious consumer", *European Advances in Consumer Research*, Vol. 8, pp. 379-380.

Vanderford, M. (1989), "Vilification and social movements: A case study of pro-life and pro-choice rhetoric", *Quarterly Journal of Speech*, Vol. 75 No. 2, pp. 166-182.

Vermeir, I. and Verbeke, W. (2006), "Sustainable food consumption: Exploring the consumer 'attitude – behavioural intention' gap", *Journal of Agricultural and Environmental Ethics*, Vol. 19 No. 2, pp. 169-194.

Viswanathan, M., Yassine, A. and Clarke, J. (2011), "Sustainable product and market development for subsistence marketplaces: creating educational initiatives in radically different contexts", *Journal of Product Innovation Management*, Vol. 28 No. 4, pp. 558-569.

Young, W., Hwang, K, McDonald, S. and Oates, C. (2010), "Sustainable consumption: Green consumer behaviour when purchasing products", *Sustainable Development*, Vol. 18 No. 1, pp. 20-31.

Index

Agenda 21 ...... 16, 17, 20, 181
Agenda setting 178, 179, 189
attitudes 191, 196, 197, 201
behaviour 54, 61
Biomimicry 152
branding 213, 214, 215, 216
Brundtland 192
Brundtland Commission 16
campaign 213, 214, 215, 216
carbon 36, 37, 39, 44, 47, 48
certification 103, 110
climate change 33, 34, 35, 36, 37, 38, 39, 41, 43, 44, 45, 47, 48, 177
Cluster 85, 86, 87, 88, 89, 95, 96, 97, 98, 99, 100, 101
Cluster Theory .. 85, 86, 87, 94, 97, 100, 101
Commons 10
community 37, 38, 40, 42, 43
Community-Based Tourism (CBT). 169
competitive advantage 123, 129, 130, 131, 132, 133, 134
complexity theory 161
consumers 209, 210, 211, 212, 213, 214, 215, 216
Corporate Social Responsibility 105, 106, 123
Costa Rica 74, 75, 76, 77
Crisis management .. 163, 171, 172, 173
curriculum 192, 195, 196, 197, 200, 203, 204
decision-making 159, 165
Declaration of Rio de Janeiro on Environment and Development... 181
destination 53, 54, 55, 57, 58, 63, 65
development politics 160

disaster capitalism 171
Drinking water 74
economic productivity 57
economics 44
ecosystems approach 140
ecotourism 125, 127, 128, 179
Education 191, 193, 194, 195, 196, 200, 203
EMAS - European Eco-Management and Audit Scheme 29
emotional detachment 165
empowerment 160, 161
energy 195, 196, 201, 202, 203, 205
environment .. 33, 34, 36, 37, 38, 40, 41, 42, 43, 44, 45, 46, 47
Environmental Impact Assessment (EIA) 13
Environmental Policy 13, 14, 15, 29
environmental tenability 57
Environmentally Friendly Tourism. 180
Europe 192, 200, 205
financial performance 123, 124, 125, 129, 130, 131, 132, 134
forestry 11, 12, 13, 15
German Sustainability Code 20
Global Sustainable Tourism Criteria 76, 78
Global Warming 179, 180
government 211
Health care equity 79
Health care professionals 71, 72, 74
health tourism 53, 54, 55, 57, 58, 60, 61, 63, 64, 65, 66, 69, 70, 71, 72, 73, 74, 75, 76, 77, 79, 80
Innovation 9
International accreditation 75

knowledge 191, 193, 194, 200, 202, 212, 214
Lifestyle of health and sustainability 177
Malleability 160, 167, 170, 174
market......209, 210, 211, 212, 214, 215, 216, 217
Marketing 214, 215, 216
mass..................... 33, 39, 42, 43, 45, 48
measures 139, 142, 146, 149, 154
media....................................... 209, 215
Medical Tourism 70, 73, 75, 76, 79
Medical waste................................... 74
National Parks 36, 47
NEPA - National Environmental Policy 13
Niche 42
perception........ 211, 213, 214, 215, 216
planning...................................... 40, 45
Politics.....159, 160, 161, 162, 163, 166, 167, 170, 171
Preventative Cycle Model 115
prevention................................... 61, 62
Pyramid of Sustainable Tourism 93
quadruple bottom line...................... 174
Quality of Service............................. 90
R10.. 155
recycling.................. 195, 197, 201, 202
resilience 140, 148, 149, 152, 154
resources..138, 140, 141, 143, 144, 146, 149, 150, 152, 153, 154
responsible tourism 124, 125, 129, 130, 131, 132
Rio+20... 14, 18
scale.137, 138, 139, 140, 141, 143, 146, 149, 150
social capital... 159, 162, 166, 168, 172, 173
social compatibleness........................ 57
social performance....................123, 124
speed 137, 138, 150
strategies 210, 211, 212, 213, 215
sustainability . 54, 55, 57, 58, 60, 63, 64, 65, 91, 96, 101, 103, 106, 107, 109, 110, 111, 112, 117, 123, 126, 127, 128, 130, 132, 133
sustainable brand labels 103
sustainable development 85, 91, 94, 167, 168, 173
Sustainable lifestyle 189
sustainable tourism ...54, 56, 63, 85, 91, 96, 101, 177, 179, 180, 181, 182, 183, 184, 185, 186, 187, 188, 189
Sustainable Travelling 189
systems theory 161
technology....................................... 194
Three-Pillar Model...........21, 22, 23, 24
tourism 33, 34, 35, 36, 37, 38, 39, 40, 41, 42, 43, 45, 46, 47, 48
Tourism Cluster 90
Tourism Clusters......................... 85, 95
Tourist industry.............................. 179
transport 34, 35, 36, 39, 44, 48
Travel Trade Industry 103, 104, 107, 117
UN Conference on Environment and Development.................. 15, 16
UNEP - United Nations Environmental Programme........... 15
university 191, 192, 193, 195, 196, 197, 198, 199, 200, 201, 202, 203, 204, 205, 206
wellbeing... 143
wellness 53, 60, 61, 62, 64, 65
Wellness Tourism 69
World Health Organization....71, 72, 75

About the Authors

As a professor of Management and Entrepreneurship at the School of Business Administration Fribourg, **Rico J. Baldegger** directs the Entrepreneurship & SME Institute and acts as academic coordinator of the Master in Entrepreneurship. He graduated from the University of St Gallen and obtained his doctorate from the University of Fribourg. He is the author of numerous publications on entrepreneurship, internationalization of SMEs and the reorganization of family businesses. Moreover, he is a serial entrepreneur, as is demonstrated by the many companies he has created.

rico.baldegger@hefr.ch

Robert S. Bristow (BS, MA, Towson University; PhD, Southern Illinois University at Carbondale) is Professor and Chair of the Department of Geography and Regional Planning at Westfield State University (Massachusetts, USA). His current research interest is in sustainable tourism planning and management. He has published papers in *Tourism Geographies, Tourism Review, Geografiska Annaler, Parks and Recreation* and has produced numerous papers for various conference proceedings.

rbristow@westfield.ma.edu

Michelle Callanan is the Assistant Dean of Tourism programmes at *University College, Birmingham*. Her extensive years of teaching both undergraduate and postgraduate tourism students have awarded her many opportunities to work on a variety of overseas and UK consultancy projects for a number of destination management and tourism organisations. These have focused on destination audits, economic impact studies, environmental audits, destination planning and control, community tourism, cultural/heritage and interpretation work. Michelle's key academic research interests to date have focussed on politics and tourism; voluntourism; border tourism; tourism and post-conflict destinations and indigenous tourism.

M.Callanan@ucb.ac.uk

Oliver Hahn, PhD, is a professor of journalism at the University of Passau, Germany.

oliver.hahn@uni-passau.de

David Horrigan led the Center of Marketing Excellence in Hospitality, Tourism, and Event Management at the *Glion Institute of Higher Education* in Switzerland from 2007 to 2012. He has been designing curriculum and delivering educational content at university level since 1993.

David has a Doctorate of Philosophy (PhD) in Educational Leadership. In addition he holds a Master of Arts (MA) in Marketing Communications from the *University of Connecticut* and a Master of Education (MEd) in Human Resource Education from *Boston University*. His Bachelor of Arts (BA) degree from the University of Massachusetts concerned multidisciplinary programs focusing on marketing, psychology and graphic design. One of David's academic interests is to bring international industry and academia together through curriculum integration and research. His research is intended to inform curricula, contribute to the academic community and offer strategic services to industry.

David has been an industry consultant for the last fifteen years concentrating on integrated marketing strategies and brand development. His professional marketing communications career began in the mid-80s with the Interpublic Group's advertising agency *Dailey & Associates*, Los Angeles and then with WPP's marketing communications firm, *Young & Rubicam*, New York City.

David Horrigan is the marketing director for EuroCHRIE, sits on the editorial board for the Journal of Vacation Marketing and is a member of Google's Global Academic Panel.

edumktg@earthlink.net

Ian Jenkins, (BSc Econ, MPhil, PhD, University of Wales) has worked in the tourism and leisure industries for the last twenty five years as a researcher, senior lecturer, consultant and director of several research units. This work has resulted in numerous publications, including industry reports, conference papers, academic articles and book chapters; he has also been a peer reviewer for journal articles. Some of the research projects he has been involved with have resulted in legislative change and improved industry standards. In addition, he has undertaken work for prestigious organisations such as UNESCO, the British Council, the British Standards Institute, Health and Safety Executive, VisitWales and CEN. His research and consultancy expertise ranges from niche tourism development through to risk management of adventure tourism products. Ian has recently been an external examiner for the University of Birmingham at both undergraduate and postgraduate level, together with being a PhD examiner at Cranfield University.

dr.isjenkins@gmail.com

Thomas Meuser, PhD, is a professor at BiTS University of Applied Science in Iserlohn, Germany, and the leader of the degree program "Green Business Management" at BiTS. He is founder of GAIA e. V. – Institut für Umweltmanagement, an institute which focusses its activities on green and sustainable affairs. His research fields are environmental management, human resource management and further education.

thomas.meuser@bits-iserlohn.de

Britt Ventriglia Meyer has enjoyed an extensive career within the travel, tourism, and hospitality sector. Most recently Britt worked for Marriott International at the North American Headquarters conducting analysis on travel demand trends and creating pricing strategies for a multi-branded portfolio of hotel properties. Britt has also consulted for a number of organizations such as CREES Expeditions (a leader in conservation and ecotourism for communities of the Peruvian rainforest), assisted with multiple ground-up hotel opening's (including California's first fully LEED Gold sustainable hotel), and has participated in multiple micro-financing projects in Africa specializing in sustainable development initiatives. Britt holds two advanced degrees: a Master in Business Administration from *Glion Institute of Higher Education, Switzerland* and a Master of Advanced Studies from *Les Roches Gruyères, University of Applied Sciences, Switzerland*. In addition she has a Bachelor of Science Degree from *California State University, Chico*. Britt's research focuses on sustainability within the travel trade industry in relation to other industries. This research was recently presented at the 2011 Cambridge Business and Economics Conference at Cambridge University, UK.

bventriglia@gmail.com

Andy Middleton is a social entrepreneur, designer and change catalyst who assists leaders and teams in business, government and the community in formulating resilience strategies for sustainability. He uses the principles of ecology and psychology, wedded to a theory of experiential learning, to help people connect what they see, know and feel to principles of working that are beneficial for long term sustainability.

He is Founder and Director of the TYF Group, a leading adventure, education and leadership business based in St.David's, Pembrokeshire, on the west coast of Britain. Andy is a board member of the Countryside Council for Wales and Associate Director of INSPIRE, the Institute for Sustainable Practice, Innovation & Resource Effectiveness. His imagination is enthused by working on city and country-scale sustainability projects and by the creative retreat centre he is in the process of building that overlooks Britain's western islands and ocean.

andy.m@tyf.com

Ruth Rios-Morales is Deputy Director of Research at *Les Roches–Gruyère*, University of Applied Sciences, Switzerland. Ruth is also the Swiss Country Director for the *EuroMed Research Business Institute*. She holds a BSc in Economics, MSc in International Economics and a PhD in Politics of International Business from the University of Ulster, UK. Before joining *Les Roches–Gruyère*, Ruth taught International Business at the School of Business Studies, Trinity College Dublin as well as International Business and Finance at the Universidad de Zaragoza, Spain. Ruth has conducted advanced research in International Business and Finance and her research has been acknowledged by both UNCTAD and the World Bank.

ruthriosmorales@bluewin.ch

Carola von Peinen, has a degree in business administration and currently focuses on sustainable tourism within the academic field of tourism. After working for nine years in business recruitment she established her own company in 2012, which specialises in recruiting staff for enterprises and organisations working in the field of sustainability and social business.

carola.vonpeinen@talents4good.org

Mark Piekarz is a Senior Lecturer in Sport Management at the University of Worcester, having taught in the subject area of Sport, Tourism and Adventure for over twenty years. His interest in tourism and politics stems from his research relating to political risk management and tourism. He has published work on a variety of subject areas, ranging from risk management and battlefield tourism to developing ethical frameworks for event impact analysis.

m.piekarz@worc.ac.uk

About the Authors

Thomas Rieger, PhD, is a professor of Sport Management at BiTS University of Applied Sciences in Iserlohn, Germany. He is also the Program Director of the Bachelor Program, Sport & Event Management and the Master Program International Sport & Event Management. His research focus is on fitness, leisure and recreational management. He serves as Chairman of the Standards Council of the European Health & Fitness Association in Brussels.

thomas.rieger@bits-iserlohn.de

Roland Schroeder, PhD, is a professor of media management and journalism at BiTS University of Applied Sciences in Iserlohn, Germany. He is also Dean of the Media and Communication Department. His research areas include online and social media issues, with an international perspective.

roland.schroeder@bits-iserlohn.de

Edmund A. Spindler, Dipl.-Ing., studied spatial planning (urban, regional and land planning) at the University of Dortmund and specialized in environmental issues from an early stage. He now works in the environmental sector, at the interface of ecology and economy. The main focus of his work is preventive environmental protection. As an expert in environmental impact assessments (EIA), he participated in the 1992 Earth Summit in Rio de Janeiro. Since then he has been intensively involved in environmental management systems (ISO-14001, resp. EMAS) and, lately, also in the subject of sustainability management (ISO-26000 and CSR). Spindler is a member of various committees (e.g. Environmental Verification Committee, VDI-guideline committee) and is a lecturer in the area of "production-integrated environmental protection (PIUS)" at the private college BiTS in Iserloh as well as at the University in Giessen. He has been a member of the Association for Sustainable Environment Management (VNU) since 2000 and is the head of the national committee of experts in "agriculture and food science". He is married with three children and lives in Hamm (Westfalen) in Germany.

edmund-a.spindler@gmx.de

Printed in the USA
CPSIA information can be obtained
at www.ICGtesting.com
CBHW050225270824
13749CB00004B/21